D1621888

THE NATURAL LAW PARTY

A Reason to Vote

◆　◆　◆

THE NATURAL LAW PARTY

A Reason to Vote

Breaking the two-party stranglehold and
bringing effective new solutions
to America's problems

ROBERT ROTH

Foreword by John Hagelin, Ph.D.
Presidential Candidate of the Natural Law Party

St. Martin's Press

New York

Book design by Paula Szafranski

Library of Congress Cataloging-in-Publication Data

Roth, Robert, date
   The Natural Law Party: a reason to vote: breaking the two-
party stranglehold and bringing effective new solutions to
America's problems / Robert Roth: foreword by John
Hagelin.
      p.   cm.
   Includes bibliographical references.
   ISBN 0–312–19304–1
   1. Natural Law Party (U.S.)   2. United States—Politics and
government—1993   I. Title
JK2391.N34R67   1998
324.273'8—dc21   98–23739

Firt Edition: September 1998

10 9 8 7 6 5 4 3 2

Contents

Contents

Acknowledgments

This is a book about exceptional people doing exceptional things to build a new political party that can make the nation a healthier, safer, more prosperous place to live. Many of these men and women are in the public eye; many labor behind the scenes.

First, I would like to thank all those from all political parties who have come before the Natural Law Party. These are men and women who have worked hard to make ballot access laws fair and to give independent and third-party candidates their rightful place in public debates and on the public airwaves. You have helped to keep the flame of democracy in America burning bright.

My deepest appreciation goes to Natural Law Party presidential candidate John Hagelin, vice presidential candidate Mike Tompkins, chair Kingsley Brooks, and founding chair Dr. Bevan Morris as well as Michael Spivak, Elaine Reding, Rafael David, and Cindy Schirmer—the chief architects of the party—for their wisdom, conviction, and persistence against incredible odds, to guide the party to where it is today. More than anyone you have given me the content and inspiration for this book.

I am also deeply grateful to Patti Breitman, my agent, who read the first eighteen pages of the manuscript and thought right away that this was a message that needed to be heard. Her ongoing wisdom and guidance through the entire process have been deeply appreciated. I feel the same for my editor at St. Martin's Press, George Witte, and George's editorial assistant, Josh Kendall. Your support for the book has meant more to me than you will ever know.

This book took its shape through the insight and dedicated efforts of many: Rona Abramson, Leslie Brooks, Laura Couture, Bill Crist, Bill Crosson, Denise Droese, Zanna Feitler, Mark Goodman, Fred Gratzon, David Hawthorne, Buck Montgomery, John Moore, Lincoln Norton, Lindsay Oliver, Sally Peden, Jane Pitt, Mark Schoenfeld, Coral Scranton, David Shapiro, Jeff Smith, and, most especially, Mike Tompkins. You did your job with care and tenacity. I trusted your judgment, and it shows.

I would also like to thank Dr. Robert Herron, Gerry Geer, and Dr. David Leffler for their invaluable assistance in helping to research and document the party's stand on the issues. This is a solid platform, and you deserve much credit. Thanks also to Linda Bedinger, Craig Herndon, and Alicia Isen for their willingness to transcribe interviews at a moment's notice.

A few of the people who have made the Natural Law Party successful are featured in this book. But there are hundreds, even thousands of people whom you will not meet. They are the party leaders, candidates, volunteers, and supporters in every state whose dedication to the high principles of the Natural Law Party makes the party go. Without their support, the successes the party has enjoyed would be significantly diminished. Thanks to all of you, including: Jeffrey Abramson, Abaan Abu-Shumays, Louise Allison, Jane Allon, Kurt Arbuckle, Elizabeth Rice Arnold, Elizabeth Ashbrook, Bill and Lois Avery, Rogers and Candace Badgett, Ron and Bonnie Barnett, Jeanie Bates, Marsh and Diana Belden, Craig Berg, Warren and Harriet Berman, Bob Beskangy, Richard and Jane Bialosky, John Black, Judy Bararth-Black, Rick Blake, Warren Blank, Shirley Boncheff, Sandi BonSell, Art Boucher, Eric and Barbara Bourdette, Carolyn Boyce, Martha Bright, Dr. Jim Brooks, Mike Busch, Dr. Veronica Butler, Jim Cahaney, Tony Camero, Tom Carlisle, Cathy Carter, Catherine Carter, Mary Jo Christian, Larry and Susan Chroman, Lauri Clegg, Donna Colby, Lane Cole, Mary Ann Cooke, Danny Corn, John Cornell, Michael and Elizabeth Cosgrove,

Patricia Cox, Michael Cuddehe, Richard and Gail Dalby, Jim and Diane Davis, Dean Draznin, Bobbi and Barbara Dreier, Kai and Julie Druhl, Bill and Helen Dunn, Billie Eastman, Tony and Mo Ellis, Annette Estes, Clarence Evjen, Tom and Roxanne Factor, Sam Farling, Paul and Josie Fauerso, George and Felicity Foster, Steven and Gillian Foster, Jonathan Freeman, Dale Freidgen, Jim and June French, Jim Gerhard, Gary Gill, Sonja and Vesna Glavina, Ira and Janet Goldberg, Ted Goldstein, Kathy Goodman, Shelley Gratzon, Sarina Grosswald, Monty Guild, Ruth Guilliard, Michael Haig, Ayres Hall, Tom Hall, Key Halverson, Ken and Carol Hardin, Sharalyn Harris, Chris and Linda Hartnett, Gail Herson, Ute Hopker, Steve and Miriam Hospodar, Michael Huddleston, Bill and Stacey Hurlin, Kent Hyde, Joe and Valerie Janlois, Charles Johanson, Chris and Ellen Jones, Richard Kahn, David Kaplan, Earl Kaplan, Barry Katz, Dick Kaynor, Ann Keith, Walter Keith, Pegi Kempner, Bruce Kendall, David Kidd, David and Eleanor Laird, Peter Lamoureux, Jane Lazzareschi, Lee Leffler, Margaret Lewis, Charley and Toby Lieb, Randall Longstroth, Randy MacKenzie, Ed and Vicki Malloy, Jay and Susan Marcus, Bob and Carol Markowitz, Curtis and Sherry McDonald, Tina McQuiston, Jane Meade, Rebecca Meisner, Mary Mellen, Patti Metten, Tony and Sharon Miles, Susan Minx, Cathy Montgomery, Barbara Morgan, Brenda Narducci, Bernie and Terry Nevas, Tom and Terry Newmark, June Norton, Martha Oaas, Gerry Ogle, Victor Pardo, Cynthia Parker, Linda Parmet, Michael and Andrea Pflaumer, Paul and Ann Pigue, Barry Pitt, Jonathan Poneman, Adam Pressman, John Pronchik, Bill and Gail Quarton, Judy Raymond, Doug Rexford, Rodney Robbins, Ernie and Barbara Robson, Chris Rogers, Alan and Susan Rosenfield, Kate Ross, Steve and Karen Rubin, Peter Salk, Barry Scherr, Becky Scott, Tom Shirah, Allan and Anne Shook, Julia Simon, Brynne Sissom, Dennis and Betsy Slotnick, Helen Smith, Rosemary Spivak, Rob Stowe, Keith and Cathy Thompson, Mark Thompson, Randall Tolpinrud, Tom Traynor, Jeff Turnbull, Christina Van Dyke, Susan Vegors, David Verrill, Gary and B. J. Wacknov, Doug and Nancy Walker, Michael Warner, Charlotte Watson, Chris and Margie Wege, Patrick West, Toni Wilder, Paul Wilson, Ron Wilson, Richard Winger, Charles Winter, Rob Wofford, Russ Wollman, Ken and Blanche Woodward, Jerry Yellin, David Zimmer, and Stuart and Moki Zimmerman.

Finally, I want to thank my family. My late father, Merall, and my mother, Susan, raised me in a loving household where politics really did matter and where conviction for ideas, and the willingness to work for them, were not options for a life well lived, but the foundation for one. I am grateful to my brothers, Bill and Tom; my sister, Ellen; and my brother-in-law, Brian, for their constant love and support and for our deep friendship. And, of course, my young nephews, Michael and Jonathan. You are the only ones to whom I would give up time from writing this book on my computer so that you could surf the Net. Thanks.

America's Great Awakening

Foreword by John Hagelin, Ph.D.

Presidential Candidate of the Natural Law Party

Few Americans who have had the opportunity to visit other countries have not returned with a renewed sense of wonder and appreciation for the magnificence of our great nation. America's unprecedented achievements—and leadership role in the world—are due in part to the great alertness and creativity of its people. We are largely a nation of immigrants, descendants of those who left their homelands and risked a perilous and uncertain journey to the new world. These were brave and hearty souls with great goals and initiative and a willingness to sacrifice for them. We are collectively the offspring of this boldness and creativity.

Another, deeper reason for America's rise to global preeminence is that the American people and the democratic institutions put forth by America's founders are in harmony with *natural law*—in tune with the laws of nature that govern the progress of the individual and society.

What is natural law? The laws of nature are the orderly principles governing life throughout the physical universe. According to science, natural law governs everything. Nothing happens that is not the direct result of natural law: from the motion of a particle to the changing of the seasons, from the emergence of life to the functioning of entire societies. *Our ability to accomplish anything, individually and as a society, is through the skillful application of the laws of nature in daily life.*

The electric light, which has profoundly revolutionized our lifestyle, is a simple application of the laws of electrodynamics. Medicines are applications of the laws of chemistry and human physiology. In a similar way, other advanced applications of natural law through chemical, electronic, and nuclear technologies are transforming the face of human civilization.

Now, to continue to progress and flourish as a nation, we must bolster our alliance with natural law. It is unfortunately true that many of our institutions, modern technologies, and patterns of behavior increasingly violate the laws of nature. Our medicines with their dangerous side effects, chemical pesticides and fertilizers and genetically engineered crops, and even some of our financial institutions are sowing the seeds of future epidemics, class warfare, and environmental disasters. We are losing favor with natural law.

Fortunately, in raising these concerns, and in promoting solutions that are forward-looking, prevention-oriented, and in harmony with natural law, the Natural Law Party is not a "voice crying in the wilderness." America is in the midst of a great awakening. Tens of millions of citizens are realizing the perils of the path we are treading and are striving hard to change that direction.

I would guess, having spoken to millions of Americans on the campaign trail, that most of you who are reading this book are already involved with preventive or alternative forms of medicine, organic and/or sustainable farming or the consumption of such healthier foods, socially responsible investing, recycling and other environmentally responsible behavior, or yoga or meditation to develop the mind and body. People everywhere are awakening to the central role that nature—natural law—plays in the growth and evolution of life and the importance of living in accord with natural law.

All that has been lacking is a political voice, and leadership, for this growing not-so-silent majority of Americans. The Natural Law Party has arisen to fill this void. Through the innovative, life-supporting policies, and the scientifically proven programs of the Natural Law Party, America can continue to grow and to prosper with even greater rates of progress—without the dangerous health, environmental, and other side effects that will prove suicidal in the long run.

America is at a crossroads and in desperate need of new leadership for its journey ahead. The path of least resistance is always the status quo—to tread the present course until our natural resources are exhausted, our soil is depleted, our food supply contaminated, our youth incarcerated. The Republican and Democratic parties appear wed to this path, bound inextricably by their corporate sponsors. Other single-issue parties, despite their valiant support for important issues like personal freedom, the environment, and certain religious convictions, lack the broad vision needed to take us into the next millennium. Today only the Natural Law Party is truly global in scope, with growing strength in over sixty countries. Its practical, field-tested programs to bring every area of national life into greater harmony with the vast organizational intelligence of nature provide a comprehensive, scientific, secure, and humane foundation for the future of civilization.

The last six years have been a whirlwind of activity for the thousands of volunteers and heroic candidates who have built America's fastest-growing grassroots party. For most of us, it has been a trial by fire, an emotional roller-coaster ride. Robert Roth's book captures the agony and ecstasy of this national drama: the agony of confronting such deeply entrenched and stultifying political resistance that it will shake the reader's confidence in America's democratic institutions; the ecstasy of gaining such overwhelming support at the grassroots level of the American people that these institutional roadblocks could be overcome.

I truly hope, and deeply believe, that this book will be merely Chapter One in the greatest epic of American history, the story of a people who reclaimed their government, and their country, from an entrenched, self-serving political-industrial oligarchy, enshrined in two parties and their corporate sponsors that, above all else, seek to preserve the status quo; the story of a people who returned their country to the profound principles of natural law upon which it was founded, the same timeless principles through which nature governs the vast and complex universe.

Your support and dynamic participation will fill the pages of this epic with tales of great victory and success. I believe that such a victory is inevitable. The Natural Law Party is riding the inexorable tide of history, the tide of natural law, which sweeps everyone and everything forward in its evolutionary path of growing truth, happiness, and ultimately, lasting fulfillment.

Preface

My father was a radiologist who dreamed the dreams of a sailor. A World War II injury kept his travels confined to day trips on the San Francisco Bay, but in the evenings I would find him in his den studying navigation charts of the high seas and tinkering with an antique sextant, a finely crafted instrument for measuring the elevation of the sun so mariners could make it safely to their destination.

Today most seafaring vessels are equipped with satellite navigation systems, as are more and more cars. The map on the dashboard shows the direction clearly: turn left on Kensington Street, take a right on Third Avenue and another right on Vine, and you're home.

Both technologies, the old sextant and modern satellite gadgetry, are based on the same principle: to get where we're going, we need a bigger picture. We have to know at every moment where we are in the context of the whole and make our next move from there. The bigger picture takes away speculation and doubt, blind conviction, and the odds-on chance of error.

We expect our leaders to have some of that bigger picture when they promise to deliver us the American dream: the best schools, a clean environment, an equal opportunity at prosperity, and a long and healthy life in a safe, peaceful world. We expect them to take a right or a left turn to steer us through the myriad detours, pitfalls, and disasters that lie ahead. We would like to trust them as we would the captain of a ship. We certainly don't expect them to take a particular turn because someone has slipped them five bucks to do so. That's not driving with the big picture. That's not even just driving crooked; that's driving dangerous.

What's the big picture when it comes to governing the nation? It's the recognition that as individuals and as a society we are, in fact, inseparable from, sustained by, and have an indomitable influence on the whole of nature. Our guiding light is our knowledge of natural law, from physics, chemistry, physiology, biology, psychology, ecology, astronomy, etc., and of how to apply the unfathomable energy, creativity, and organizing power that pervade every grain of creation in ways that are life-supporting, evolutionary, and nourishing for all.

The knowledge of how to use nature wisely is already available, proven through extensive scientific research and tested in our schools, on our farms, in our factories, hospitals, and prisons. This is knowledge that can fulfill the American dream for everyone. It can bring far better health and far greater comfort and prosperity to everyone—without hazardous side effects.

The knowledge is there, but too many of our leaders just aren't paying attention—out of either ignorance or political expediency. The Natural Law Party was founded in 1992 to provide a powerful political voice for the tens of millions of Americans who have grown concerned, frustrated, even angry at the reluctance or inability of our leaders to navigate by a bigger picture.

The Natural Law Party: A Reason to Vote is about that bigger picture. It's about how nature functions and how people are applying this knowledge to benefit the nation. It recounts how difficult it is to get a new party off the ground and bring it to the awareness of the American people. It provides a glimpse into what the Natural Law Party stands for, who the candidates are, and why they run for office. Lastly, it highlights some of the unique policy positions the party takes.

This book has been written by an unabashed advocate of the role of third parties in America, who is also an enthusiastic supporter of the Natural Law Party. It is an honest account of the start of a remarkable journey to give a much-needed new political direction to our country. As such, I hope it provides you with a feeling for where we are heading as a nation and where we still need to go.

The Battle

1

Does Politics Matter Anymore?
(Yes, More Than Ever)

No one cares about politics anymore; at least that's what the polls show. Televised presidential debates don't draw viewers. Campaign commercials don't change voters' minds. It's not like the old days when you could get into a good heated exchange over dinner with an uncle or a neighbor over the president's stand on civil rights or foreign policy, what Congress was going to do next, and whether the media were reporting from the left or right. Or when college campuses were teeming with political activity—radical, reactionary, and stay-the-course. *Opinions* mattered; *involvement* was a must; *caring* was paramount. Those days are pretty much gone.

Political commentators tell us why. They say that voters see government as out of touch with the concerns and values of the people, in the pocket of special interests, and now, when the country is flourishing economically, increasingly irrelevant. Business is booming, crime is down, and America is playing a leading role in the family of nations. But for most people the national transformation appears less the by-product of government leadership and more the result of American ingenuity, creativity, and self-reliance.

True or not, this good news has had at least one chilling side effect. It may be lulling us into a political deep sleep with dangerous consequences. Are these good times numbing us? Recent polls indicate that we don't care that much about the campaign finance scandals. We seem to be reconciled to the fact that the high-stakes, highly objectionable deals between public and private sector leaders are an inevitable, if not acceptable, part of Washington life. Such deals are of little immediate consequence to our own lives, the polls suggest. If the economy is good, life is good. And if life is good, there is nothing to worry about. Let Washington do as it wishes; it won't affect us, not really.

Don't believe it. Those deals aren't just for money to win elections; those deals are to cut in stone the direction of public policy in America and the world for decades to come.

The fact is we, the American people, have lost, or are in extreme danger of losing, our power to set the public policy agenda for our government, for the nation. How did we lose it? Principally, in two ways: the buyout of the politicians and the buyout of the press. Those hefty PAC and corporate contributions certainly do influence our leaders' decisions. Special interests often do take precedence over national interests, particularly on the big-ticket items, such as health care reforms, energy policies, corporate subsidies, and biotech regulations. Also, the fact that many of these same special interests are buying up the major media outlets does dictate, or at least severely restrict, the scope and depth of information about the issues that reach the American people. But for my money, the most damaging development, which is tied inextricably to special interest influence and the media buyout, is the shutting down of third parties in America. I know that sounds odd because most people these days hardly consider third parties. And that is the problem.

2

Ruminations of a Third-Party Operative

I can tell you a lot about starting a new political party, far more than you may ever want to know. For example, I can tell you how many volunteers you will need standing in the parking lots of how many Wal-Marts in how many Texas towns each collecting how many signatures to pass the threshold of 43,963 valid signatures required to put your candidate on the ballot in that state.

I can tell you how to plan a campaign stop in, say, Cleveland, to get the most media coverage. (Press conferences are risky. If there is a fire downtown, you are out of luck; that's a much better photo op. Lectures in university political science classes always seem to attract newspaper reporters. Check the president's itinerary, and don't send your candidate there if he's in town. Trust me, no one will show.)

I can point out the laws passed by Republican- and Democratic-run legislatures in almost every state just to keep new parties and independent candidates off the ballot and out of the political debate—and to make your job as impossible as possible.

I can also tell you that even if what I say does not particularly interest you right now, it will soon. The way the two main parties are discrediting themselves in the public eye, within the next one or two election cycles, third parties are going to be a confounding, if not altogether revolutionary, force in America.

Who am I to tell you so much about third parties? As the press secretary for the Natural Law Party, the fastest-growing new party in America, I have worked for the past six years with an ever-expanding cadre of friends and colleagues to build what we hope will be the next-generation mainstream political party in America. We started late in 1992 and against considerable odds we are making remarkable headway. In 1996 we ran four hundred candidates on the ballot in forty-eight states—a huge accomplishment for a new party. We had little money for paid advertising, so we relied primarily on word of mouth, and it worked—for now. Together our candidates totaled several million votes. Dr. John Hagelin, a Harvard-trained quantum physicist and our presidential candidate, was the only third-party presidential candidate to qualify for federal primary matching funds (about half a million dollars), a feat not even Ross Perot accomplished and a testimony to John Hagelin's broad-based grassroots support. We have also developed a platform that most Americans, when they hear about it, endorse.

Many diehard Republicans and Democrats say that we (and all third parties) have an impossible task, but the times are on our side, and we are bullish about our future.

To give you a better idea of what I do and to introduce you to the Natural Law Party and what we stand for, I offer these five brief episodes that took place during four days in Washington, D.C., October 7–10, 1997.

"USA Today Is Here"

Tuesday, October 7, 1:00 P.M. I am standing in the back of a room at the National Press Club, keeping out of the line of sight of a television camera crew. The room is small and stuffy, with about forty people jammed into chairs facing a podium in the front or squeezed in at the back, standing up in the doorway. We needed a larger room for this news conference, I say to myself. Assembled in the front are the leaders of America's largest third parties, representing the votes of nearly ten million Americans during the 1996 election and the sentiments, I believe, of tens of millions more.

This is the first time in U.S. political history that the leaders of third parties have united with a common cause: to push for sweeping campaign and election law reforms. The event has been organized by the Natural Law Party, and the press turnout has been good, larger than I expected, considering that there is a campaign finance scandal in progress and Harold Ickes, one of President Clinton's closest aides, is testifying on Capitol Hill.

John Hagelin, the Natural Law Party's presidential candidate in 1996, is at the podium, introducing the other leaders who stand in a semicircle behind him: Ralph Nader of the Green Party, Harry Browne of the Libertarian Party, Howard Phillips of the U.S. Taxpayer Party, and Russ Verney, representing Ross Perot of the Reform Party.

It strikes me, amid the frenzy of a news conference, that this is a good day for the Natural Law Party and a great day for democracy.

Each political leader at the podium has set aside his own ideological differences to support two bills introduced by U.S. Congressman Ron Paul, a Republican from Surfside, Texas, who wants to overturn election laws and debate regulations that keep independent and third-party candidates out of the political arena.

The obstacles are significant and outrageous when you consider that they were enacted by Republican and Democratic lawmakers. Here are a few: An independent or third-party presidential candidate must collect 701,089 valid signatures to get on the ballot in all fifty states, which is twenty-eight times the number needed by a Democratic Party presidential candidate and thirteen times the number needed by a Republican. Third-party candidates also have to meet sizable discriminatory filing fees, filing deadlines, and restrictions on who can circulate and who can sign the petition—regulations that are not required of the major parties.

Paul's Voter Freedom Act of 1997 (H.R. 2477) would set fair and uniform ballot access standards for federal elections and prohibit states from erecting excessive ballot access barriers. The Debates Freedom Act of 1997 (H.R. 2478) would prohibit recipients of taxpayer-funded campaign matching funds from participating in debates to which all qualified candidates are not invited. Any presidential candidate who is on the ballot in at least forty states is guaranteed inclusion in the debates.

Everyone of course speaks eloquently and with considerable passion in support of the bills, but Ralph Nader's comments stick with me throughout the day. Ralph can see that there is a good media turnout, but he is not overly impressed.

"In 1920 America's black leadership held a major news conference in Washington, D.C., to call attention to the unfair and discriminatory laws that blacks must overcome to participate in the political process," Nader says. "The *Washington Post, New York Times*, and *Wall Street Journal* did not attend that news conference. The parallels are striking between black participation in the political process then and third-party participation today. I would like to ask now, Is anyone here from the *Washington Post, New York Times*, or the *Wall Street Journal?*" There is a painful moment of silence when no one answers, until Andrea Stone, who covers third-party politics for *USA Today*, says, "Well, *USA Today* is here."

"It Shouldn't Be Easy to Exclude Third Parties"

Wednesday, October 8, 11:45 A.M. I am standing on the steps of the U.S. Supreme Court, and very fortunately, today is not a hot and muggy day, because I am in the midst of a crush of media. Television camera crews, photographers, and print reporters balancing tape recorders and notepads all are jockeying for position. Their target: Ralph Forbes, a boyish-faced, heavyset middle-aged man from Arkansas who has become a thorn in the side of public television.

Forbes is suing Arkansas Public Television because the station refused to let him participate in a televised debate it sponsored during the 1992 campaign. Forbes was an independent candidate for U.S. Congress in Arkansas's Third District. He was a legitimate candidate in the eyes of the state; he had gathered the necessary petition signatures to put his name on the ballot. In fact, two years earlier, in a 1990 statewide race, Ralph received 47 percent of the vote. But Forbes was not a Republican or a Democrat, so the editorial staff at the station decided Ralph was not really legitimate, had little chance of winning the election, and therefore barred him from the debate.

Forbes took Arkansas Public Television to court and lost. He didn't go away. He appealed to the Eighth Circuit Court of Appeals, and won. His argument was simple. Commercial television is privately owned, must concern itself with ratings, and must answer to advertisers. Therefore commercial television may make an excuse for not inviting every candidate to its debate. But public television is government-owned and is under no such constraints. The journalists who work for public television are government employees, and they should not be the editors in chief for America's 180 million eligible voters, deciding what ideas, candidates, and political parties are worth hearing about and what are not. That is the right and responsibility of the American people.

(Certainly you cannot have fifty or a hundred candidates participating in a publicly sponsored debate. There has to be some criterion to determine what makes a candidate viable. But such a criterion is already in place: getting on the ballot. If a candidate is able to surmount the considerable obstacles to ballot access put into place by state lawmakers, then let him or her talk.)

The court of appeals agreed with Ralph Forbes, overturning the lower court's decision. Arkansas Public Television disagreed with the new ruling, appealed to the Supreme Court, and that's why I am here today.

It is my job to host Ralph Forbes for his court appearance. The case is a big one. Several hours before the 10:00 A.M. hearing, there is a line of two hundred or more people, many of them law students, stretched across the courtyard in front of the Supreme Court steps, each waiting for a chance to get in for a five-minute glimpse of the case in process.

The hearing goes surprisingly well. I am sitting next to Forbes in the audience, and his face is registering waves of shock and amazement as his lawyer's arguments gain a positive foothold in the minds of many of the justices. Justice David H. Souter worries that if public television wins the case, it is just another way of saying that "a distinctly minority candidate always loses." Justice Ruth Bader Ginsburg says, "Debate is for the public. It shouldn't be so easy to exclude third parties." Justice Sandra Day O'Connor says that criteria for participation in a debate should not be arbitrary, left up to the opinion of a government employee after the fact, but should be made clear ahead of time to all candidates.

The case has far-reaching political ramifications, beyond simply whether public television can pick and choose its own debate guests. According to Richard Winger, the editor of *Ballot Access News* and an expert on U.S. election laws, third parties have been the principal source of most of the good ideas that have shaped our democracy, from the abolition of slavery to the right of a woman to vote to basic child labor laws. How will similar new ideas reach the public arena in the future if all media outlets, including public television, shut out small, but potentially powerful, new voices?

The hearing ends at 11:00 A.M., and Forbes's lawyers are quietly exuberant. We step outside into the bright sunlight for a news briefing that draws a big media turnout, and it pushes on for over an hour—a lifetime by Washington standards. This time reporters for the *Washington Post* and the *New York Times* are here, along with *USA Today*, Associated Press, *Christian Science Monitor*, ABC, CNN, and NPR.

The air is clear and crisp, the news briefing is going well, my job is done, and I am relaxed. Behind me is the U.S. Capitol building, where President Clinton's staffers are under interrogation for a campaign finance scandal that won't go away. The significance dawns on me as I watch the camera crews pack up their gear. Over there, across the street, the Republicans and Democrats are severing whatever thread of trust and credibility remains between them and the American electorate, while just one hour ago, up the steps from where I stand, in the chambers of the Supreme Court, the most fundamental and precious tenet of our democracy—the constitutional right to free speech—was on trial in the highest court in the land. The justices will decide in the coming months whether third parties have a seat at the table of our political process and, not coincidentally, whether our democracy regains much of its former vitality and vigor.[1]

It is clear that we are at a crossroads in the political future of America. Given a level playing field and an equal chance under the law, it is also clear that third parties are destined to play an ever-larger and more powerful role in the years ahead.

"Thank God for C-SPAN"

Wednesday, October 8, 2:00 P.M.   I am on the phone to Mimi Hall, White House reporter for *USA Today*. She covered third parties during the 1996 campaign, and now she covers the White House. We talk about our news conferences at the National Press Club yesterday and at the Supreme Court earlier today. She has a few moments to chat, so I tell her about a phone call I recently received from a political science professor from the University of Virginia. He was working on a textbook on third parties, and he wanted to know if I had any thoughts on how the press treats us. I asked him how many ninety-minute cassettes he had for his tape recorder. He laughed, thinking that I was joking. I was not. I have a lot of thoughts on the subject, and few of them are flattering.

First, let me give you some personal background. I have been in the public relations field for twenty-five years. I make certain that the story I pitch to a reporter is legitimate, newsworthy, and worth taking up the few moments that a writer can spare to hear about it. Moreover, even though every PR guy is used to hearing noes from reporters who are on deadlines or working on other stories, as a rule I have always received an open ear and a fair hearing. I took this confidence with me into my role as press secretary with a new political party in 1992.

Looking back at it, I see that I was incredibly naive.

Science reporters, education reporters, environmental reporters, crime reporters, even business reporters always seem interested in something new. For instance, given the chance, most health reporters will do a serious story on an unusual yet now highly credible subject like the use of natural medicine to treat chronic diseases. But for some reason, and it still baffles me why, that is not the case with most political editors. They do not appear interested in anything outside the two-party system; worse, many of them seem to have a highly personal stake in preserving the two-party system, a stake that can sound like religious zeal.

Here's a third-party scorecard: During the entire 1996 campaign, neither John Hagelin nor any other third-party presidential candidate (other than Ross Perot, who is in a different tax bracket) appeared on any network NBC, CBS, or ABC news show. *Time* covered the third-party presidential candidates once, with just two weeks left in the campaign, summing up each candidate's entire campaign message in a one-inch caption. Nothing in *Newsweek*. The *New York Times* gave the candidates scant coverage, including one easily missed roundup story that appeared on the bottom of page 11 in the Saturday, October 5, 1996, edition. (This was from the newspaper that sets the daily editorial agenda for all the network television news shows.)

Similar scant coverage was given by many other national and metropolitan dailies. In Iowa an editor at the *Des Moines Register* actually said his paper has an editorial policy *not* to cover any third-party candidates. This policy was taken to the extreme during the 1994 campaign for Iowa attorney general. The Natural Law Party's candidate, Jay Marcus, an attorney and the author of a highly regarded book on criminal rehabilitation, participated in a spirited public debate with the Republican and Democratic candidates. The next day the *Register*'s coverage of the debate included extensive quotes from the two major-party candidates. Jay was not mentioned until the very last sentence of the article, where the reporter wrote, "Also participating in the debate was Jay Marcus of the Natural Law Party."

So why aren't third parties covered in the national press?

Colman McCarthy, a journalist and nationally syndicated columnist for the *Washington Post* for thirty-five years, addressed that question in a column on October 1, 1996, on what he perceived to be an unholy alliance between some members of the press and politicians and a deep-seated unwillingness to entertain new ideas.

"Presidential debates ought to be about the choices of ideas in the marketplace of politics, with the aisles as wide as possible," McCarthy wrote. "If the political views and reforms of today's allegedly minor candidates—so labeled over drinks at the National Press Club or faculty lounges—are seen as 'fringy,' perhaps it is because the two major parties, with their shared monopoly on what is safe, stale, and sterile, fear freshness."

There may be other reasons why new parties receive such little press coverage. In his best-selling book *The Media Monopoly*,[2] author Ben Bagdikian points out that something very dangerous is happening to our newspapers, magazines, and television and radio stations—and not many people recognize it. Our locally owned and operated press outlets are being bought up by huge corporations and turned into media conglomerates. On a national level, NBC is owned by General Electric, CBS by Westinghouse, ABC by Disney. This means, Bagdikian says, that information and news, once precious knowledge-based commodities that could move our society forward, are fast becoming entertainment-based commodities subject to heavy pressure from the bottom line. Also, news or information that is not a ratings grabber or does not enrich the bottom line of the corporate owner may no longer be viewed by management as being news or information worth publicizing. Both General Electric and Westinghouse, for example, are major manufacturers of nuclear power and nuclear weapons technologies. Should it be surprising, therefore, that neither network invited John Hagelin, a Harvard-trained nuclear physicist who is solidly opposed to nuclear power, as a guest on any of its many news shows? Is it mere coincidence that National Public Radio's highly regarded program *Science Friday*, which is underwritten in part by Archer Daniels Midland, one of the nation's largest producers of genetically engineered crops, has given comparatively little coverage to the growing concern over the safety of genetically engineered foods, a stand supported by some of America's foremost scientists and doctors and endorsed by the Natural Law Party?

Fortunately, all the news on the media is not sour. Times are changing. More and more journalists are recognizing the newsworthiness and importance of third-party voices and giving them more airtime and more ink. Much credit goes to Larry King for his airing of two third-party presidential debates immediately following the network televised debates between President Clinton and Senator Dole. In addition, other reporters, such as *USA Today*'s Mimi Hall, Knight-Ridder's Brigid Schulte, and CNN political news reporter Kim Kleine, made extra efforts to see that the message of third parties reached the public.

However, it was a small but avidly watched (at least in Washington) cable network that set the standard for what can happen when third-party ideas are brought to the American people. Or, as we at the Natural Law Party said throughout the campaign, "Thank God for C-SPAN."

As I said, Natural Law Party candidates received several million votes during the 1996 campaign, and John Hagelin estimates that a majority of those votes came from C-SPAN viewers. That is because C-SPAN let third-party candidates give their messages, for up to an hour at a time and on many different occasions. Voters had a chance to meet new candidates, bring them into their living rooms, watch them under the scrutiny of debates and interviews and the glaring eye of an unblinking camera lens. C-SPAN aired live the Natural Law Party's national nominating convention for four hours and rebroadcast it on several occasions; aired several news conferences with John Hagelin on a range of platform planks; broadcast two third-party presidential debates and one vice presidential debate; and hosted several in-studio roundtable discussions with the candidates. The most mail the Natural Law Party received from voters came following C-SPAN broadcasts. The letters expressed inspiration, relief, and satisfaction from our message. Just about everyone asked that same, painful question: "How come you are not in the news more often?"

"Who Are You People?"

Thursday, October 9, 2:00 P.M. "Just who are you people? How did the Natural Law Party start? Where does the money to fund your party come from?"

I hear these questions all the time. This time they come from a woman who is a member of the Center for Visionary Leadership, a national networking organization of writers, teachers, scientists, environmentalists, and political activists who want to bring a more spiritual, humane approach to politics. On their own (because the center is a nonprofit organization) they are meeting with members of the executive committee of the Natural Law Party, curious to see if there may be a meeting of the minds.

John Hagelin answers. He explains that the Natural Law Party, founded in April 1992, has grown quickly and attained a national status with millions of people voting for the party, signing its petitions, and supporting its platform because it encompasses the individual values and public policies supported by a majority of the

American people. These policies include using prevention-oriented natural medicine in the health care system to reduce disease and promote health; preserving the environment through renewable energy technologies, such as solar and wind; and safeguarding the food supply through use of sustainable agricultural practices, to grow crops without hazardous chemical fertilizers and pesticides.

The money to grow the Natural Law Party, Hagelin says, has come from grassroots support; from individual contributors across the country, usually in the $25 to $100 range. The party refuses all PAC contributions, he points out. This obviously handicaps the Natural Law Party when it is trying to compete with the major parties, but the party has been successful nonetheless. This can be seen in the fact that John received federal matching funds. (To qualify, a presidential candidate must receive a minimum of $5,000 from each of at least twenty states in contributions of $250 or less. This $100,000 threshold is intended to demonstrate broad-based popular support.) All of the Natural Law Party's contributions and financial transactions are public record.

Everyone seems satisfied with Hagelin's answers. Then someone asks each of us on the executive committee to talk about why we joined the Natural Law Party. I chime in.

"I was raised a lonely Democrat in a strong Northern California Republican stronghold," I say. "I worked idealistically for Robert Kennedy in 1968, when I was a high school senior. Following Kennedy's assassination and my subsequent years as a student at U.C. Berkeley, where I quickly grew disillusioned with the political movements of the day, I disappeared from active politics. I did, however, maintain my desire to improve the lot of society. While at Berkeley, in my spare time, I studied the stress-reducing Transcendental Meditation® technique, became a teacher of it, and lectured widely. I then taught TM® to prisoners in San Quentin Prison, students and teachers in inner-city schools and colleges, and executives and employees in Fortune 100 companies. I even wrote a book about it[3] and did several nationwide book tours. I enjoyed speaking about it. But I also felt passionate about many other issues, such as educational reform, protecting the environment, urban renewal, and crime prevention. I sensed that my political fire, dormant for decades, was rekindling. When I heard about the Natural Law Party, I realized that here was an ideal forum for the issues that were important to me, a forum I did not find in any other political party."[4]

When I finish telling my story, I look around the room. I can see many people nodding in agreement. It must be that my political path has not been unique.

A Glimpse into America's Political Future

Friday, October 10, 9:00 A.M. "What do you think is the future of the Natural Law Party? Is John Hagelin going to run again in 2000?"

I am having breakfast with Kim Kleine of CNN at a coffee shop next door to the network's studio. We spoke often during the 1996 campaign because I called CNN a lot and because Kleine, a reporter for the network's political desk, was always interested and polite and asked good questions. She is now a producer at CNN's *Moneyline*, where she is working harder than ever. CNN has been covering the campaign finance hearings live on Capitol Hill, and Kleine is in charge of the production. Her first love is politics, and over breakfast she wants to hear all about the Natural Law Party.

I tell her that the national political trend is on our side, that the future of the Natural Law Party looks very bright, and that I assume John Hagelin will run for president again in 2000 and be our candidate, if he receives the party's nomination. Our conversation then moves to a larger discussion on the future of politics in America. Kleine wants to know if I have any opinions, which of course I do. This is what I see:

1. A deep-seated backlash mounting against the Republicans and Democrats.
2. A growing grassroots movement among voters away from the two main parties toward a political newcomer.
3. The realization that to get the government we want, the Republicans and Democrats must have genuine competition at the ballot box. For that, we need campaign finance reform to get special interest money out of politics and reforms of election laws to allow independent and third-party candidates equal access to the political mainstream.

4. Our country's best and brightest citizens, until now alienated or disillusioned by public life, taking a more active role in the political process. You don't have to look far for evidence. The Natural Law Party ran more than four hundred candidates during the 1996 campaign, and most of them—doctors, professors, business leaders, homemakers et cetera, of all ages, races, and religions—had never run for office before.

This is one very real, very positive scenario I see emerging everywhere I go in America, I tell Kim Kleine. But I also tell her that for this to happen in our lifetime, there are considerable voter misconceptions yet to overcome and some oppressive laws and institutions yet to change.

3

Are Third Parties a Threat to Democracy?

December 23, 1997   I am sitting across from my cousin Hank at an Italian restaurant in San Francisco. Hank is a physicist on the faculty at the University of California at Berkeley. Ours is a big family dinner, a birthday party for my sister, not a great scene for serious discussion about anything other than perhaps sports and politics. We opt for politics. I tell Hank that I am writing a book on third parties in America, specifically the Natural Law Party. He is surprised and intrigued. He is also blunt. He does not believe in third parties. "Third parties are a threat to our democracy," he says. "I believe in a democracy where you have two strong political parties, each one representing positions clearly distinct from the other. Third parties confuse the issue."

Hank is digging a fork into his dinner salad as he says this, unaware, I am sure, of what is about to hit him. I have come to this meal fresh from six years on the campaign trail and an equally long time learning about the role third parties have played historically in America, the fundamental right of freedom of speech afforded them in the Constitution, the laws that have gradually usurped that right, and the battles waged past and present to reclaim what has been lost. I am about to download on dear Cousin Hank a deluge of facts, figures, citations, and examples to convince him otherwise. Fortunately he is ready to listen, and to his credit, he stays with me for the ninety minutes until the birthday cake has been served and consumed.

This is what I say. I agree with Hank that in a winner-take-all system like ours, there may always be two dominant political parties. There is a difference, however, between two dominant political parties and two dominant political parties that are healthy, vigorous, and independent, that represent two clearly distinct viewpoints—and that are open to new ideas. We don't have that right now, I say. Hank nods in agreement. This is because the Republicans and Democrats exercise a virtual monopoly over the political process. The upside for them is they own the keys to the castle; they control the power. The downside for the country is that they have closed themselves off to the infusion of new ideas; they exist in isolation. With few exceptions, both parties are starting to look and sound much the same, like two sides of the same coin.

Hank is waiting for my punch line. I make the same point I make dozens of times every day to reporters. Traditionally the role of third parties has been to inject new ideas into the political debate. Abolition of slavery, a woman's right to vote, and crucial child labor law reforms all have come not from the two parties in power but from outside the mainstream, from strong third-party movements. Hank's eyes widen. I can see this comes as a bit of a surprise. I add that our democracy was most vital and attracted the largest voter turnout more than a hundred years ago, when there were no laws restricting third-party participation in the political process and, as a result, there were several vibrant smaller parties. Voter turnout was 80 percent. Since then, as new ideas and third parties have increasingly been squeezed out of the fold, voter participation has steadily declined until now less than 50 percent of eligible voters cast ballots in presidential elections and less than 40 percent vote in off-year elections.

So rather than confuse the issue, I say, third parties actually are a source of powerful new ideas that refocus the issues.

I look closely at Hank as I talk. He is family, and I want to be invited to his house in the future, but I can see he's genuinely interested. He asks a question as I load up for another round.

Why don't people care as much about politics? he asks.

Bingo. I say that people don't care because they've heard the same political rhetoric for so many years, and somehow these days it just lacks relevance, it lacks meaning, it lacks life. Substantive new ideas can't make it into the national debate because third parties are basically banned from the political process.

Hank asks for a specific example of ideas that don't make it into the public arena. I cite genetic engineering, and proving the point, Hanks admits that he knows little about it. Billions of dollars from the biotech industry are being poured into technologies that fundamentally alter the genetic blueprint of all of the foods we eat, not only in America but throughout the world. Such foods, purely for the sake of argument, may or may not be safe—scientists are not at all in agreement—but the American people will never know if the foods they are eating have been genetically engineered. Such foods will not be labeled, according to the official policy of the United States Department of Agriculture. I ask Hank, Might the altered content of the foods we eat be of some national consequence that merits more discussion? He nods yes. I say that only a third party, in this case the Natural Law Party, has brought this issue to the American people, not the Democrats or Republicans (who have received millions of dollars from the biotechs). But the Democrats and Republicans have written the ballot access and debate participation rules to keep such new ideas out. In 1998 and 2000 the Natural Law Party—along with the Reform, Libertarian, Green, and U.S. Taxpayer parties—will spend most of their time and resources just to get on the ballot. Little time will be left for serious campaigning. This is very dangerous and very debilitating to democracy.

Hank waves off generalizations. He challenges me for specifics: Give an example of a tough ballot access law. I tell him: Florida. The number of signatures required for a new party to get on the ballot in Florida alone exceeds the signature requirements that a new party would have to collect if it wanted to get on the ballot in all the countries in Europe, as well as Canada, Australia, and New Zealand *combined*. In fact, for each third-party candidate to get on the ballot for statewide office, Florida requires two hundred thousand signatures per candidate. Oh, yes. The Republican and Democratic candidates do not have to collect any signatures to get on the ballot in Florida.

Hank argues that such laws were enacted to keep too many new parties off the ballot. Actually, I tell him, such laws were first passed in the 1930s to keep out the Communist Party, and the laws were toughened again in the late 1960s, after Alabama Governor George Wallace received nearly 13 percent of the vote for president. The laws went through two more rounds of stiffening after independent—and moderate—presidential candidate John Anderson's strong showing in 1980 and Ross Perot's 20 percent vote count in 1992. The problem has never been too many parties or candidates on the ballot. (Mississippi and Vermont, among other states, have open laws for new parties, and neither state suffers from a glut of names on the ballot.) The problem has always been competition for the Republicans and Democrats. Sizable voter turnouts in the past stole support from the two main parties. It scared them so much they changed the rules in state legislatures across the country. It may be true that George Wallace was an extremist who did not deserve to be president. But who makes that decision? In a democracy that sacred choice should be left up to the voters. Who gave the Republicans and Democrats the authority to change the laws and basically relegate all third parties to the nether reaches of the political arena? You won't find it in the U.S. Constitution because it's not there. The answer is not a mystery: No one gave them the authority. The Republicans and Democrats just took it. The problem now in America is not the threat of third parties. The problem is that no new ideas can find their way into the national debate, no new party can make a dent in the political process.

America would have been a different country if today's laws had been in place 140 years ago.

Abraham Lincoln Was a New Party Candidate, but He Certainly Wasn't Fringe

Fact: Abraham Lincoln is widely regarded as one of our greatest, if not the greatest, president in U.S. history.

Fact: Abraham Lincoln was the presidential candidate of a political party, the Republican Party, that was only six years old when he won the 1860 election.

Fact: If the Republican Party in 1854 had to face the same laws to get on the ballot that new parties face today, it's a safe bet that Abraham Lincoln would not have been president in 1860, and the nation and the world might look nothing like they do today.

I know this because now I am talking with Richard Winger, editor of *Ballot Access News* and arguably the nation's leading authority on laws that allow—or, more likely, prevent—new parties access to the ballot. We are in the living room of his home in the Marina district of San Francisco. Books on politics are stacked everywhere—on coffee tables, on bookshelves, on the dining room and kitchen tables. Winger is a national treasure for third parties, a storehouse of information that can steer party leaders and their lawyers through an impossibly complicated web of arcane regulations, financial hoops, and logistical obstacles. Since 1965 Winger has immersed himself in researching ballot access regulations, mastering the study of legal precedents and absorbing the content of countless newspaper clippings about changes in ballot access laws that date back to the 1800s and early 1900s, records he digs up in the U.S. Library of Congress. Winger shows me his tiny office. More books and papers are strewn everywhere; a computer is on the desk. It is from here that he is changing the face of America's elections. By his own estimation he has directly influenced the liberalization of ballot access laws in more than half the states in the country. He has done this through letters, such as the one he wrote in 1994 to the secretary of state of Kansas, in which he claimed that the deadline for submitting petition signatures was too early and subject to a legal action. The secretary of state immediately asked the state legislature to improve the law, and it did. Winger has also testified before Congress and many state legislatures. But his most far-reaching influence is felt through the counsel he gives leaders of third parties.

Winger says the story of the Republican Party is a prime illustration of how restrictive and stagnant our democratic process has become. The Republican Party was founded in July 1854, when there were no restrictions to third parties participating in the political process. Voters responded vigorously to the party's ideas, and on election day, just five months after its formation, the party won more races for governor and sent more representatives to Congress than any other political party. If the Republican Party had to start up today, it is highly unlikely that the party could get off the ground as fast—if at all. More likely, I imagine, the party would merit but a passing mention in *USA Today*'s political roundup column. This is because today new parties are buried in regulations.

I ask Winger to comment.

"Our great-great-grandfathers, if they were American voters, had a greater opportunity to change public policy with their votes than we do today," he says. "It is a paradox that as the proportion of Americans permitted to vote has increased over the past century, the power of those votes has diminished. The rights of voters to organize new political parties, and to vote for candidates of their choice, are weaker today than they were seventy-five years ago."

Winger says the golden age of our system may have been during the 1870s and 1880s, when there was high voter turnout at the polls (an average of more than 80 percent), an absence of gridlock, and a frequent exchange of power between the two major parties. During that same period, he says, there were "many vigorous and powerful third parties," including the farmers' parties, such as the Greenback Party, the Union Labor Party, and the People's Party.

"These groups forced the two major political parties to pass significant antimonopoly legislation as well as important labor legislation," he says. "They also brought new voters into the process. The presence of viable alternatives beyond the two major parties kept voters involved in the democratic process."

What happened? I ask. Why don't we have more viable third parties?

Winger tells me that Democratic and Republican state legislatures have passed laws that have made it exceedingly difficult for third parties to get on the ballot in many, if not most, states. "There has been no grand conspiracy to change the laws all at once," Winger says. "They crept in slowly over time; they didn't emerge overnight."

He gives me a ballot access history lesson:

- Before 1888 there were no ballot access requirements.
- From 1888 to 1931 ballot access laws were generally unobtrusive.
- In 1924 only fifty thousand signatures were required to place a new party's presidential candidate on the ballot in all forty-eight states, a figure that represented 0.15 percent of the number of people who voted in the prior election.
- During the 1930s ballot access laws became far more restrictive, requiring new parties to gather more signatures and file for application earlier and earlier in the campaign year.
- It was not until the 1960s that compliance with ballot access laws became extremely difficult.
- Now, in 1998, if a new party wants to contest all the federal, state, and county partisan offices up for election, it will need to collect more than five million valid signatures. By contrast, the Democratic and Republican parties will not need to submit any signatures to get themselves on the ballot, and their candidates would need to collect less than 20 percent of the third-party totals to place themselves on the primary ballot. In fact, the United States now has the most discriminatory election laws of any democracy in the world. (See table on page 25.) Most democracies treat all parties the same in each election and have minimal ballot access requirements, if at all.

Winger sends me out the door into the brilliant Bay Area sunshine with this final message: "The fact remains that active and vigorous third parties play a vital role in maintaining the health of our two-party system. In order to keep our political system healthy, we must allow people the freedom to vote for the qualified candidate of their choice. Such freedom is not only essential to the health of our government, it is also our right as citizens of the United States."

Signature Requirements for a New Party to Get on the Ballot

COUNTRY	SIGNATURES REQUIRED	DO ALL PARTIES HAVE THE SAME REQUIREMENTS?
United States	**5,141,472 total**	NO
Australia	0	YES
Austria	2,600 total	YES
Belgium	200–400 per candidate*	YES
Canada	25–100 per candidate	YES
Croatia	0	YES
Finland	0	YES
France	0	YES
Germany	200 per candidate	YES‡
Great Britain	0	YES
Greece	0	YES
Ireland	0	YES
Netherlands	190 total	YES
New Zealand	2 per candidate	YES
Norway	0	YES
Poland	75,000 total	YES
Portugal	5,000 total†	YES
Spain	0	YES
Sweden	0	YES
Switzerland	2,500–10,000 total	YES

*Or three signatures from sitting members of parliament.
†This is a one-time-only requirement.
‡If a party has elected one member of parliament, no signatures are required.

Ballot Access Blues

When people ask me what I do with the Natural Law Party, I say that I write press releases, talk on the phone to reporters—and worry about ballot access. No matter what anyone else does in a third party—give stump speeches, raise money, file reports with the Federal Election Commission (FEC), put up posters for events—during the heat of a campaign, everyone is always worrying about ballot access. It's a fact. But Kingsley Brooks is the one person in the Natural Law Party who has to do more than worry. As the chairman he is responsible for actually doing something about it, for getting our hundreds of candidates on the ballot. It's a mammoth, almost military undertaking that requires conviction, persistence, thick skin, the ability to pull money out of a hat, an easy demeanor, and laserlike focus. It's a task that should be dropped in no one person's lap.

For the eighteen months leading up to the 1996 election, you could hardly see the paint on the walls in Brooks's office. He had maps—state, congressional, district, and county maps covered with circles and arrows and dates—graphs, posters, and charts taped and tacked everywhere as well as long lists of the numbers of petition signatures that would be needed to get the party on the ballot in each state.

Now it's February 1998, and Brooks is at it again. Every morning he wakes up to a barrage of ballot access problems—and it's going to be that way until September. When you see what he goes through—and what every other third party goes through—you know that we need to do more to revitalize our democracy than just stop illegal campaign contributions coming from Asia into the White House. We need to stop these outrageously unjust laws that block legitimate political voices from the political debate.

How tough is it for third parties? As Richard Winger said, in most states Republicans and Democrats have written the laws that grant themselves automatic access to the ballot. On the other hand, in 1998 a new party must collect more than five million valid signatures to run a full slate of candidates nationwide.

How tough is it? Those five million-plus valid signatures are spread out among the fifty states. Each state has completely different rules, completely different procedures to get on the ballot, and completely different requirements for each office sought—U.S. president, U.S. Senate and House, state assembly, etc.

How tough is it? Ralph Nader, with a strong base of national support, could get on the ballot in only twenty-two states as the presidential candidate of the Green Party in 1996.

So while Kingsley Brooks should be spending his time building the state parties, recruiting candidates, overseeing campaign itineraries, raising money, and keeping a vigilant watch over all the campaign activities to be sure the election law rules are being followed to the letter, he spends 75 percent of his time and the party's money on signature drives and looking for more money to pay for them.

Ballot access involves four steps: (1) deciphering the requirements; (2) meeting the requirements; (3) preparing for the legal fight after you meet the requirements; and (4) getting geared up to repeat steps one, two, and three in the next election.

1. DECIPHERING THE REQUIREMENTS. To collect signatures you need a crash course in election-speak, and each state, sometimes each county, has its own particular dialect. You'd better become fluent fast, or else it could cost you your place on the ballot. You will be speaking with county clerks and state officers to learn about the rules, and you don't want to lose anything in the translation.

The first big problem you will encounter comes in learning the proper meaning of key words such as "valid," as in "five million valid signatures." What does the word *valid* mean? It depends on what state you're in when you ask. While some states have reasonable rules and require that you only be a registered voter in the state to sign a petition, far too many states have rules obviously rigged to make the job of collecting "valid" signatures next to impossible.

- In West Virginia *valid* means that the signature must be from a registered voter whose signature is determined to be identical to the signature on the voter's original voter registration form (e.g., if the voter accidentally leaves off the middle initial, it is out). Voters must also swear neither to vote in the next primary election nor to sign any other petition, and they will be prosecuted under penalty of law if they do. Not surprisingly, only about one in three signatures is ever approved. To run a full slate of candidates, you're going to need a total of 28,345 valid signatures; that means you must collect nearly 90,000 to get on the ballot. Not only that, the people who are collecting your signatures—the petitioners—must live, vote, and collect signatures only in the district where the candidate lives and must notify all potential signers that they will be violating the law if they sign the petition and then vote in the next primary election. Petitioners in West Virginia reported that a gun-toting deputy from the secretary of state's office stood by as they collected signatures to make sure that they were collecting them properly. Some petitioners were actually jailed for petitioning incorrectly. Republicans and Democrats collect no signatures.

- In Texas *valid* means that the signatures collected must be from registered voters whose legible signatures are accompanied by printed names, street addresses, county names, zip codes, and congressional district numbers; who did not vote in the last primary election or sign any other petition; and who will be prosecuted under penalty of law if they did any of these things and then go ahead and sign your petition. Moreover, before anyone can sign the petition, you need to read that person a long paragraph that describes his or her liability if he or she does sign your petition. Your job is to find 43,963 Texans who meet that description, and you've got only ten weeks to do it. Oh, and don't forget to notarize your petitions. Republicans and Democrats collect no signatures.

- In New York in 1996 *valid* meant that the signatures must be from registered voters whose legible signatures are accompanied by printed names, street addresses, county names, zip codes, congressional district numbers, and precinct and ward numbers. Off the top of your head, do you know your precinct and ward number? Maybe you do, but our experience is that most people don't. If you want all your candidates on the ballot, you have 6 weeks to go and find 608,981 who do.

- In Florida *valid* means that the signatures must be from registered voters who live in the same district in which the candidate is running. Each voter must fill out a separate petition. For all your candidates, the total number of valid signatures—and separate petitions—required: 883,148. (That's a lot of pieces of paper.) Because of this, there has been no third-party candidate for governor on the ballot in Florida since 1920. Republicans and Democrats collect no signatures.

2. MEETING THE REQUIREMENTS. I am going to confess something here. In my six years of working full-time with the Natural Law Party I have never collected a single signature. It's true that I've had my excuses—I direct media campaigns for all our candidates—but they're not the real reason. The real reason is I just can't do it. I simply can't park myself, clipboard in hand, in front of a harried woman as she's coming out of a supermarket carrying several bags of groceries, with two young children in tow, and say, "Excuse me, ma'am, would you please stop right there and listen to what I have to say? Then would you answer my questions about where you live, what political party you belong to, what congressional district you're in, and whether you voted in the last primary? Oh, and please show me your driver's license. And you should also know that in some states if you vote in the next primary election after you sign my petition you could go to jail. Now then, how about signing my petition?"

Maybe I could do it once or twice, but a thousand times a day, for months on end? I could talk all day long to reporters in bad moods before I could do that to a thousand people.

Question: Is collecting ballot access petition signatures a fair or accurate way to measure voter interest?

Answer: No. It's actually a very effective way to bug the heck out of people who are busy. Besides, it's such a waste of time.

In theory, signature gathering is supposed to be a measure of widespread popular support. But truth be told, it's a costly, time-consuming, world-class, migraine headache that just keeps new candidates and new ideas out of the political arena. Signature requirements can be so outlandishly high that few independent or third-party candidates or initiative sponsors could ever imagine mobilizing enough volunteers to do the whole job. So they hire people to do it for them. To our knowledge, every major petition drive for every initiative and candidate—and this includes those rare Republican and Democratic candidates who actually have to collect some signatures for themselves—is conducted in whole or in part by paid signature-gathering companies.

The bottom line is that third parties and independent candidates, usually with scarce resources, are forced to pay anywhere from one to five dollars per signature—valid or invalid. In the few states where Republicans and Democrats have to collect signatures, the signature companies somehow get them to pay five to twelve dollars each. Perhaps that's their just desserts. In every case, though, for third parties and major parties alike, as the deadline comes near, the price goes up.

The Natural Law Party was fortunate to have volunteers willing to collect signatures for next to nothing and also that professional signature gatherers liked our platform so much that they would often carry our petitions for well under the going rate. I imagine this is true as well for some other third parties and independent candidates. Still, getting on the ballot comes down to money—lots of it. That means that basically, money decides what ideas you hear about in the political debate.

The irony of it all is that most Americans sign a petition not so much because they support a particular candidate or issue but because they like the idea of more choices on the ballot. You don't need millions of signatures to prove that.

An argument can be made for setting basic ballot access signature requirements that are the same for all candidates—Republicans and Democrats as well as third parties and independents. Many bills have been introduced in Congress that move in that direction, including Representative Ron Paul's (R-Texas) bill, the Voter Freedom Act of 1997. Unfortunately such a bill, which has been languishing on Capitol Hill in one form or another for more than a decade, has never made it out of committee, much less been voted on.

Once you have your volunteer and for-pay petitioners lined up—

once you know how many troops you have—it's still only the beginning. Now you have to strategize. You have to figure out which candidates to try to get on the ballot. It's also time to be a realist. You can forget about running a full national slate of candidates as the Republicans and Democrats do. There's no way. Signature requirements have grown so outrageous in the past seventy years that no third party has even come close to running a full slate. The fact is, ballot access laws are so skewed in favor of the two main parties that third parties are forced to limit their options severely in order to get at least a few candidates on the ballot.

For example, in Illinois the Natural Law Party had nearly one hundred people—doctors, businesspeople, teachers, retired people, etc.—who wanted to run for office in 1996. But here's the brick wall they ran up against: In Illinois, the land of Lincoln, there is no procedure for a new party to get on the ballot. Instead candidates would have to run as independents and altogether collect a total of 827,055 valid signatures for a full slate. (As a rule, you need to collect twice the required number of signatures to survive any state's validity check.) Let's say you're the third-party leader in Illinois supporting these candidates and you have to decide what to do. The first 25,000 valid signatures will put a presidential candidate on the ballot. Or it will put two congressional candidates on the ballot. Or eight candidates for state assembly. It's a tough decision because while a presidential candidate will bring you the most media attention, local candidates can get closer to the people and are better able to address local concerns. The result: Voters in Illinois are denied the opportunity to hear ideas from more new voices.

Kingsley Brooks has to make these kinds of decisions every day, for all fifty states, for months and months. Moreover, nothing is set in stone. If Texas is going slowly, he has to send more people there. If his petitioners lose several thousand signatures in North Carolina (it happens), he's got to work like crazy to catch up. Utah is a breeze, so he can send two extra petitioners to West Virginia (if they meet the state's requirements). If five petitioners quit in the morning in San Diego—a common occurrence for every signature drive everywhere (and who can blame them?)—Brooks has to be sure his local organizers are training new petitioners in the afternoon. In the midst of all this madness, when a relatively simple decision comes along, such as in Kansas—does he go for putting the whole party on the ballot with 16,418 signatures (due date: June 1) or just the presidential candidate with 5,000 signatures (due date: August 5)?—it can feel like the proverbial straw that broke the camel's back.

3. PREPARING FOR THE LEGAL FIGHT AFTER YOU MEET THE REQUIREMENTS. Once you've turned in your valid signatures exactly as specified, don't expect to be greeted by a welcome wagon. Count on more resistance. Some examples (the names of the states have been left out because of concern that they might make it even more difficult for the Natural Law Party—and other third parties—to get on the ballot in the future. The concern may be real or imagined, but why take the chance?):

- The general counsel for the secretary of state in one state told David Shapiro, the Natural Law Party's national ballot access coordinator, that her boss was not enthusiastic about having another opponent run against him in the November election and she would need the party to provide her with "a very solid argument" to convince him to allow the Natural Law Party on the ballot.
- The secretary of state in a southern state told Patricia Cox, the party's regional coordinator in that area, "We don't care what the rules say; we're not putting you on the ballot."
- The ballot access rules in another state require that a new party fulfill its requirements by motivating people to register at just one of four locations in the state. Many people who tried to register with third parties were told by the county clerks: "We only register Republicans and Democrats in this state." The voters complained to the secretary of state and were told, "We can't control every clerk. They're free to do what they want."
- One attorney general told third-party organizers: "We don't approve of what you're doing. We don't want you here, and we're going to do everything we can to keep

you off the ballot. And if we had our way, we wouldn't allow even Republicans on the ballot."

With rugged determination and a thick skin you can try to overcome such barriers. When that doesn't work, you go to court.

- In South Carolina the state refused to put the Natural Law Party's candidates on the ballot even though the party followed every written state rule to the letter. The party filed suit. Fifteen minutes before the court hearing was scheduled to begin, the state agreed to put the Natural Law Party's candidates on the ballot—and thus avoid embarrassment in court.

- In Georgia the Natural Law Party collected sixty-two thousand signatures and submitted them before the ballot access deadline in early July 1996. However, the party didn't hear back from the state until September 3, when the secretary of state notified the Natural Law Party and the U.S. Taxpayer Party that neither party's candidates would be allowed on the ballot. The state used an obscure court ruling to invalidate the notarized signatures. The "logic" goes something like this: If a notary collects any signatures for a party, the notary must be considered biased and therefore *all* petitions notarized by that notary are invalid. No exceptions. (There is, by the way, a constitutional right to petition that is being ignored here.) It turns out that both the Natural Law Party and the U.S. Taxpayer Party used the same three notaries for most of their signatures. Those notaries innocently collected some signatures themselves. No one in the state government had told either party about this rule, nor is it in the state guidelines for getting on the ballot. The case went to court, but the judge refused to hear the case. It's an election law speed trap that Georgia used in 1996 to keep new parties off the ballot. The Natural Law Party got caught in that one.

- In Alabama, in the middle of the Natural Law Party's ballot access drive, the required number of signatures was increased from twelve to thirty-six thousand, effectively barring the party from the ballot. The move was clearly illegal and was made despite considerable protest, including public hearings at which third-party leaders condemned the action, editorials in the state's major newspapers opposing the action, and letters from citizens that flooded into local newspapers and government offices. The Natural Law Party prepared a lawsuit. On the day the lawyers were to file their suit in Montgomery, the secretary of state's office asked the Natural Law Party to give the state a day to reconsider. The next day the Natural Law Party was on the ballot.

- In Texas the Natural Law Party collected seventy-five thousand signatures. The state accepted a challenge to our petition. (If just one person in Texas challenges a new party's petitions, the state will then evaluate all of the party's signatures.) The state claimed it studied the petitions and concluded that most Natural Law Party signatures were invalid. But the Natural Law Party had copies of voter registration records that made it clear that most signatures were in fact valid. The Natural Law Party headed for court. Just before the case went to trial, the state admitted its records were outdated and it was unsure whether our signatures were, after all, invalid. The Natural Law Party was put on the ballot.

Yes, there may be victories, but consider this sobering thought. Even when a third party wins, it loses. In both Alabama and Texas the Natural Law Party had to pay its own legal expenses, and it lost precious time and resources that should have gone into getting its message out to voters. Yet the state suffered no penalties whatsoever. In the next election the state can turn around and put the Natural Law Party or any other party through the same costly rigamarole without any repercussions.

4. GETTING GEARED UP TO REPEAT STEPS ONE, TWO, AND THREE IN THE NEXT ELECTION. Once you get on the ballot, don't celebrate too long because the work is just starting. Now you have to start fighting for your right to be heard—to participate in the public debates and

gain access to the media. Even more distressing, you have to start gearing up for the next election's ballot drives. You have to do the whole thing, all over again, every two years.

"It's a vicious cycle that just keeps going—and it will keep going—as long as voters continue to elect Republicans and Democrats into office," Brooks says. "The U.S. government fights for democratic reforms in every other country; it's time the government fights for them here as well."

Taking on Institutions That Take on Third Parties

If you are a third-party or independent candidate and you believe that you have been wronged by the Republicans and Democrats, where do you run for help? Nowhere safe. Unfortunately it's a bit like one of those old *Twilight Zone* television shows in which everywhere the guy runs for help to get away from the weird people, all he meets are weird people. Like that, everywhere a frustrated third party looks for help to get away from the Republicans or Democrats, all it finds are the Republicans and Democrats.

For example:

- FEDERAL COMMUNICATIONS COMMISSION. This is the federal government's watchdog organization to oversee the public airwaves. It's supposed to ensure that all qualified political voices—Republicans and Democrats as well as third-party and independent candidates—have equal access to this most important channel of communication.

  THE PROBLEM. Members of the FCC have their jobs courtesy of the Republicans and Democrats. Members are appointed by the president and confirmed by the Senate. Maybe this explains why, in the past sixty years, there has been a steady erosion of third-party access to the airwaves. (And you wonder why you don't hear more from third parties—or even know they exist.)

- FEDERAL ELECTION COMMISSION. This is the watchdog

organization charged with monitoring campaign spending and punishing offenders. It also sets the rules for
sponsoring political debates.

THE PROBLEM. The FEC comprises three Republicans
and three Democrats. Maybe that explains why it
looked the other way when the Commission on Presidential Debates denied two legally qualified third-party
candidates, Ross Perot and John Hagelin, their rightful
place on the stage in the 1996 presidential debates.

- THE COURTS. Judges hear cases that challenge laws that
  keep third parties and independent candidates off the
  ballot and out of debates.

  THE PROBLEM. Judges themselves are appointed by
  Democrats or Republicans, and many judges are wary
  of rewriting the system that has been put in place by
  the two main parties.

So how do you bring about reform? It's very tough, says Mike
Tompkins, the Natural Law Party's vice presidential candidate in
1996, who has witnessed his fair share of court hearings. "America's
system of checks and balances only works when there's healthy
debate. But that's not the case with campaign finance reform, nor
is it the case with opening up the system to new parties. In both
cases the two parties are on the same side of the issue: They don't
want the reforms; they don't want to change."

So where does a third party look to redress its claims? Good luck.
The American system is based on the principle that no interest
should judge its own case. Yet there is no truly independent agency
in place to police Republican and Democratic campaign finance ir-
regularities and to review laws they make that unfairly keep out
third parties.

Still, third parties keep appealing their case. During the 1996 election I sat in on several Natural Law Party attempts to open the doors
to national debate for all legitimate third party voices. Here are a
few instances that give you an idea of what third parties are up
against.

GOING HEAD TO HEAD WITH THE FCC

June 25, 1996, 10:00 A.M. The scene seems right out of a John Grisham novel. A high-level government commission is holding a public hearing to determine the fate of a controversial issue. Surrounded by a phalanx of media types, television lights, and cameras, an august panel of politicians, lobbyists, network executives, and Washington insiders argue in favor of the plan.

Only one man dissents. Yes, on the surface the plan appears to be a good one, the man agrees, but on another, deeper level the fallout will be something else entirely, something very insidious.

Commission members listen to the man politely, almost deferentially, it seems. Maybe too politely, too deferentially.

I'm sitting two rows back in the press section of a room at the Federal Communications Building on M Street in Washington, D.C. The FCC is holding an en banc hearing to decide whether or not you will hear Bill Clinton and Bob Dole speak for free on commercial and public television during the final weeks of the 1996 campaign, a gift, free of charge, from the networks to the Clinton and Dole campaigns and to the American people. The offer is being spearheaded by Rupert Murdoch, chairman of Fox Television, who is concerned that there may be too much money being spent in the presidential campaigns, a fact, he worries, that may be turning off voters. He wants to let the candidates speak for free on his network, a few minutes each night or at least once a week. Give the message straight to the American people. No pesky interviewers, no big bucks shelled out to pay for advertising time. PBS has also joined the Murdoch bandwagon, and other networks are watching closely to see how the whole thing plays out.

The problem for Murdoch, though, is he can't just give away the airtime for free. He has to get permission from the Federal Communications Commission. Otherwise it would, rightfully, be considered a sizable campaign contribution to the Clinton and Dole camps.

The problem for the FCC is that Fox and the other networks want to give the free time only to Clinton and Dole and cut out everyone else. For that, Fox is asking the FCC for an exemption of its sixty-year-old "equal opportunity provision" that guarantees free airtime to any presidential candidate on the ballot in ten states, a provision that would include Ross Perot, John Hagelin, and two or three other candidates. Fox isn't willing to abide by that provision. The network states that if it is forced to open up the offer to any other candidates, it will withdraw the offer.

That's why the FCC is holding a public hearing today. Commissioners want to hear both sides of the issues before making the decision. Twenty panelists are invited to testify in support of the proposal; only one who opposes it is invited. Those who praise it include Murdoch, U.S. Senator Bill Bradley (D-New Jersey, now retired), Senator John McCain (R-Arizona), Frank Farenkhopf (former chairman of the Republican National Committee), and Frank Manet (former chairman of the Democratic National Committee). John Hagelin is the one person invited who dissents.

Hagelin is given three minutes to speak. He acknowledges the spirit of the network offer, but he believes strongly that the FCC must uphold the law. It must protect the rights of the American people to have freedom of choice by ensuring that all legitimate parties have the opportunity to present their message to voters. He tells the FCC that the yearning for third-party ideas is greater than ever.

"Polls show that eighty-five percent of the American people do not believe that the Republicans or the Democrats have the answer to our nation's problems, and a majority favor a third-party alternative," he says. "The democratic process stagnates when it is denied third-party ideas. According to many scholars, ninety percent of the key ideas that have shaped our democracy came from third parties."

Hagelin argues that objective criteria must be used to determine which candidates receive access to the airwaves. "The criterion set by Congress requires a candidate to be on the ballot in ten states. If the FCC wants to restrict access further, then increase the number of states to twenty, thirty, or even forty. Or use the criteria recently suggested by the Federal Elections Commission for the presidential debates, which included ballot access and federal matching funds. But party affiliation, standings in the polls, or subjective assessments made behind closed doors—these must not be the criteria," Hagelin says.

In comments directed toward network executives and leaders of the Commission on Presidential Debates, Hagelin says the decision on who merits airtime must not be left in their hands. "Networks are for-profit entities with their own vested interests. Networks should not be left to determine what ideas should be heard and what ideas should not be heard. The decision about airtime should also not be in the hands of the Presidential Debates Commission. The Debates Commission is not a government agency, but a private committee composed entirely of former Democratic and Republican party chairmen.

"Americans are so turned off to politics that our democracy is in crisis. We now have the lowest voter turnout of any democracy in the world. Many Americans feel that our democracy has been usurped by two parties that are out of ideas and no longer represent the people. To restrict access to the airwaves to Bill Clinton and Bob Dole will simply force-feed Americans more of what they already don't want. Bring Americans back into the political process. Set objective criteria that will open the door to legitimate third parties," Hagelin says.

Three months after the hearing, the FCC announces that Hagelin's request has been denied and grants Fox and the other networks an exemption. But the matter is far from dead. As this book goes to press, Natural Law Party lawyers are preparing suits intended to restore equal opportunity rights to legitimate third-party and independent candidates.

SUING THE COMMISSION ON PRESIDENTIAL DEBATES

October 3, 1996, 9:00 A.M. I'm sitting in the second row, on a hard wooden bench, in the Federal District Court Building in Washington, D.C., waiting to hear the fate of the political aspirations of Ross Perot and John Hagelin this year. Three judges will decide whether or not Perot and Hagelin will join Bill Clinton and Bob Dole in the two nationally televised presidential debates. The first debate is scheduled to be held in three days.

I'm jammed in next to some lawyer types that are scratching notes to themselves in spiral binders. To my left, across the aisle, I see familiar faces: reporters from the *New York Times*, *Washington Post*, *USA Today*, ABC, NBC, CBS, and CNN. These are people I have been talking to for months, hoping to get them to cover the Natural Law Party. Finally they are here, for this. All of us are awaiting the arrival of Judge Laurence H. Silberman, Judge A. Raymond Randolph, and Judge Judith W. Rogers, from the U.S. Court of Appeals for the District of Columbia Circuit.

The stakes are high. You don't get this media turnout for nothing.

The Commission on Presidential Debates (CPD) has already said no to Perot and Hagelin. The commission claims that the two candidates do not have a "reasonable chance of winning the election" and therefore will not be included in the forums. It says this despite the fact that the two men have actually met the difficult, clearly defined, preestablished objective criteria for participation proposed by the Federal Elections Commission.

I marvel at the audacity of the CPD. First, it claims to be an independent, nonpartisan organization even though it is headed by the former chairman of the Republican Party and the former chairman of the Democratic Party. (The commission stakes its claim to a nonpartisan status so that it can receive generous tax-deductible donations from special interests, such as the Phillip Morris Tobacco Company, to put on the debates.) Second, I marvel at the commission's audacity to exclude Ross Perot from the 1996 debates, even though he received close to twenty million votes in the 1992 election. He's not a serious candidate? Twenty million people are a lot of people. Love him or loathe him, do you want the former leaders of the Republican and Democratic parties to decide for you whose ideas are worth listening to?

I've heard the projected downside to opening up the debates to more candidates. It will crowd the platform and keep the major party candidates from a serious discussion of the issues. But the other side of the argument makes more sense. We're talking about setting up only two more chairs on the stage, not ten or one hundred, as some detractors like to disinform us. Besides, during the Republican primaries, there were televised debates with as many as eight candidates. Those debates were far livelier, and the candidates were far more candid and forthcoming, than in those canned affairs where just two candidates rattle on in their standard campaign-speak. The argument also goes that the debates should be for the two candidates with a realistic chance of winning. I hate to break the news, but did Bob Dole have a realistic chance of winning? Did Michael Dukakis? Barry Goldwater? Walter Mondale? Ideas are primary in a democracy, and the Republicans and Democrats do not have a monopoly on ideas.

So why are lawyers for Hagelin and Perot here in court? The following timeline just scratches the surface of the obstacles faced by legitimate third parties to get their presidential candidates into the debates, but it gives you an idea.

- *February 8, 1994.* After years of fact-finding and research, staff members at the Federal Elections Commission propose to the commissioners new regulations that would guarantee equal opportunity for all qualified federal candidates to participate in debates. The report states that any sponsoring agency for a presidential debate would have to adhere to preestablished objective criteria:

  1. The presidential candidate satisfies the eligibility requirements of the Constitution, including being at least thirty-five-years old and a native citizen.
  2. The presidential candidate is on the ballot in enough states to have a mathematical chance of obtaining an electoral college majority.
  3. The presidential candidate is eligible to receive matching funds from the Federal Elections Commission.

A major plus for third parties is that the report also explicitly states that which political party the candidate belongs to as well as all subjective criteria, such as chances of winning and standings in the polls, is not acceptable.

- *November 1995.* The Democratic- and Republican-run Commission on Presidential Debates publishes its criteria for including candidates in the 1996 presidential debates. Republicans and Democrats get automatic invitations while other candidates will be evaluated us-

41

ing three objective criteria (similar to those cited above) along with a long list of subjective criteria.

- *February 1996.* The FEC commissioners reject their own staff's proposal and instead decide to allow the sponsoring agency—in this case the Commission on Presidential Debates—to come up with its own preestablished objective criteria. However, this new ruling makes the CPD's subjective criteria illegal.
- *September 9, 1996.* The Natural Law Party faxes a letter to the executive director of the Commission on Presidential Debates, Janet Evans, informing her that John Hagelin has met all of the commission's objective criteria.
- *September 13, 1996.* Three days before the commission will formally announce its decision on who is in the debates, the word leaks out in Washington, D.C., that Hagelin is definitely out, Perot is probably out. Hagelin files three preemptive suits to stop the commission from applying subjective criteria. The suits are filed with:

  1. The IRS to revoke the Debates Commission's 501(c)(3) nonprofit status for acting in a partisan manner.
  2. The FEC over the Debates Commission's use of illegal and discriminatory subjective criteria.
  3. The federal district court in Washington as an injunction to stop the Debates Commission from using subjective criteria.

- *September 16, 1996.* The Debates Commission gives its official no to Perot and Hagelin. Reform Party lawyers are on the phone immediately with Natural Law Party lawyers to join in the lawsuits.
- *September 27, 1996.* John Hagelin and Ross Perot's case goes to the U.S. District Court for the District of Columbia. The presiding judge, Judge Thomas Hogan, likens the importance of this case to that of the Pentagon Papers in its potential to affect the history of America.

Lawyers for the Debates Commission argue that subjective criteria are a fair and legitimate means to decide participation. Lawyers for Hagelin and Perot argue that such criteria are unfair and discriminatory and are designed to block permanently legitimate third parties from the national debate. Judge Hogan considers the case for a day and then refuses to slap an injunction on the Debates Commission. He says that it's not his decision to make; his hands are tied by the Federal Election Campaign Act, passed by Congress, which requires the FEC to study any election complaint for a minimum of 120 days *before* it can make a judgment. The act states that the courts can intervene only after all administrative review processes have been exhausted. Hello? The election is less than 40 days away. Judge Hogan's decision means that by law, there will be no decision before the election. Who wrote such a law? Republicans and Democrats.

- *September 28, 1996.*   Hagelin's and Perot's lawyers request an immediate appeal, but scheduling difficulties postpone the hearing several days. The issue stays hot in the press, however, and Hagelin gives more interviews over the next three-week period than he has done for months up to that point. He's on the front page of the *Washington Post.* On NPR's *Talk of the Nation*, Hagelin debates Paul Kirk, chairman of the Debates Commission and former head of the Democratic National Committee. Not one person calls in to support the commission's decision. In fact, one caller tells Kirk, "You could wait for the entire two hours of this show and no one will call to say what you did was right." On CNN's *Burden of Proof*, Hagelin debates the former head of the FEC and a lawyer for Bob Dole's campaign. The mood of the people is the same: Open up the debates. We want to hear new ideas; we deserve to hear new ideas; we have the right to hear new ideas.

- *October 3, 1996.*   John Hagelin and Ross Perot's case goes to the U.S. Court of Appeals in Washington, and that's where I am right now. The room is packed. No television cameras are allowed in, so artists for networks, sitting across the aisle to my left, will transmit the mood of the proceedings in colored chalk.

Thomas Newmark, a partner in the St. Louis law firm of Gallup, Johnson, and Newman, is the lead counsel for Hagelin. He owns this case with a passion. He opens his remarks by reminding the judges that both Hagelin and Perot have met the Commission on Presidential Debates' preestablished objective criteria to appear in the debates. He makes the point that such ballot access criteria are a very formidable requirement for a third party and show considerable popular support. "At no time in the history of the United States have more than three third-party candidates met that daunting requirement. It sets the bar very high," he says.

Newmark wants the judges to be bold, to make a strong statement in support of democracy, to break the grip of the two parties. "In all respect, Your Honors, if not now, then when? We have the debates in just a few days. And if we are forced to exhaust administrative remedies that will take at least one hundred twenty days, and that cannot give us relief, then the American people are the losers."

I have sat in on many court battles over third-party access to the election process. These judges seem informed and ask penetrating questions. But in the end it appears that Newmark asks too much in Washington's politically charged climate. The judges too refuse to circumvent the FEC's administrative review process. They also deny Hagelin and Perot any form of justice. I read their decision, which is released to the media a day later, while standing in an empty hallway outside the press offices at the U.S. District Court Building. I have to keep reminding myself that this is the United States of America, the greatest democracy on earth, not some little mock-democratic country, where laws are passed conveniently to serve the lawmakers, not the people.

It turns out, however, to be a hollow victory for the winners. The debates go on with just Clinton and Dole and receive the lowest Nielsen ratings of any debate since 1976. In the San Diego debate one woman in the audience asks Dole, "Where are the third parties? Where is the Reform Party, the Natural Law Party, the Green Party?" Dole's answer is vague, something about being willing to debate anyone at any time.

For Hagelin, the experience proves to be a victory of another sort. He and his cause grab national headlines, and that helps put the Natural Law Party on the map. Polls show that nearly 70 percent of voters want the debates opened up to new voices. People don't like being told whom they can hear and what ideas they can be exposed to.

Like the FCC decision barring third-party presidential candidates from access to the public airwaves, the issue over participation in the presidential debates is far from over. Hagelin and Perot say they are prepared to keep fighting until the FEC alters its policy and mandates that debates include all legitimate candidates who meet the preestablished objective criteria.

Epilogue.   Eighteen months after the three judges funneled John Hagelin and Ross Perot's complaint to the FEC's four-month administrative review process, on March 11, 1998, the FEC decided in favor of the Commission on Presidential Debates. The Natural Law Party and the Reform Party have now appealed the decision. Regarding Hagelin's suit with the Internal Revenue Service, the IRS has told the Natural Law Party that it does not discuss any pending case. Eighteen months later, still no decision.

Third Parties Fight Back

November 7, 1996, 5:00 A.M.   Roll the tape to four days after the 1996 election. My muscles and bones ache. It's been a twenty-month sprint from the start of the Natural Law Party's first ballot drive in

San Diego, California, to the celebration party on election night held at the Mayflower Hotel in Washington, D.C. The telephone jars me out of a deep slumber. It's John Moore, the Natural Law Party's director of ballot and media access. He's calling from Vienna, Austria, and he wants to tell me some good news. He's excited, and I'm disoriented. What's he doing in Europe, and how did he get there so fast?

John Moore is a boon for America's third parties. He has organized more than thirty court cases and other legal fights to gain access to the ballot and candidate debates for third-party and independent candidates since 1992. He was also the driving force behind the lawsuit against the Commission on Presidential Debates on behalf of all third parties. Like all of us, he has been frustrated by the lack of response from government authorities to third-party election and campaign law complaints. So he's in Europe, taking the case to the world court of public opinion.

Moore is leading a delegation representing thirty-three nongovernmental organizations from twenty-seven countries, including the Nonpartisan Committee for Political Debates, which itself represents the Natural Law Party, Reform Party, Libertarian Party, Green Party, and U.S. Taxpayer Party. He is in Vienna to speak at the review meeting of the Organization for Security and Co-operation in Europe (OSCE). The OSCE grew out of the Helsinki Accords that began in the 1970s. Once every two years the OSCE holds a heads of state summit with leaders from fifty-five nations. One month before each summit, the OSCE hosts a review meeting attended by ambassadors and delegates from those fifty-five nations, to evaluate human rights conditions throughout the world and to prepare a resolution for the heads of state to sign. This year that review meeting is in Vienna.

One of the key missions of the OSCE is to promote and ensure fair and open elections throughout the world. In fact, in 1990 in Copenhagen fifty member nations signed the Document of the Copenhagen Meeting on Human Rights, pledging themselves to "respect the right of citizens to seek political or public office, without discrimination," and to "respect the right of individuals, and groups to establish, in full freedom, their own political parties or other political organizations and provide such political parties and organizations with the necessary legal guarantees to enable them to compete with each other on a basis of equal treatment before the law."

The United States signed that document, continuing its long tradition of carrying the torch of democracy throughout the world. One purpose of the OSCE summit will be to consider any violations of the Copenhagen agreement in any country in the world. At these meetings the United States is usually the chief finger pointer. This time, however, it will be on the receiving end.

John Moore is there to talk about unjust campaign and election laws in the United States that clearly violate the Copenhagen Accords. He is invited to make his case to ambassadors and delegates in the grand assembly hall at the Hofburg Palace, headquarters of the OSCE. He distributes thirty pages of documentation, irrefutable evidence of third-party claims.

"The United States enforces fair elections on all the other countries, but at home it has the most discriminatory election practices of any democracy," Moore says. "The U.S. has two sets of rules: one, fair and equal opportunity for Republicans and Democrats, with automatic access to the ballot, the media, and the debates. And two, rules that present huge obstacles to prevent new parties and independent candidates from participating in the election process. This is in complete violation of the very accords that the United States is forcing on the rest of the world."

The hall is silent. Everyone listens carefully.

"While America's once model democracy of openness and fairness has faded, most democracies in the world still have consistent ballot access requirements for every party and candidate in each election. And most countries, including Russia, give all qualified candidates equal airtime and include them in the televised debates.

"Every year the U.S. State Department compiles a detailed report on human rights violations for every country in the world, but it is forbidden from evaluating democratic conditions at home. If the U.S. is to be a world leader, it must at least uphold the same democratic principles that it insists other countries follow. Discriminatory election practices must be ended immediately. Americans and the world community must no longer tolerate bad politics."

The next day U.S. senator Timothy Worth (D-Colorado), who is representing the Clinton administration at the meeting, shows up to proclaim America's commitment to open and fair democracy in the United States and throughout the world. The staff director from the FEC, John Surina, shows up to rebut Moore's testimony and defend U.S. election laws. He agrees that America's election problems are large but says that although there are many problems, it's not the fault of the federal government; it's the fault of the fifty states.

Moore is given a chance to respond the next day. He expresses his appreciation to Senator Worth for voicing America's commitment to open, free, and fair elections, and he says he looks forward to the State Department's annual report evaluating human rights conditions in every country in the world—especially the United States. He then expresses surprise over the FEC's premise that the responsibility for electing the president of the United States and the entire federal government is not the responsibility of the federal government. He asks, "Was the U.S. delegation suggesting that the United States withdraw its membership from the OSCE and have it replaced by fifty states so that they could come and accept responsibility for election law violations?"

John Moore has a high-profile role at the OSCE meetings. In addition to forty-five minutes of testimony, he meets with twenty-one delegations and speaks at five international news conferences.

"What's amazing is that no one knows the extent of our unfair election laws—not U.S. State Department representatives, not members of the Helsinki Commission, and certainly not delegates from the other nations," he says.

Moore found great receptivity, but he also ran head-on into political reality. "More than one ambassador told me, 'There's no way we will ever bring sanctions against the U.S.—or even speak out about these violations—because we are afraid of retaliation.' "

BRINGING THE BATTLE TO THE HOME COURTS

December 14, 1997, 2:00 P.M. It's a year later. John Moore is at it again. This time he's sitting at a long oval conference table in a meeting room at the Sheraton Hotel in Washington, D.C., surrounded by thirty people, some of America's hardest-working and most influential experts on election reform.

The meeting has been called to establish the "Fair Elections Commission"—a new "FEC"—a nonpartisan, nonprofit organization dedicated to working for fair and open elections in America. Moore is the founding chairman of the commission. Also present are Mike Tompkins and Kingsley Brooks of the Natural Law Party; leaders of the Reform, Libertarian, and Green parties; active Republicans and Democrats; and independent political leaders, such as John Anderson, candidate for president in 1980; Rob Ritchie, executive director of the Center for Voting and Democracy; Nancy Ross, a longtime Washington lobbyist for campaign reform; Ernie Robson, another lobbyist who worked on FCC issues; Bill Warner, a D.C. attorney who has represented Democrats in court against the FEC; and Richard Winger.

Moore calls this a "historic moment" when representatives of all political parties will move together for a common cause: to revive the American spirit and open the marketplace of ideas once again.

In his inaugural talk Moore says that decisions are being made that are heavily influenced by special interests. "Only by eliminating the undue influence of money in our elections and opening up the ballot and the public airwaves to new ideas can the public interest be served. Because the way it is today, the whole campaign system is legalized bribery.

"Even with the best intentions, over the course of time, a society can be found drifting from its high democratic ideals," Moore points out. "Sometimes it's necessary to step back and take a fresh look at the direction we may be going. At this moment, who is guarding the public good? America is adrift, and Congress, the Justice Department, and the courts must be held responsible. They have failed to protect our democracy."

Moore says that the first duty of the new commission will be to offer "that independent, nonpartisan mechanism to ensure that the will of the people is expressed through the election process.

"We will immediately begin an integrated campaign to educate elected leaders, the public, and the media about the problems of current election and campaign laws, and we will organize whatever legal action necessary in order to correct these problems, including the following: one, massive legal action to eliminate discriminatory ballot access laws; two, filing antitrust violations against the Republican and Democratic parties; three, challenging the Federal Communications Commission for misuse of the public airwaves in not providing equal access to all parties and all qualified candidates; and four, challenging, and eventually replacing, the Federal Election Commission for not upholding fair election practices in America.

"Together we will restore the high standards of democracy that our nation's founders envisioned," Moore says. "And together we will revitalize America's political process to ensure that government is serving all the people."

The Message

4

Media Tips from the Front Lines

My job was to get the Natural Law Party's message out, whatever the message may have been during a given day or week on the campaign trail: crime, Bosnia, soaring health costs, etc. Here are a few lessons I have learned over the past six years.

All candidates live and die by the press. It doesn't matter if you're a major-party candidate with a thirty-million-dollar war chest in a race for the U.S. Senate or a third-party candidate with (comparatively speaking) pocket change to run for the same seat. The difference is—and it's huge—Republicans and Democrats can use their thirty million dollars to buy their exposure and craft their images any way they see fit. On the other hand, a third party has to rely on the whims of the free media for exposure and credibility. For that you actually have to be newsworthy. You need new ideas and new solutions to costly old problems that just won't go away (spiraling health costs, juvenile gangs, falling test scores). You need substantial local voter support, good people who will stand up for you and your ideas. You need to be persistent. For some reason, every minute of every news day something HUGE always seems to be happening—and that's your competition. So you have to be persistent but not be a pain. Stay with your story, make friends with the press, and in time you'll get covered. Maybe not on this trip through town, but perhaps on the next.

Here's no surprise: Television makes the biggest impact. I always tried to get our candidates on the local evening news—one or two minutes at 6:00 P.M. or 11:00 P.M.—to make a splash. But for real impact on a national level, go for the Larry King show or even an hour on C-SPAN. (Obviously network television is the best, but third parties were shut out of that one. The closest John Hagelin and other third-party presidential candidates came was an interview scheduled with Tim Russert on NBC's *Meet the Press*, but Israel and the Palestinians got into a verbal skirmish, and the interview was scrapped.) The returns from television are immediate. Hagelin was walking down a side street in the town of Westminster, Pennsylvania, when a woman in her thirties, with her two children at her side, walked up to him with a stunned look on her face. "I can't believe that you're campaigning in Westminster," she said. "I've been following you on C-SPAN and just love what you have to say." The morning after he appeared on *Larry King Live!* in Atlanta in late October, Hagelin got off a plane at Dulles Airport outside Washington, D.C., and started heading for baggage claim. A man in a suit walked up to him and said, "Good job last night; I'm going to vote for you." There were many other knowing nods as he made his way down the hall.

Newspaper articles are okay, depending on their placement, and they do have a long shelf life; you can make copies and send them to members of the media in other cities. The producer says, "Oh, the *Los Angeles Times* thought this was big news, so maybe it should be news here in Peoria. Let's have this guy on the show." But as far as content goes, newspapers are at the bottom. Space limitations. You do a two-hour interview, you spill your guts, and all that shows up the next day are three or four sentences of your words, a quote from someone who says you make sense, a quote from someone who says you don't, and maybe a few lines taken from an old newspaper article the reporter lifted off the Internet or out of the paper's archives.

Radio is better, although early-morning drive time radio is a zoo. Chatter and banter, and nothing serious. ("What color socks does a Natural Law Party candidate wear? Our survey shows Republican candidates wear gray socks, Democrats wear blue.") Who wants politics at 6:52 A.M. anyway? The best shows are the issue-driven hour-long phone-in talk shows. With a good host and an informed audience you can really get some substantive ideas out. A great example is the *Ronn Owens Show* on KGO in San Francisco. Of course, my opinion has been colored by the fact that Owens, the most listened-to talk show host in California, liked John Hagelin a lot and had him on his show several times during the 1996 campaign. ("I'm going to have Bill Clinton and Bob Dole on my show because I have to. I'm going to have John Hagelin back on my show because I want to," Owens said over the air.)

The Internet is great—and getting better. The Natural Law Party's Web page (www.natural-law.org) received hundreds of thousands of hits a week toward the end of the campaign; Hagelin was interviewed several times live by *Time* on-line, CBS on-line, and ABC on-line; and we received a flood of E-mail from supporters. I'm sure other third parties had similar experiences.

But ultimately nothing beats one-on-one, particularly if you want to build a strong grassroots organization and not just be a vaporous, media-driven phenomenon. For that you need to get out of the broadcast booth and onto the road. You need to meet people face-to-face to inspire them to become candidates, to collect petition signatures (that horrendous task), and to take responsibility for the party in their area. We would set up lunches or dinners for Hagelin or Tompkins with a handful of local movers and shakers, hold a living room talk for fifteen or twenty guests, or rent a meeting hall or a ballroom in a hotel for hundreds of people. That's where I am right now, at the Doubletree Inn in Houston.

5

"The Best-Kept Secret in America"

August 30, 1996, 8:15 P.M. The people John Hagelin is speaking to tonight in Houston are the types of people he believes are his voter base: everyone—conservatives, liberals, old, young, employed, unemployed. He says that the ideas he is proposing are ideas that transcend demographics and party affiliation and appeal to all. "Commonsense ideas" he calls them, ideas that you don't need to be a quantum physicist to understand.

Hagelin is talking tonight about prevention, shifting the focus of government from crisis management to preventing problems before they arise. "An intelligent and cost-saving solution to runaway spending," he says. He talks about conflict-free politics: "Yes, politics is about debate, but the level of negativity and partisanship in government often puts Republican and Democratic party interests above national interests. Voters don't like it, and the whole country suffers." He talks about moving our public policies away from supporting many of the highly toxic approaches of modern medicine, fossil fuel energy sources, and high chemical input agriculture to programs that are scientifically proven and in accord with natural law, supporting, for example, prevention-oriented natural medicine; renewable energy sources, such as wind and solar; and organic agriculture. He talks about harnessing America's most precious resource—the creativity and intelligence of its 260 million citizens—"to promote a healthier, more forward-looking, more self-governing nation."

Ten years ago Hagelin the scientist would probably have been talking to an audience of physicists and graduate students. Now Hagelin the presidential candidate is speaking to an audience of educators, doctors, scientists, environmentalists, students, homemakers, retired people, and community leaders.

I'm in the third row, and I look around the room. There's no one apathetic in this group. They all are involved-in-the-community types. To my right is Brynne Sissom, a thirty-something former aide to a Republican Texas state legislator. Sissom will head off to Albania as a Peace Corps worker immediately after the election. In the meantime she has mobilized an army of signature gatherers to put the Natural Law Party on the Texas ballot—no small feat since Texas has some of the most difficult laws for third parties. Sissom has described herself as a "political seeker." The room is filled with political seekers, America is filled with them. It doesn't matter what their education, their religion, or which end of the political spectrum they call home; these are people who are looking for depth, for something real in politics, not something slick, prepackaged, and spin-doctored, like what is being offered up for popular consumption by the two main parties.

Hagelin is a big, strong presence at the podium. He's about six feet tall, weighs 190 pounds, with thinning, sandy-colored hair (almost bald on the top), clear blue eyes, and a wide open oval face. The camera loves him, as more than one producer has told me.

Hagelin is happy with the way things are shaping up for his party, including the massive "sea change" in the nation's attitude toward things natural and the enthusiastic letters and E-mail the Natural Law Party receives after a candidate gets on TV or the radio. (Don't think that that doesn't make a huge difference to third-party volunteers because it does. You work hard for something, and when your message goes out and you hear back from a lot of very good people—from both ends of the political spectrum—it's fuel for the soul.)

Hagelin feels the support. "Here's a statistic which bodes well for the Natural Law Party's success," he is saying. "There are now seventy million voters who are what one Stanford researcher calls cultural creatives. These are people who are concerned about the environment, responsible investing, women's rights, natural foods, animal rights—the kinds of concerns that are in harmony with natural law. That's why we find that wherever we speak, the programs that we promote and the ideas that we espouse are naturally resonating with people.

"The Natural Law Party researches and supports programs and policies that work. We're building a platform that is so comprehensive, so scientifically sound, so defensible, and so obviously right that most Americans can't help but support it. And we're doing this with programs that are more effective, more humane, more cost-effective, and far more fair and just than programs currently in use," he says.

While it's true that third parties didn't get anywhere near the media attention they deserved, I did enjoy watching hard-bitten political reporters interview John Hagelin or Mike Tompkins.

I remember back to December 1995, when veteran CNN political reporter Marc Watts spent a day with Hagelin and Tompkins at the party's headquarters in Fairfield, Iowa. Watts had been on the campaign trail for months covering Bill Clinton and the Republican front-runners. He had waded through the crowds, listened to endless stump speeches, and heard straight from the people what they were saying about their government. After one day of listening to Hagelin and Tompkins, he was shocked.

"You are the best-kept secret in the country!" Watts told me. "What you're saying is what the American people want to hear. If you keep saying what you are saying and doing what you are doing, you are going to succeed; it's just a matter of time, but you are going to succeed."

I remember another interview late in the campaign that Hagelin had with Ronnie Bennett, a CBS on-line reporter, in her office in Manhattan. Bennett told me later that in her thirty years in the business she had never talked with any presidential candidate who gave such deep and thoughtful answers. She said that most reporters are used to fifteen-second sound bites.

The fact is, there are no fifteen-second sound bites to describe the Natural Law Party. Believe me, I kept trying to come up with one, because reporters usually give press secretaries about that long to pitch a story—that is, if they're not on deadline. Then it's considerably less.

Right or wrong, when you think Democrats, you think more government. Republicans, less government. Libertarians, no government. Reform Party, balanced budget and campaign finance reform. Greens, green. But the Natural Law Party doesn't fit a pigeonhole. You could say, natural medicine, you could say developing consciousness, you could say renewable energy, you could say campaign reform, and you'd be partially right, but that doesn't get the big picture.

The best answer, which requires another answer, is "life in accord with natural law."

What Is Natural Law?

What is natural law, and what does it have to do with a political party? This is what I tell reporters: The law of gravity is a good example of a law of nature. If you hold up a baseball and let it go, the ball drops. If you do it a thousand times (anywhere on earth), it will drop a thousand times. The earth keeps spinning on its axis and orbiting the sun, and the sun keeps moving through our galaxy, and our galaxy keeps moving through its cluster of galaxies in the same way, day after day, year after year, aeon after aeon—all according to laws of nature. Everywhere you look—with a microscope, telescope, or the naked eye—you see natural law at work. The hormone cortisol is secreted into your bloodstream to wake you up every morning as the sun rises in the east following laws of nature. Billions of synapses in your brain fire in concert so you can brush your teeth or solve a math problem, and they do so following laws of nature. These things don't happen by chance. Natural law nourishes the seed in the soil, transforms sunlight in chlorophyll, produces energy out of wind. Natural law creates, maintains, and evolves millions of different species on earth.

This is what Hagelin the physicist tells the audience in Houston: "Over the last several centuries modern science has identified myriad laws of nature governing behavior at all levels of the physical universe: on subatomic, atomic, molecular, biological, geological, astrophysical, and cosmological scales. Nothing happens that is not the direct result of natural law, from the motion of an electron to the evolution of life to the functioning of entire societies."

Hagelin adds that we rely on natural law for everything: "Everything we accomplish is achieved by applying natural laws. We have the electric light courtesy of technologies that apply natural law, a man walked on the moon and a rover scoured the surface of Mars because of technologies that harness natural law, and we treat our sick with medicines that utilize laws of nature."

The problem is that technologies can be used for good or for bad. For example, wind and solar energy technologies versus nuclear technologies. A bigger problem is that industry is churning out technologies so fast that government regulators can't keep up—even if they were so equipped or so inclined. With so much money invested in the research and development of new technologies, these technologies often get shoved into the marketplace before they are adequately tested for safety. To protect their investments, these industries also pour megabucks into the treasure chests of both the Republican and Democratic parties.

"That means our leaders, whom we entrust with the responsibility to look out for our common good, instead all too often capitulate to the short-term, bottom-line corporate interests," Hagelin says.

In response, Hagelin proposes an almost shockingly simple formula for assessing new technologies for public policy: Independent scientific research should demonstrate that these technologies actually work, and they are safe, that they are in harmony with natural law. He says this formula is not a step backward into some more primitive epoch but rather is based on a great leap forward in our scientific understanding of how nature, including the human body and the environment, functions.

John Hagelin is an intelligent man, an articulate and compelling speaker, and he has organized a litany of the hazardous side effects of modern life into a very powerful presentation. As I sit here listening to him speak, I realize that much of what he is saying millions of Americans already know. What is significant, however, is that for the first time a national political platform is being created that will give these toxic problems, and their solutions, a powerful voice. The influence of that voice will surely grow stronger as more people are educated about these issues and wake up to their primary importance.

Hagelin pauses for a moment. There are one or two questions; someone wants a clarification of the Natural Law Party's stand on nuclear energy (against) and tax reform (yes to sweeping changes). Hagelin looks at his watch, takes a drink of water, and says that if no one minds, he would like to take the discussion of natural law and government one step farther and talk more about recent discoveries in physics and the insights they can provide in improving the administration of society.

No one minds.

Hagelin paints a picture of a universe structured in layers of existence, from tiny to huge, from microscopic to macroscopic, from the subatomic world of elementary particles to the large-scale structure of stars, galaxies, and the universe. He says that not only do these levels have vastly different time and distance scales, but each level also has its own laws.

I look around for glazed eyes but see none. This is definitely not a "bash your opponent" stump speech. Hagelin is trying to educate people.

He describes the building blocks of the universe, the four fundamental forces at the basis of all matter, all energy, you, me—of everything in nature. These forces are electromagnetism, the strong interaction, the weak interaction, and gravity. At deeper levels of nature, such as the atomic or subatomic levels, there are "unparalleled levels of energy and dynamism." At the deepest level of nature the energy is so enormous that the energy density in a single cubic centimeter of empty space exceeds, by several orders of magnitude, the entire mass energy of the visible universe.

Hagelin finishes painting his picture of nature, describing the recent discovery of completely unified field theories: "a single, universal field of nature's intelligence at the basis of all forms and phenomena in the universe—the fountainhead of all natural laws."[1]

But what does this have to do with public policy, with government? I can imagine people asking themselves. Hagelin senses it too. He makes the connection between the purely abstract and the very concrete. He says that this most modern scientific understanding of how nature functions reveals three things relevant to government.

First, it provides a cutting edge, awe-inspiring picture of the all-powerful, all-pervasive nature of nature and gives added impetus to why it is that we, in our personal lives and in public policy, must work *with* nature, not against it, to fulfill our aspirations.

Second, it provides the best example anywhere of a good government. "Look through a microscope and look through a telescope, and see how perfectly nature administers the universe. Look at a typical forest ecosystem. There are millions of diverse plant, animal, insect, and microbial species coexisting in a perfectly organized, intricate web of mutual interdependence. In this nourishing forest habitat, species emerge, thrive, reproduce, and evolve in magnificent concert with one another.

"Now, consider that each time we utilize a natural law—draw in a breath, digest a meal, turn on a light, compute a math problem—we are putting nature to work for us. We are harnessing the intelligence of natural law that functions everywhere around us and within us. We are, in effect, employing ourselves with the same government of nature that administers the vast and complex universe, with billions of galaxies and millions of species on earth.

"To mirror the efficiency and effectiveness of the government of nature [Hagelin likes this term because it captures the whole of nature, not just an isolated plant here, a mountain there, or a star above], our government must promote policies and technologies that are in accord with natural law, that take maximum advantage of the organizing power of nature to promote our health, grow our food, fuel our cities, and enlighten our minds—without hazardous side effects.

"But there's still a sizable problem," he says. "Government can't make people eat right or behave in a way that is naturally law-abiding. And educating people with reams of information about what is good or bad often isn't enough. Witness the countless posters hanging up in innumerable high school cafeterias in an effort to wake up students to the very real, very deadly dangers of cigarette smoking and alcohol and drug abuse. Studies indicate that the impact of such campaigns has been marginal, at best."

This brings Hagelin to his third point. We have to do something to wake people up. "You can tell people what is right, but they won't behave differently unless they want to, unless there has been a change in their attitude. We need to educate people in such a way that they *want* to live—and *do* live—*spontaneously* in accord with natural law, so they don't make themselves sick and suffer, so they have the good health, natural creativity, and intelligence they need to fulfill their own desires. Education must do more than inform; it must enlighten as well."

Hagelin says we don't have to look far to discover how to promote this change in attitude, this change in consciousness. He points out that the laws of nature that govern our environment and run the universe are the same laws that function within each of us, that pervade our physiology and govern our cognitive functioning.

"The human physiology and psychology are a rich laboratory of natural law. There are modern educational programs that provide direct experience of, and develop intimate familiarity with, the laws of nature through the inner exploration of consciousness [see chapter 12, Science, Consciousness, and Public Policy].

"Research shows that as a result of using these educational programs, people act spontaneously in ways that are more in harmony with natural law; they automatically shy away from actions that damage the body, that undermine personal relationships, or that damage the environment. These powerful programs get to the root cause of all problems of the nation: the widespread violation of natural law and the tragic underutilization of our precious human resource. The Natural Law Party supports any scientifically proven program that promotes life in accord with natural law and the development of consciousness—full human potential."

I like to watch people's reactions at these events. I try to figure out who is still the skeptic and who is the eager receiver when the talk is done. This time, when John Hagelin finishes, nobody moves. Everyone has been through a lot tonight, mentally a bit depleted from exercising long-dormant brain cells to follow the physics, emotionally drained from expressing outrage at government impotence to halt dangerous technologies, and deeply recharged from the clear scientific understanding that each one of us enjoys an immutable connection to the deepest realms of nature.

I cannot speak for anyone else, obviously, but something remarkable happened that night that hadn't happened to me before on the campaign trail, and I remember it clearly today. It was a familiar feeling, though; I had experienced it in the silence of meditation, in moments of inspired writing, and in special times spent with my family. For some reason Hagelin's talk that night—it could have been the content, delivery, audience, coincidence, or all the above—provided me with a moment of transcendence, a window of calm and tranquillity. Sitting there afterward, reflecting on the considerable problems confronting our nation, I realized again, somehow more profoundly than before, that we don't have to go it alone. We don't have to fabricate from scratch an elusive miracle drug in the hope that it will cure everything that ails us or manipulate the genetic code of an aeons-old plant form to keep the insects away so we can feed the hungry masses. We have an ally on our path to a healthy, harmonious, richly diverse, prospering society (not an enemy), and that ally is nature, which is bigger than we are, which is more powerful than we are, which is all of us.

That is the fundamental contribution of the Natural Law Party to politics in America. It doesn't fit nicely on the liberal-conservative axis; instead it is, I believe, what people are looking for in the stewardship of our country.

6

Preparing for the
Vice Presidential Debate

Mike Tompkins is talking and pacing, talking and pacing. He stops to think, picks a few grapes out of a bowl, and then resumes his talking and pacing. He paces across the kitchen where I am sitting at a breakfast table. Out the door into the dining room. Across to the living room, and back around through a swinging door into the kitchen. Tompkins has to leave the house in less than twenty minutes for the third-party vice presidential debate being held at American University in Washington, D.C., and he is doing some last-minute fine-tuning of his answers. His target response: sixty seconds, informative, punchy, to the point.

I throw out a question; the second hand sweeps across my watch. Too long, I say when he goes past the minute mark; you have another five seconds, I say when he stops short.

This is Tompkins's first foray into nationally televised (C-SPAN) debates. Hagelin has already done five or six on CNN and C-SPAN. Tompkins, who has spent much of the past four years on the road building the party, recruiting candidates, speaking on college campuses, and doing lots and lots of local media interviews, is pumped. He'll be debating Jo Jorgenson of the Libertarian Party and Herb Titus of the U.S. Taxpayers Party. The event is sponsored by the

American University Student Union and will be moderated by Allan Lichtman, American University professor of history and one of the most respected political analysts in the country.

Health care, I say to Tompkins. He replies: "We boast that we have the world's best health care system, certainly the most costly, but our health statistics are among the worst in the developed world. Fifty percent or more of our disease is preventable, self-inflicted by our own unhealthy behaviors. We spend only one percent of our health care dollars on prevention, and yet we are mystified that there has been a thirty-nine percent increase in infectious diseases in recent years. We can incorporate right now cost-effective, natural, prevention-oriented health care programs shown by extensive scientific research to prevent disease and promote health and thereby reduce health care costs by more than fifty percent."

Special interests: "Partisan politics and special interests have taken priority over the good of the nation. Our approach is an 'all-party government,' bringing together the best ideas, programs, and leaders from all political parties and the private sector to solve and prevent problems. We also support essential campaign finance reform to eliminate special interest control of government. In addition, we advocate an end to negative campaigning, which demeans the political process and relegates important social and economic issues to the back burner."

Food and agriculture: "Our agriculture is a great triumph, we can feed the world, but for how long and at what cost? In this century half our topsoils have blown away in the winds of our own neglect, and now agrochemicals are poisoning our water, polluting our foods, sterilizing our soils, and spawning a greater demand for genetically engineered seeds, the consequences of which on the global food supply are entirely unknown and very likely catastrophic. The Natural Law Party supports natural, organic agricultural practices proven to produce healthy, high-quality food grown without hazardous chemical fertilizers and pesticides. At the same time these practices preserve the environment for future generations."

Energy and the environment: "Every year we load a ton—a ton—of hazardous waste onto the earth for every man, woman, and child in our country. We're running out of places to put it, no one wants it, so we export it to other, less fortunate lands, as we export the chemical pesticides we have outlawed here in our own country. We need to put into place renewable energy production and energy conservation practices that are shown to be environmentally clean and cost-effective."

Education: "We Americans say that we are a country of education; everyone in America can get an education, grow up, and become vice president. Right? Yes, spending on education has jumped one hundred and twenty-six percent in the last ten years, but test scores have plummeted. Several years ago we actually downgraded the SAT scale, establishing a lower mean, because our children's scores had been consistently declining over the years. We can improve education through programs that develop the inner creative genius of the student. Research shows that these programs increase IQ, improve learning ability and moral reasoning, and decrease substance abuse."

Foreign policy: "The U.S. is the largest arms dealer in the world. We confront our own weapons in Somalia, Bosnia, Desert Storm. We are sowing the seeds of resentment and hate all around the world. No wonder we are a principal target of terrorism. We must shift our foreign policy away from the export of weapons toward a more life-supporting policy based on the export of U.S. know-how in business and entrepreneurship, education, and agricultural and environmental technologies. Then we will make friends in the world, not enemies."

Tompkins stops pacing and sits down at the table. We have to leave in just a few minutes. He reviews his opening three-minute speech, reading notes from index cards. You'd better memorize that, I say, pointing to the words on the cards. You may not be able to have notes. You'll be stuck. (No truer words were spoken during the campaign.) But there's no time to spare. Tompkins has just come in to Washington from three full days of campaigning in the Midwest and hasn't had a moment to pull everything together.

The debate is being held in a large chapel on campus. Ten minutes before airtime the rows are filled with several hundred students, camera crews, and some print journalists. There's a photo shoot of the three VP candidates at two minutes before eight, and then everyone takes his place behind the podiums. Tompkins is doing a last-second scan of the index cards. No more than fifteen seconds before Professor Lichtman is to give his welcome comments, a student organizer slides across the stage and asks Tompkins to put his cards away. He hesitates for a split second, then puts them on a shelf inside the podium and casts a quick smile in my direction. The television cameras roll, and he doesn't forget a thing.

Here is how Mike Tompkins opens the debate: "I stand to represent Dr. John Hagelin and the hundreds of candidates of the Natural Law Party who are on the ballot in forty-eight states and also here in the District of Columbia. One question we are often asked is, Why do you call it the Natural Law Party? Well, before the Republicans, before the Democrats, before all the other political parties there was natural law. One of the founders of our country, John Adams, called natural law 'the Great Legislator of the Universe.' And in the Declaration of Independence, Thomas Jefferson, in the very beginning of the document, derived our very existence as a country and also all our rights from what he called the 'laws of nature.'

"So what is natural law? It is the order, the intelligence in the universe. It governs everything, from our bodies to the larger world environment. Our founders believed that if we could gain knowledge of natural law, of how it operates both inside us and all around us, then we would grow as individuals and also as a nation. In fact, it's when we violate the laws of nature that we create our problems. But when we are able to live in accord with natural law, then we meet with success and fulfillment in life.

"Let me give an example. In health care, if I don't look after my body, if I don't eat properly, don't rest properly, if I abuse alcohol and drugs, I compromise my immune system, and I fall sick. And in fact, more than fifty percent of illness in this country results from such violations of natural law. Well, if we can learn how to prevent illness simply by keeping our immune system strong, then we have the solution to many of the problems of our health care system. To give people the knowledge and incentive to do this is to practice preventive government.

"Government's approach to solving problems has always been superficial. It's been an outside-in approach. Look at crime. The outside-in approach to reducing crime is all about prisons, gun control, capital punishment, mandatory sentencing. It's about how to impose law on ourselves from outside. But what about preventing crime by connecting people to the source of law inside themselves—natural law? People become spontaneously law-abiding. Again, look at our health care system. The outside-in approach is all about the financing and delivery of disease care services. The inside-out approach emphasizes prevention: strengthening the immune system from within and empowering people to take better care of their own health. This is something everyone can support, both liberals and conservatives alike: liberals because prevention improves the health of the people; conservatives because it does that and it saves money. Solving problems at their bases through preventive solutions satisfies everyone.

"The Natural Law Party has built a broad platform of many scientifically proven solutions, a platform where the whole of America can stand together comfortably and share a strong, common political voice. You will see that yes, we are for preventive medicine and organic agriculture and renewable energy and energy conservation and consciousness-based education and preventive criminal justice and more socially responsible business and industry and sound economic policy and political reform and all of that.

"But more important, we are for government that works from the inside out, for awakening ourselves to our true identity as Americans rooted in natural law. In this way we become self-governing individuals and a self-governing society living spontaneously in accord with natural law. The result will be a healthier, more prosperous, more richly diverse, and yet more harmonious nation for us all. This is the commitment of the Natural Law Party."

The Issues

7

Genetically Engineered Foods: The Hazards of Tinkering with Natural Law

Technically speaking, you cannot really violate a law of nature. You cannot exceed the speed of light, and for every action there will always be an equal and opposite reaction, no matter what. You can, however, run afoul of natural law and create problems for yourself and others. You can eat things that make you sick, put chemicals in the soil that make it barren, release substances into the air that kill off life. Such may be the case with genetic engineering, which, according to a growing number of credentialed scientists, represents a pervasive and highly dangerous tinkering with natural law that could jeopardize the health of the whole earth. Surprisingly few people really know much about the danger.

In the 1950s nuclear energy was billed as the answer to all our energy needs, as well as a miraculous new technology that would forever transform the way we live. Edward Teller, one of the fathers of the H-bomb, enthusiastically promoted the idea of "geological engineering"—using nuclear explosions to restructure "safely" the geography of different aspects of the earth's surface. His first proposal: Carve a huge harbor out of the shoreline of Alaska above the Arctic Circle. Unbelievable as it may seem today, it was only an effort by a group of scientists from the University of Alaska and the

Eskimos who would be displaced that captured the attention of the American people, and the project was halted at the eleventh hour because of intense public pressure. For decades the nuclear power industry claimed that nuclear energy was safe, clean, and inexpensive and could provide all the energy requirements of a rapidly growing society. What we didn't discover until much later was that there are huge life-threatening pollution and waste problems associated with nuclear technology. Now, because of these problems, no new nuclear power plants are under construction in the country and nuclear power is no longer considered a viable solution to America's future energy needs.

It is true that society marches ahead on technological advancements. It certainly can be argued that far more technologies have proven beneficial to society than not. But it is those few exceptions, those highly hyped technologies, that turn out to endanger life seriously—nuclear energy, DDT, and such "miracle" drugs as thalidomide, to name a few—that teach us a valuable lesson. We have not been vigilant enough to investigate promotions that oversell potential benefits and that ignore, or cover up, very real hazards.

Genetic engineering—technologies that alter the genetic code, the very building blocks of an organism—is one such case. Proponents claim it can produce more abundant crops, create more nutritious foods, eradicate certain diseases, and thereby improve the quality of human life on earth. Not everyone agrees. Many scientists claim it's a technology that presents serious health and environmental risks,[1] and many consumers feel the same concern. In response to pressure from such consumers, the European Union has passed a law requiring all genetically engineered foods for sale in member nations to be clearly labeled "genetically engineered." Austria and Luxembourg have even placed an outright ban on genetically modified corn. Many Japanese food retailers have told U.S. farmers to send over only genetically natural soybeans.

What's the story in the United States? We have no such laws, no such restrictions, no such precautions. In fact, some state governments have passed laws *forbidding* such labeling. Experts estimate that since the approval of the first genetically engineered food by the FDA in 1994, 60 to 70 percent of the processed foods now available in the U.S. market contain genetically engineered ingredients, such as high-fructose corn syrup, soy-based products, and genetically engineered versions of virtually every fruit, vegetable, grain, and legume.* Experts predict a flood of these man-made species will inundate our food supply in the next few years.

How do we know that genetically engineered (GE) foods are safe? Because the Food and Drug Administration says so. How does the FDA know? In almost every case, it knows only because it asked the biotech industries, the corporations that, for a hefty profit, manufacture these foods. It's true. An editorial in the *New England Journal of Medicine* pointed out that the testing of genetically engineered substances at present is largely voluntary; more than 90 percent of genetically engineered foods are not required to be tested before they enter the market.[2] Consequently, the details of the testing programs are left primarily in the hands of the developers—namely, the biotech industry. We've left the fox guarding the chickens.

Speaking as a press secretary, I am astounded that there is no burning debate in the United States, as there is in other countries, over the intrusion of GE foods onto our grocery store shelves. It's a modern-day miracle of information management, or spin-doctoring, by the biotech industry. Instead of healthy, heated public debate, in which both sides air their differences, there is no public discussion at all. The biotech industry makes the food, the FDA virtually rubber-stamps its approval, and we buy it unknowingly, unlabeled, off our grocery shelves. Whatever controversy does remain is being fought in the organic market, where biotech interests are trying to penetrate that small but fast-growing and highly lucrative market, but where they are meeting considerable resistance from the natural foods industry.

---

*Genetically engineered foods approved by the FDA(•) or awaiting approval or under development: abalone•, alfalfa, apples, asparagus, barley, beets, broccoli, canola•, carrots, catfish•, cauliflower, cheesemaking enzymes (chymosin)•, chestnuts, chicory, corn•, cotton (cottonseed oil)•, cucumbers, flaxseed, grapes, kiwifruit, lettuce, melons, papayas, peanuts, pepper, potatoes•, prawns•, raspberries, rice, salmon•, soybeans•, squash, strawberries, sugarcane, sunflowers, sweet potatoes, tomatoes•, walnuts, watermelons, wheat.

At first glance, the subject of genetically engineered foods can appear too complicated to grasp and perhaps is best left in the hands of the experts. But the Natural Law Party strongly disagrees. Genetic engineering is not too complicated, nor should it be left in the hands of the "experts."

Taking a Stand against Genetic Engineering

November 7, 1994. My introduction to genetic engineering came from John Fagan, a Cornell-trained molecular biologist, who had spent twenty years conducting research on gene regulation and the molecular mechanisms of carcinogenesis, which is basically the role genes play in cancer. Fagan had spent seven years at the National Cancer Institute and been the recipient in the past seven years of more than $2.5 million in government grant money to conduct his research.

Fagan was calling me for help with a press conference. He was about to return $614,000 awarded him by the National Institutes of Health and withdraw grant proposals worth another $1.25 million. The reason for this surprising—and, it turned out, unprecedented—decision was his growing concern about how his own research findings could be used by other scientists for potentially dangerous genetic engineering applications. More than that, he had become increasingly disenchanted with the whole direction in which biomedical research was going—in particular, the misapplication and overpromotion of genetic engineering.

Fagan said he wanted to hold a press conference "to set the record straight. I want to point out the serious risks that are associated with genetic engineering, in biomedical research as well as in agriculture and in the environment."

At first it was all new to me; in fact, it was all pretty indecipherable. But Fagan was a good teacher, and it didn't take me long to grasp both sides of the issue. Fagan is a quiet and humble type, but he was eager to use this opportunity—maybe a once-in-a-lifetime chance—to bring widespread public attention to an issue that had little or none.

Our press conference, unlike the extravaganzas I have seen put on by the biotechs, was a shoestring operation. Overnight we wrote up a press release and faxed it out to hundreds of media outlets in Washington. That was three days before Fagan's news conference was scheduled to be held at the Capitol Hilton Hotel on November 12, 1994.

We had no idea what to expect. The dangers of genetic engineering were then, and are now, not well understood by the public or the press. (If you want to show the dangers of the atom bomb, you can point to a picture of Hiroshima. With a genetically engineered tomato, you can point to, well, a tomato.)

The first response from the D.C. press was tepid at best. I worried that the news conference would be a bust. But then Rick Weiss, health writer with the *Washington Post,* read the release, convinced his editor it was a story of national consequence, and wrote a powerful piece that appeared prominently in the *Post* on the day of the news conference. The story, entitled "Genetic Engineering Breeds Costly Protest," was better than I could have dreamed. In the article Weiss writes, "In a move that has become the talk of the scientific community, John Fagan has returned $614,000 in grant money to the National Institutes of Health, while withdrawing his previously filed request for an additional $1.25 million in support. He is doing so to protest what he sees as rampant and unwise genetic tinkering with plants and animals and the release of these novel organisms into the environment."

At 10:00 A.M. the news conference room was packed. Thirty-five journalists from the national and international press corps, including *Science, Nature,* and *BioTechnology,* showed up to hear John Fagan talk about his decision and how the government should better patrol the biotech industry. Their stories were all great—fair and even-handed—and four days later the *Washington Post* wrote an editorial praising Fagan's stand, entitled "Scientist's Qualms." The editorial concludes: "Fagan's bigger point is that the excitement of these and other commercial possibilities could outstrip researchers' own caution and get beyond even the existing safety features. His gesture, and the attention it has drawn, could flash a useful yellow light on the stampede."

That news conference not only made "a statement" but also made Fagan a much sought-after spokesman on the potential dangers of genetic engineering worldwide. Since then he has traveled to more than twenty countries, primarily throughout Europe and Asia, where he has met with high-level government leaders in health, agriculture, and the environment, as well as with leaders of some the largest food companies and food manufacturers in the world. His work has been considered instrumental in educating and mobilizing the European Union against genetic engineering.

Fagan's message to lawmakers wherever he goes is simple: "You are getting only one side of the story, the biotech side, but there is more to the issue. While it seems safe to base your decisions about genetic engineering on rigorous scientific evidence, you need to be aware of the environment within which a scientist works. If a scientist is funded by the biotech industry—and most molecular biologists are, directly or indirectly—it's very hard for him or her to be scientifically unbiased and to give a balanced evaluation of this technology."

Fagan advises decision makers in government and in private industry to take a prudent and commonsense approach and access a broad spectrum of scientific expertise in order to ensure that they get balanced information from all sides.

January 21, 1998. It's been more than three years since the D.C. news conference. Although our paths crossed several times during the 1996 campaign when he spoke out against genetically engineered foods, this is the first time that I've had the chance to sit and talk at length with John Fagan about recent developments in genetic engineering. Now, though, we are not in a hall packed with reporters but in a laboratory filled with instruments. In addition to his global travels, Fagan is spending as much time as possible in his laboratory, developing cutting edge technologies that will allow governments and food industry leaders to test plants or seeds and determine if they have been genetically engineered. Fagan's technology has become the international industry leader and is being used by the U.S.-based company Genetic ID to run tests for international grain traders and large food manufacturers worldwide that want to screen for GE crops and products.

Right now Fagan is standing in front of a long black table with test tubes and beakers and pots and pans stacked on two shelves.

On the far corner of the table are dozens of containers filled with soybeans, each container labeled with a tape with a series of numbers. Soybeans come in from all over the world to be tested at the lab, which also tests soy products and corn and corn products, including tofu, baby formula, baco bits, veggie burgers, cornflakes, and corn chips. A lab assistant leaves the room carrying a tray of tiny plastic test tubes, each a half inch tall by a quarter inch wide, filled with a grainy brown substance. "Ground-up soybeans," Fagan says. They are about to have some of their DNA removed through a chemical extraction process, the second step in a twenty-four-hour procedure that will identify whether or not the soybeans have been genetically engineered and determine whether or not a shipment of these soybeans will be allowed into Europe unlabeled. As Fagan maneuvers around the lab, he defines some GE terminology—basics, such as what is a gene and what is genetic engineering.

"Genes are like the architectural blueprints of life," Fagan tells me. "They form biological structures that compose DNA and give rise to the specific characteristics that define a particular living organism. Genes make a tomato a tomato and a fish a fish. These structures, or genetic codes, have evolved over millions of years in perfect harmony with all the other genetic codes that make up life on earth.

"Genetic engineering allows scientists to remove genes from one organism, say, a flounder, and transfer those genes into any other organism, say, a tomato. The transfer of genes changes the genetic blueprint of the tomato and reprograms its cells to produce different material, which in turn creates new characteristics within the tomato. Through this process, researchers can change the traits and characteristics of an organism as they see fit. For instance, they can engineer a tomato to be frost-resistant by inserting into it 'antifreeze' genes from a flounder. Or they can make soybeans that are resistant to herbicides or corn that has its own built-in pesticide."

At first glance the promises of this technology seem wonderful and unlimited, Fagan says. "Researchers have become very excited about using genetic engineering to produce more abundant crops, to create more nutritious foods, to eradicate certain diseases, and thereby to improve the quality of human life on earth."

But the downsides are considerable. "Genetically engineered

foods may contain toxins and allergens or be less nutritious," he says. "In fact, consumers have become sick and even died from such toxins already. Worse, genetically engineered organisms may multiply and crossbreed with the natural, nongenetically engineered population, creating irreversible biological changes throughout the earth's ecosystem."

I'm familiar with some of the hazards of GE foods, but I confess to Fagan that I am confused. How could something so potentially dangerous, as Fagan and many other scientists claim, be viewed with such optimism by so many other scientists and by the U.S. government? Is Fagan being a doomsayer? Is he antitechnology? I say that at least once a week *USA Today* runs a news story about a major breakthrough in gene research that holds promise for curing a terrible disease or a minor problem, from cancer to Alzheimer's, from obesity to baldness. Yet there is nary a word to indicate the possible downsides of these findings. Even my mother, who is a highly informed seventy-six-year-old (she watches C-SPAN instead of network sitcoms), is surprised to hear me talk of the possible risks of genetically engineered food. "Why," she wants to know, "would they sell something if it's dangerous? The government says it's safe."

Fagan answers: "No scientist can speak from the platform of scientific objectivity and claim that some new technology is a cure-all or is absolutely safe. When nuclear technology was developed, nobody knew that within a few years the human race would be threatened by mutually assured destruction. Nobody knew when nuclear energy was harnessed to produce electricity that we would be left with millions of tons of radioactive waste that could remain highly toxic for tens of thousands of years. Nobody knew, but we leaped ahead and created serious long-term problems for ourselves and for future generations.

"So how can the biotech industry possibly know that genetically engineered foods are completely safe, so safe that they don't need to be labeled? The answer is, it doesn't know.

"It took millions of years for life on earth to evolve into the highly balanced, dynamic ecosystem with its countless life-forms that we know today. Now, in a generation or less, most of our important food crops are being radically changed through genetic engineering, and this change will seriously impact on the ecosystem as a whole, jeopardizing human health as well. Until a genetically engineered product is proven safe, then there's a question about it. The implementation of genetic engineering should be guided by rigorous scientific safety standards, not by the profit motive."

We walk across the lab through some double doors into another room where there is still more equipment. Here is a machine, about the size of a desktop photocopier, that amplifies, or makes millions of copies, of the extracted soybean DNA molecules. (This type of equipment is also used in court cases to match blood types.) In the room next door another machine, through a process called electrophoresis, completes the procedure by determining whether a new gene has been engineered into the genetic code of the soybean. Fagan makes a few adjustments to a meter. Standing off to the side, out of his way, I ask him how his technology works.

"Basically the test works like a word search on your computer. If you have a two-thousand-word document and you want to find if the word *good* is in your document—and how many times it appears—you give the command to your word processor, and it searches for the word *good*. We simply use a genetic word search procedure to identify whether a soybean, corn, or any other crop has been genetically engineered."

I must not look entirely enlightened, so he elaborates. "When scientists engineer a plant, they're actually adding new genetic information. It would be as if you had a Shakespearean sonnet and then were to cut into it a phrase from another poem, say, a poem by e. e. cummings. It changes the information content. This test searches through the genetic information of a plant to identify if any new information has been added."

Fagan is working on new technologies that will speed the process up to around thirty minutes. He also hopes to make the equipment portable, so that tests can be done anywhere.

"This will allow developing countries, where there are few laboratory facilities, to be able to monitor incoming foods and make sure that they're not genetically engineered or to at least determine if they are. This is important because otherwise these countries cannot control what's coming across their borders," he says.

We leave the lab and walk into his office. He sits on a stool, his back to a bank of computer monitors. Is it true, as proponents claim, that genetic engineering is simply a natural, but more precise, extension of traditional breeding practices—practices that mankind has been using for thousands of years to improve our food?

Fagan shakes his head, no. "The fact is that genetic engineering is not natural," he says. "It's a radical, revolutionary, and highly artificial approach to changing our foods. Is this a natural extension of traditional breeding practices? Absolutely not. Traditional breeding makes use of natural reproductive mechanisms and must respect the natural reproductive barriers between species. But genetic engineering uses artificial means aggressively to penetrate those barriers. Genetic engineers can isolate genes from virtually any organism on the planet and introduce those genes into any other living thing on earth. When you introduce a gene from a fish into a tomato, or from a bacterium into corn, or from a virus into a squash, you're doing something that would never happen in nature."

The biotech industry also claims that technologies for manipulating genes are exact, I say.

Fagan says they're not. "It's true that scientists can cut and splice genes very precisely in the test tube. But that's only half the battle. Once an artificial gene has been constructed in the test tube, it must be inserted into the food-producing organism. And that's a highly imprecise process whose results are extremely unpredictable and uncontrollable, at times producing dangerous toxins and allergens and reducing the nutritional value of the food."

Fagan refers to genetic engineers in Japan who altered the genes of a bacterium to make it produce large amounts of the food supplement tryptophan. The engineers had been using this bacterium as "little factories" for tryptophan production and hoped to make this process more efficient, and therefore more profitable, through genetic engineering.

"They succeeded in souping up these bacteria so that they produced trytophan much more efficiently, but unexpectedly their genetic manipulations also caused the bacteria to produce a powerful toxin," Fagan says. "The genetic engineers had no idea that their tinkering had created this deadly contaminant until the supplement was put on the market and people started getting sick and dying. Altogether fifteen hundred Americans were permanently disabled and thirty-seven died from this defective product.[3] Because it was not labeled genetically engineered, it took months to track down the source of the problem and take the product off the market."

Fagan cites a well-documented near-miss horror story: "Genetic engineers at Pioneer Hybrid International introduced a gene from Brazil nuts into soybeans to improve their nutritional content. However, to their surprise, the Brazil nut gene also caused the soybeans to be allergenic to certain people. Fortunately this problem was detected before these soybeans were placed on the open market, and no harm was done. In the grand scheme of things, Brazil nuts are much more closely related to soybeans than a flounder is to a tomato or an insect is to a squash. Just think how much more impossible it is to predict fully the outcome of mixing genes from such distantly related organisms."

Another argument in favor of genetic engineering is that it will lead to reduced pesticide use, I say.

"Oh, yes, proponents do say that," he says. "But the reality is that most of the genetically engineered crops developed to date not only perpetuate but actually extend the chemical approach in agriculture. This approach is depleting our soil, diminishing the nutritional value of our food, and tainting it with toxic and carcinogenic substances.

"Nearly fifty percent of all genetic manipulations of crops have been carried out to make them resistant to herbicides. For example, Monsanto markets a pesticide called Roundup and a genetically engineered soybean called Roundup Ready. Herbicide-resistant crops allow the farmer to spray the fields heavily to kill weeds, knowing that the crop plants will not be hurt. This seems convenient, but in fact, it will increase the use of these toxic chemicals at least threefold. Already eighty percent of America's groundwater is polluted by herbicides and other toxic and mutagenic agricultural chemicals. Chemical companies engineer these herbicide-resistant crops to stimulate sales of their herbicides, but we don't need the increased pollution caused by such high-tech crops. In the long run, these crops will also create more work for farmers by generating herbicide-resistant weeds."

Fagan says that the reliance on genetic engineering and other high-tech approaches in agriculture "is regrettable because it is so unnecessary. These approaches have stunted the implementation of organic, sustainable farming approaches that are capable of growing crops more efficiently and cost-effectively."

I ask him about religious concerns over genetically engineered foods.

"It's a very big problem," he replies. "Many people hold religious beliefs that include dietary restrictions. Should a person of the Jewish or Muslim faith be asked to eat a tomato that has pig genes? Many people believe that genetic engineering across different species violates the natural reproductive boundaries set in place by God. Others find the patenting of life-forms blasphemous. Without product labels, these consumers will not be able to avoid foods that conflict with their religious and spiritual orientations."

Fagan looks at his watch. He has a lot of work ahead and a lot of travel. Tomorrow morning he will fly to São Paulo, Brazil, to meet with retailers from Europe, a local food-testing company, and one of the largest soy processors in the world. The purpose of his visit is to set up a third-party certification system so that Europeans can import soy products grown and processed in Brazil that are guaranteed to be natural and not genetically engineered. Four days later Fagan will return to the United States to speak at a two-day conference of organic farmers and organic food manufacturers from throughout the northern plain states that will be held in Aberdeen, North Dakota. He then will turn around and, with his wife, Susel, fly to Perth, Australia, where he will transfer Genetic ID's testing technology to a laboratory that will use it to test grain products being exported to Europe and Japan. Just about the time the Fagans get over that jet lag, they will head back to Wisconsin, where John Fagan will speak at the largest organic conference in the country.

Before leaving, I have a quick question about his research. What got him started on it?

"I kept reading in the newspapers about how the promoters of genetic engineering from the U.S., including Secretary of Agriculture Dan Glickman, were speaking all over Europe, saying that genetically engineered soybeans are just like the natural ones: They're just as safe, they're just as nutritious, they're identical; you can't tell them apart.

"When I heard that, I knew as a molecular biologist that you could tell them apart, that any competent molecular biologist with a decent lab could set up a test to do it. So I just took the time to develop that test, and over the years we have refined that test and made it more effective and more sensitive. But the tests that we do right now are not something that is a Nobel Prize–winning discovery. It was simply applying known technology to a new problem, and it works."

Mobilizing Grassroots Support
for Mandatory Labeling

December 6, 1997.   Laura Ticciati is on the telephone from her hotel in Florida, talking to a reporter about her efforts to do something that's never been done: pull together a powerful coalition of U.S. senators and representatives, scientists and doctors, clergy, and leaders of the U.S. health food industry that can stand up to the biotech interests. As executive director of Mothers for Natural Law, a nonprofit educational organization that she spun off from the Natural Law Party in 1996, Ticciati and a handful of volunteers have spent two years working nonstop to mobilize the forces. Their work is paying off. A year ago few people had ever even heard about genetic engineering. But that is changing quickly, as the issue moves to the front burner, at least in the health food market. The shift is due, in large part, to the efforts of Ticciati and her associates.

Ticciati hangs up the phone and walks into a room filled with two hundred natural food retailers attending a regional trade show of the natural foods industry at the Omni Rosen Hotel in Orlando. She is a keynote speaker. For those who are not up to speed on the issue, she defines terms, gives a balanced account of both sides of the argument, and outlines an action plan to collect one million signatures in health food stores nationwide calling for mandatory labeling of all genetically engineered foods. This, she says, will send an unambiguous message to policy makers about citizen unrest over genetically engineered foods and attract considerable media coverage along the way.

It's the holiday season, and Ticciati uses the holidays as a launching point for her talk. "As we gather with our families this year, we can still give thanks for a safe food supply," she says, herself a mother of two young children. "In 1998 that may not be the case. Genetically engineered foods are taking over a larger share of the market. By the year 2000, the FDA estimates that one hundred to one hundred fifty new GE foods will be on our grocery store shelves.

"Last year European consumers and food retailers united and gained government support for stricter policies and labeling of GE foods. And a few months ago Japanese retailers collected one million signatures demanding labeling. It's time America got on board!

"We have always taken the position that whatever the challenge, there's always a solution. Right now the challenge is to get the word out fast. Our Right to Know petition is a simple way to accomplish this. Grassroots organizers in Japan gathered in just a few months one million signatures from citizens concerned about the safety of their food supply. Here in America we intend to do the same.

"How can we accomplish this? Through commitment and organization," she says, breaking down the total into manageable chunks. "One volunteer in a high-traffic location can realistically collect several hundred signatures in a few hours. Multiply that effort by a dozen friends, and a dozen Saturdays between now and next spring, and you could easily organize delivery of thirty thousand signatures from your community. What greater contribution could you make to the health of the planet? What greater favor could you do to protect yourself and your children from the unknown dangers of these untested manipulations?"

Ticciati has been on the road a lot. For example, in the past year she testified at a hearing of the National Organics Standards Board in Indianapolis; she addressed a national meeting of the Social Ventures Network, an association of CEOs and other top business leaders who are concerned about socially and environmentally responsible investments; and she was a featured speaker at National Products Industry Expos in Baltimore, Anaheim, and Las Vegas.

Ticciati talks about recent legal victories, and that draws applause. "Ben and Jerry's, who make superpremium ice cream and yogurt, won a First Amendment lawsuit against the state of Illinois and the city of Chicago that will allow the company to voluntarily label its dairy products as being free of the controversial bioengineered growth hormone rBGH. Ben and Jerry's was joined in the suit by Stonyfield Farm, a manufacturer of yogurt and ice cream;

Whole Foods Market, the nation's largest chain of natural food supermarkets; and Organic Valley, a farmer's cooperative selling milk, cheese, and butter products."

Ticciati concludes on a heartfelt note: "We are at a crossroads on this earth where we can no longer afford to violate laws of nature in a mad dash for profits. We must make a decision to embrace technologies that support *all* of life, technologies that not only uphold and promote our growth as a society but also do not damage anyone or anything in the process.

"There is an order in the universe, a seamless web that nourishes and connects us all—from the tiniest seed, to the beating of our hearts, to the stars in the galaxies," she says. "Every time we act without regard to that underlying intelligence of nature, we harm ourselves and we harm our planet. If we align ourselves with the nourishing power of nature, we will create a society that upholds the integrity and dignity of life for all of us, for all times to come."

The Natural Law Party's Policy on Genetic Engineering

1. SAFETY TESTING. Rigorous, premarket safety testing by an independent scientific review board of all genetically engineered organisms.

2. MARKET SAFETY. Removal of all products containing genetically engineered organisms currently on the market that have not been safety-tested by an independent scientific review board.

3. MANDATORY LABELING. Clear and accurate labeling of all foods derived from, processed with, containing, or consisting of genetically engineered organisms before they are released into any and all commercial markets.

4. BAN ON RELEASE OF GE ORGANISMS (Best-Case Scenario). A fifty-year moratorium on the release of genetically engineered organisms into the environment until they are proven safe by an independent scientific review board.

8

Putting Health Back into
Our Disease Care System

On the surface, it appears that America has the finest health care system money can buy. We have sophisticated diagnostic procedures that can identify such deadly disorders as heart disease and cancer; surgical procedures that can repair a ruptured spleen and replace a degenerated hip; immunizations that can prevent such horrible diseases as polio and smallpox; and antibiotics and other drugs that can treat infections, both minor and deadly.

At first glance, it appears that all we need to solve the health care crisis is to find either more money to pay the bills or new ways to cut the costs. That way as many people as possible will have access to our current health care system, and everything will be fine.

True or not true? Not true. It turns out appearances are misleading. There is more to health care than emergency procedures, and there is more to the health crisis than a lack of money. In fact, America ranks near the bottom in overall health compared with twenty-nine other industrialized nations, and that ranking has been on a downward spiral for nearly forty years. This is despite the fact that we spend—by a very wide margin—the highest percentage of our gross domestic product on health care.[1,2]

If you listen to a growing number of insiders—medical doctors trained in some of our best medical schools—then you know that the problem with our health care system is one not just of economics but, more crucially, of *content*.[3] The public as well seems to know something is wrong because an estimated 30 percent of them have visited a health care professional other than a medical doctor for their health complaints, according to a study published in 1993 in the *New England Journal of Medicine*.[4] And those statistics are from back in 1990.

The consensus seems to be this: Whatever's good about our modern health care system needs to be much better. Increasingly, health care professionals are recognizing the need to change the focus, reverse the current trend away from a disease care system, and emphasize, instead, prevention of disease and keeping people healthy through natural, nontoxic medicine. It's a commonsense approach that is supported by compelling scientific evidence, and it also makes sense for reasons both economic and humane. But like the issue of genetic engineering, this debate has not made it anywhere near the top of the agendas of the two main political parties, so there's not much serious discussion about it in the political arena.

Fortunately many physicians are working to make it an issue of national concern. Two are profiled here. Through their research and experience you can see more clearly what is wrong and what needs to be done.

Barry Charles, M.D., is executive director of the Physicians' Association for Eradicating Chronic Disease, an organization of hundreds of doctors who are concerned about both the alarming rise in the number of people who suffer from chronic diseases and the inability of modern medicine to treat these diseases effectively. These doctors are establishing medical centers to treat chronic disorders using a comprehensive approach to health care that includes natural medicine.

Dr. Charles is a graduate of the New York University School of Medicine. He has spent the last twenty years working to educate government agencies and members of Congress, doctors, health insurance leaders, medical schools, and the public about the deficiencies of modern medicine and the need for a prevention-oriented approach to health care. He has organized national and international medical conferences and has supervised the training of medical doctors worldwide in new modalities that would keep people healthy and be more effective in treating those with chronic diseases.

Barry Charles knew he wanted to be a doctor when he was a child. He comes from a medical family in New Jersey. His father is a pediatrician, and his brother is a radiologist; other relatives are doctors or work as health professionals. For Dr. Charles, the failings of modern medicine are a bitter pill to swallow. But what is far more galling, he says, is that millions of people suffer unnecessarily from these failings and that this suffering is not being addressed by the medical establishment or the government.

June 14, 1997, Washington, D.C. Dr. Charles is testifying before the Department of Education's Office of Postsecondary Education. The purpose of the meeting is to get rubber-stamp approval for the licensing agency that accredits medical colleges, the Liaison Committee for Medical Education (LCME). Barry Charles is there to object. He is given five minutes to speak and tells the department why. He makes four points:

1. Our current health care system causes very serious health hazards, and this is substantiated by thousands of studies published in leading medical journals, such as the *Journal of the American Medical Association* and the *New England Journal of Medicine*.[5]

2. Nevertheless, the Liaison Committee for Medical Education continues to accredit the same medical curricula that propagate this flawed system.

3. Medical schools need to develop new curricula that will educate medical students properly in prevention and include the most up-to-date knowledge of how to avoid disease at its source.

4. The LCME is made up solely of officials of the AMA and the association that represents the medical colleges themselves, both of which have vested interests to maintain the status quo.

For these reasons, Dr. Charles says that the LCME should be replaced by a new, independent committee open to approaches that can safely and effectively prevent disease and promote good health.

I talked earlier with Barry Charles about his testimony, so he calls me afterward to give a report. He says that several committee members asked good questions and acknowledged that chronic disease is a major problem in America. But they were unwilling to give the status quo a budge, not even just a little. The department voted unanimously to renew the committee's accreditation authority.

Dr. Charles isn't surprised. He's been through this for twenty-five years. He knows, however, that in spite of whatever happened—or did not happen—in Washington on that June day, change is in the air. In the past few years there has been an enormous shift in the nation, among both doctors and patients, toward natural, preventive medicine. He believes it's just a matter of time before policy makers recognize the inadequacies and hazards of modern medicine and adopt a humane, cost-effective, safe, commonsense approach to health care.

It's now July 20, a month later, and I am in Bonn, Germany, listening to Dr. Charles speak at an international conference of leaders of Natural Law parties. There are a thousand people here—business leaders, physicians, scientists, educators, lawyers—representing sixty countries. He is elaborating on the testimony he gave before the Department of Education, and it seems to be striking a chord with people from all these countries. (It turns out that what everyone knows is true: The world is shrinking. The problems—environmental pollution, health care costs, crime, drug abuse, etc.—are much the same in every country, and the solutions are much the same as well.)

As I listen to Dr. Charles speak, I have to admit that when I first heard him talk about the serious dangers of modern medicine, without hearing all the facts, the whole notion sounded a bit extreme. But when you consider the facts all at once, in one sitting, as Barry Charles is giving it out tonight, the case is *overwhelming*.

Dr. Charles clicks on a slide that fills a massive screen behind him. The profile of a man appears standing next to a huge stack of papers. "This is actually a stack of several thousand medical articles on the hazards of medical treatments," he says, pointing an arrow at the screen. "They have been collected from the most prestigious medical journals in the world. And this stack of articles—this high heap of hazards—is growing higher every day."

Dr. Charles holds up one journal that reports on the epidemic of chronic disease in America. "One hundred million Americans suffer from a chronic disorder, and the numbers are predicted only to get worse," he notes, citing a study in the *Journal of the American Medical Association* in November 1996.[6]

I look around the hall. Translators with headsets are busy converting his words. But still not that many people really react, probably, I think, because not many people are certain exactly what a chronic disease is.

"A chronic disease is a disease for which modern medicine says there is no cure, including heart disease, asthma, arthritis, menstrual disorders, migraines, diabetes, multiple sclerosis, ulcerative colitis, thyroid disease, Alzheimer's, and Parkinson's," Dr. Charles explains. "These are terrible diseases that linger on for years, many of them cause recurrent pain, and all that modern medicine can offer people with these diseases are *palliative* treatments—treatments which suppress the symptoms or slow the progress of the disease, often with very dangerous, even fatal side effects."

The problem, according to Dr. Charles, is that modern medicine doesn't fully understand the causes of such diseases and, as a result, can't offer any cures. Another problem is that most diseases are in some way caused by behavioral factors, such as diet, stress, health habits, and environmental influences, and our current health care system can't do anything about that either.

"Modern medicine treats diseases on a superficial level, not at their source," he says. "Nevertheless, chronic disorders in the U.S. account for four hundred thirty-five billion dollars in costs, including about 80 percent of all hospital stays and sixty-nine percent of all hospital admissions.[7]

"What does that show?" he asks rhetorically.

I say to myself that it shows that not many people must think there are treatment choices to what modern medicine offers.

Dr. Charles says something equally true. "It shows that our health care system is sick."

I look around again, and now people are reacting, taking notes;

a few are raising their hands with questions. It does sound appalling, when you think about it, that 40 percent of Americans suffer from serious diseases with no known cures.

He lists more statistics:

- More than 180,000 people die in the United States each year partly as a result of medical treatment, a number "equivalent to three jumbo jet crashes every two days throughout the year." He is quoting from an article in the *Journal of the American Medical Association* that originated at the Harvard School of Public Health.[8] (How would the public react and how quickly would the FAA respond if crashes happened three times a week? I wonder.) Another *JAMA* article points out that this number is far more than the annual automobile mortality rate of 45,000 and accounts for more deaths than all other accidents combined. In fact, more people are dying today from problems associated with medical treatment than from AIDS.

- More than 3 million people are harmed each year because of medical mistakes (e.g., a patient is given the wrong dose of medication[9,10] or has the wrong appendage amputated[11]). In response, the AMA has just founded the National Patients' Safety Foundation to deal with just this problem. By the AMA's own research, over 40 percent of Americans will be impacted by medical errors, some of which last a lifetime.

- The overuse of antibiotics is creating germs that are drug-resistant to antibiotics, leaving health authorities with the very real threat of an epidemic of diseases for which there may be no treatment. Doctors are now alarmed by the appearance of a common bacterium that is resistant to even the most powerful antibiotic; they worry that this is a harbinger of a future medical disaster.[12,13] In fact, the infectious disease death rate in the United States between 1980 and 1992 increased 58 percent,[14] in part due to the growing number of germs resistant to antibiotics.[15]

93

- Commonly prescribed drugs can cause a wide range of such side effects as skin rashes, nausea, headaches, and gastrointestinal disorders as well as abnormal heart rhythms, angina, immune system dysfunction, serious blood disorders, liver or kidney toxicity, depression, deafness, and even death.[16]

"Put all the statistics down on one piece of paper, and they're staggering," Dr. Charles says. "A significant number of people are being harmed by medical treatments. It's a horrible epidemic in its own right, and it shows clearly how urgently we need to change our health care system."

A man standing at the audience microphone asks if there isn't something good to be said about modern medicine.

Dr. Charles nods and says that yes, obviously, there are aspects of modern medicine that have been very successful, even miraculous, especially in acute care and trauma. "But when we take a close look at all the research we have to conclude that there are serious limitations to this approach that should not be ignored. We have to recognize these inadequacies and work to remedy them—especially when people are being harmed."

What can be done? another man asks.

"It's clear that there are elements missing from modern medicine," he answers. "There are decades of research on safe and effective therapies based on profound new discoveries of how the body functions from its most fundamental level, which allow us to treat and prevent disease at its source. These include diet, exercise, herbs, daily and seasonal routines, environmental influences, the effect of consciousness on health, and collective health measures. These should be available in our health care system."

Prevention. I think back to my childhood and the friends I grew up with. For us, prevention was—and it probably still is today—going to bed early, eating a balanced diet, wearing warm clothes in the winter so we didn't catch a cold, doing limbering-up exercises before basketball practice so we didn't pull a muscle, shots for mumps and measles, and, in my case, regular tetanus shots because of my frequent encounters with rusty nails.

But now it's also clear that while there are shots to prevent those childhood diseases, there are no shots to prevent adult diseases, such as hardening of the arteries, many types of cancer, Alzheimer's, rheumatoid arthritis, and Parkinson's disease. Modern medicine has few answers there, but the need is clear.

Consider heart disease. This is the leading killer in the Western world. Medical specialists now recognize that heart disease can be prevented, yet it continues to be an epidemic. For example, Dr. Alexander Leaf, former chair of the department of preventive medicine at Harvard Medical School, describes the current approach to coronary heart disease as "inadequate, despite massive efforts to apply costly treatments after the disease is clinically manifest. Doctors are too preoccupied with measures that only lessen symptoms and which will do nothing for the next generation of thirty-, forty-, or fifty-year-olds, dooming them to the same heart disease."

Also consider cancer. According to a recent Harvard study, at least 60 percent of all cancers are preventable.[17] But the thirty-year, twenty-six-billion-dollar war against cancer in America is being lost, according to an article in the *New England Journal of Medicine*. The author of the article, Dr. John Bailar, an internationally respected researcher, concludes that the key to controlling cancer is prevention.[18]

What do doctors mean when they talk of prevention? Barry Charles says that when we speak of prevention in modern medicine, "we talk of how women over forty should get a mammogram or men over forty should have a prostate examination. But this is not true prevention; this is really just early detection. In truth, there are three levels of prevention":

- **Primary Prevention.** "This means we do something that actually prevents the onset of the disease, that keeps the body in balance so that even very small imbalances don't crop up that lead to a disease," Dr. Charles says.
- **Secondary Prevention.** "The second level means basically detecting a disease at its earliest stage, before it causes any significant health problems, and then doing whatever we can to prevent that disease from progressing. For example, conducting tests and finding that an

individual has atherosclerosis and then putting that person on a diet and exercise program so that he doesn't have a heart attack."

- **Tertiary Prevention.** "At the third level the person already has significant health problems, and we do something to prevent the problems from getting worse. For example, a man already has had a heart attack, and now we want to prevent him from having a second one. Or he has diabetes, and we want to keep him from going blind and losing his leg."

The crime in all of this, Dr. Charles says, is that even though most of disease and death is preventable,[19] including 60 percent of cancers, there is little or no emphasis on prevention in our health care system. In fact, America spends less than 1 percent of its trillion-dollar health budget on prevention.

What about health maintenance organizations, HMOs? a woman asks. Don't they offer prevention?

"That was their intention, but in reality they don't offer anything new or different," Dr. Charles replies. "HMOs were created to make the delivery of health care more efficient and thereby reduce costs. It was a good idea, and expenditures dropped at first, but now costs are going up again. In 1998 the increase for most plans is projected to be five to seven percent, with other, smaller plans as much as thirty percent. That's because HMOs put the cart before the horse. They try to reduce costs by limiting treatments and diagnostic procedures and by reducing reimbursements to doctors, but that'll never work. The only way to reduce costs is to make people healthier. Then you can actually reduce health care utilization. And the only way you can do that is through effective approaches to prevent and treat disease at its basis."

Even from the standpoint of the delivery of conventional medicine, there are serious flaws with HMOs, he says. "What kind of health maintenance or insurance would pay only when a person gets sick, and not provide services to keep someone healthy right from the beginning of his enrollment?

"Health care authorities have to wake up and realize that modern medicine has serious limitations and that a new knowledge is ur-

gently needed. We have to do more than pay lip service to prevention, and we have to look seriously at other therapies that work and
are safe, even if they come from outside the usual knowledge base
of allopathic medicine."

Barry Charles says that if we seriously want to reform health care
in America, we can't simply reform its financing and delivery. We
must reform the treatment that gets delivered and paid for. For that,
laws that grant a monopoly to the current system and that govern
medical practice have to be changed.

"For people to be denied access to treatments of their choice that
are effective, especially when the current system is inadequate, is a
clear violation of human rights," Dr. Charles points out.

" 'Health freedom' legislation and 'access to medical care' legislation have to be enacted," he says. "Congress and state governments have to mandate support for prevention. They have to change
the emphasis of the system. The heath care system has to be opened
up to all therapies that are effective, even if they are not a part of
modern allopathic medicine, and this includes natural medicine. And
medical educators have to give doctors training in this."

Dr. Charles tells his listeners not to look to the American Medical
Association to push for these changes. "The AMA is a political organization dedicated to maintaining the status quo. The political action committee of the AMA consistently ranks among the top ten
spenders on Capitol Hill, and they spend to keep the current system
in place.

"To expect the AMA to take a leadership role and change the
system, all of a sudden to produce a prevention-oriented system with
safe and effective therapies, would be a waste of time. Even many
doctors are no longer looking to the AMA for leadership. In fact, the
AMA is losing members. In 1996 less than thirty-five percent of doctors belonged to the AMA—down from ninety percent in the 1960s.
If doctors aren't looking to the AMA for leadership, the public
shouldn't look to the AMA for change."

Where should we look for true health care reform?

"We have to demand it ourselves," Dr. Charles answers. "We have
to demand it from the government, from doctors, from health in-
surers and HMOs, and from medical educators. But we also have to
take responsibility for our own health rather than wait until we fall

sick and then see a doctor. Much of sickness is caused by violations of natural law: unhealthy diet, poor sleep habits, et cetera. We can't play a passive role. The shift to prevention and natural medicine is being driven by the public. We must vigorously continue to push our disease care system into becoming a true health care system."

Barry Charles points out that today thousands of doctors, on their own, are investigating therapies and modalities that can provide a safer, more complete and effective system of health care. In 1997 many of his colleagues opened medical centers for treating chronic diseases through natural medicine. Many more such centers are slated to open in the future. In Dr. Charles's opinion, these facilities cannot be opened quickly enough. "When modern medicine declares a disease to be chronic, it damages the patient psychologically to think that there's no possibility of a fully effective treatment. For someone who is sick, every day is a terrible burden. And as doctors we can't go on saying, 'Oh, gosh, this patient has a chronic disease that we can't treat, so we'll just give him some more pain medication.' And we can't be satisfied with therapies that have serious side effects, even if there are benefits in the short term. The knowledge now exists to bring health to every American. If there's something available that works, then we should make it available—widely available."

Enlivening the Body's Inner Intelligence to Prevent Disease and Promote Good Health

January 16, 1998. Dr. Stuart Rothenberg is taking my pulse. He's resting the first three fingers of his right hand on the radial pulse of my right wrist. After thirty seconds he applies just a bit more pressure. He's not counting heartbeats. Instead he's "looking for patterns of imbalance" in my body. This is hardly a high-tech procedure. It's thousands of years old. But more and more medical doctors are learning this ancient science of pulse diagnosis as an accurate, non-invasive way of detecting disease in its earliest stages. I am healthy, Dr. Rothenberg says. To stay that way, he will prescribe an herbal compound that researchers at the Ohio State University Medical

School have found to be a potent antioxidant, he will make modifications in my diet that include my steering clear of hot, spicy foods, and he will make a pointed admonition to get more rest.

Dr. Rothenberg is the medical director of the Center for Chronic Disorders in Dallas, one of the nation's first medical facilities to integrate natural approaches in the treatment and prevention of health disorders. I'm here at Barry Charles's suggestion. If I had been here for a regular doctor's appointment, Dr. Rothenberg would also have put me through a standard medical checkup. But I'm not. I'm here for just a few minutes to find out more about the shift toward natural medicine and the programs offered at the center.

Stuart Rothenberg, forty-nine, is a busy man. He oversees an in-residence program for people suffering from chronic diseases, and he administers an outpatient rejuvenation program for people who want to stay healthy. In recent months he has also become a focal point for doctors in the Dallas area who are interested in learning more about natural medicine and possibly collaborating on research. In fact, he and a group of doctors are now applying for a grant from the National Institutes of Health for research on natural medicine treatments for chronic disease. The group has already received eight million dollars from the NIH for research on the effects of natural medicine modalities on heart disease. The application process alone can be a full-time job.

In 1974 Dr. Rothenberg graduated from New York University School of Medicine and went into family practice. He has been board-certified in family practice by the American Board of Family Practice since 1978, and he has been a Fellow of the American Academy of Family Physicians since 1983. He has also served as a member of the clinical faculty in family medicine at the University of California at San Diego School of Medicine.

Dr. Rothenberg has incorporated natural medicine into his family practice since 1983 and is now one of the most experienced medical doctors in natural medicine in the world. He has lectured internationally on natural medicine at the National Institutes of Health in Washington, D.C., the Institute of Preventive Medicine of the Soviet Union in Moscow (in 1990), the Hadassah-Hebrew University School of Medicine in Jerusalem, and the First International Conference on Ayur-Veda, sponsored by the All-India Ayur-Veda Congress in New Delhi.

It's a crystal-clear day. Through the window in his office I can see the sprawling Dallas skyline stretch out for miles. I ask Dr. Rothenberg if attitudes toward natural medicine are changing in Dallas, which has traditionally been a conservative bastion of the country.

"At lightning speed," he answers. "Five years ago you couldn't say you were practicing complementary medicine and be taken seriously by the medical community. Now it's become an issue of intense, positive interest."

Why the sudden interest?

"It's driven by the health care consumer. The public is demanding alternatives to conventional care. Modern medicine has not been successful in addressing the root cause of most of the serious disorders that afflict people, so the public is driving the change."

I ask Dr. Rothenberg what prompted him to make the shift to integrate natural medicine into his practice.

"My patients," he says. "So many of them had health problems that I wasn't able to help with conventional medicine alone. Often all I could do was to prescribe a drug that would suppress or temporarily alleviate a symptom, but it wouldn't get to the root cause of the disease. And often the medicines that I prescribed created side effects."

I ask for an example.

Dr. Rothenberg offers a common, but often deadly, example: high blood pressure, a disorder that afflicts close to fifty million Americans and is a leading risk factor for heart disease, the number one cause of death in the country.

"When I prescribed blood pressure medication to a patient, I would have to prescribe it for life," he says, "because if the medicine would be withdrawn, the blood pressure would come back up. The medication wasn't getting to the source of the problem; it was just suppressing the symptoms.

"Another problem was the side effects, which ranged from fatigue to depression to gastrointestinal upsets to life-threatening arrhythmias. More than half the people who are prescribed blood pressure medicine stop taking it. I didn't find out until later that a large percentage of my patients also just stopped taking the medication because of unpleasant side effects."

I ask Dr. Rothenberg, If I were a patient with an ulcer or headaches and went to see him before he began to use natural medicine, and if I went to see him today, how would he approach my disease differently?

"There is no comparison," he replies. "Previously I wouldn't have had the knowledge or framework to get to the source of your problem. If you complained of a chronic headache, I would have prescribed a pain reliever to suppress temporarily the pain. Or if you had a chronic digestive system problem, I might prescribe an antacid, such as Zantac or Tagamet, to suppress the secretion of stomach acid. I would just be treating at the symptom level.

"But today I would treat your headaches or ulcer with approaches that have been tested for thousands of years to enliven your body's own inner capacity to create health from within."

How, I ask, does that work?

"The body has its own inner intelligence, which governs its normal physiological processes at every moment. That means it has its own inner self-repair, self-healing, balancing mechanisms. In modern medicine, we call them homeostatic and self-repair mechanisms."

For example?

"Look at the immune system. If a streptococcus germ enters the body, the immune system has a remarkable ability to identify it as a foreign invader. This sighting triggers a myriad of responses. Immune system cells communicate instantaneously with each other throughout the body through chemical transmission molecules and mobilize an army of killer immune cells to destroy the invaders.

"This is the essence of the healing response," he says. "Unfortunately there's little emphasis in modern medicine on the body's own capacity for healing. That is why there are so many diseases we can't cure and why health care has become so costly. But the main goal of natural medicine is to enhance, promote, and enliven these natural self-repair mechanisms by awakening the body's inner intelligence."

Dr. Rothenberg tells me that many of the natural treatment programs offered at the center are based on work done by neuroscientist Tony Nader, M.D., Ph.D., whose analysis of human physiology, he says, "linked the structures and functions of the body to an inner intelligence that underlies and administers all these functions."

He pulls out a chart that shows forty different approaches of treatment grouped in four categories—mind, body, behavior, and environment—and discusses the underpinnings of natural medicine:[20]

- MIND. "The mind is very powerful in creating health or causing disease. If the mind is balanced and calm, then it becomes a powerful promoter of healing responses. This is not just a subjective experience: it is scientific fact. Every thought, every feeling that we have produces powerful chemicals in the nervous system, called neurochemicals, including neuropeptides, which promote either health or disease. We teach people how to access the quietest, most refined level of the mind and to develop inner reserves of healing, orderliness, and integration for the body."
- BODY. "Diet has a considerable impact on health, much greater than we imagine in conventional medicine. Our approach to diet is individualized; it's tailored to the needs of the specific patient. To help us to determine the proper diet, we use pulse diagnosis to determine the patterns of imbalance in the body that are the root cause of disorder. We can either do this as a preventive tool before a person falls sick, so we can provide him or her with measures that would be helpful to prevent the disease from emerging, or if a person is already ill, we can diagnose the pattern of imbalances that is at the root of the illness and then prescribe diet and other measures to help to reverse those imbalances.

  "We also draw upon the knowledge of thousands of herbal preparations that are used traditionally to enhance the body's own healing responses.[21] In addition, we recognize that many chronic disorders have their root in impurities that have accumulated in the tissues of the body and suppress the body's natural immunity and other repair mechanisms. So we use physiological purification procedures to rid the body of toxins that come from the food we eat and also from environmental pollution. And we offer an exercise program that includes exercises that integrate mind and body."

- BEHAVIOR. "The body has an internal clock that is aligned with the cycles of nature, such as the twenty-four-hour cycle of day and night, the monthly cycle of the moon's rotation around the earth, and the annual cycle of major seasons. There are daily and seasonal routines that can promote balance and synchrony with the rhythms and cycles of nature—key factors in preventing disease and maintaining good health."
- ENVIRONMENT. "Conventional medicine generally overlooks the critical influence that the environment has on health. We use knowledge of how to construct the home and workplace using only nontoxic materials," he says, citing a recent article in the *New England Journal of Medicine* entitled "Building-Related Illnesses," on the growing evidence that toxic building materials can cause the so-called sick-building syndrome.[22] "But more than nontoxic materials, we use traditional knowledge of how the proper layout and orientation of the building on the site can promote health. This means, for example, that for the maximum well-being of the occupant, a building should be constructed along a north-south/east-west grid, with the most ideal entrance coming from the east or north. And for the distant environment, we recognize that we're not in isolation from the universe. In fact, as we know from modern science and learn from the traditional systems of natural medicine, we're very much influenced by the cycles of the distant environment, including those of the sun, moon, planets, and stars—what have been called our cosmic counterparts—and we provide approaches to promote harmony between the individual and the distant environment."

Dr. Rothenberg has to take a phone call in the next room. I wonder, When he was in medical school, what exactly did he learn about health. When Dr. Rothenberg returns, I ask him.

"Actually we learned a lot about disease, but very little about health," he says. "You have to understand, modern medicine is part of a reductionist system of Western science. That means that scientists try to break things down to find out their component parts. For example, we can break the physiology down to the cellular and the subcellular levels, and this has yielded enormous progress in our understanding about disease. The problem is that health is a holistic phenomenon; it is more than the sum of all these different component parts. It transcends the parts. So if your approach is reductionistic, you lose the ability to create health. What you gain is the ability to create temporary, isolated effects in certain parts of the body, but you do that at the risk of creating problems in other parts. Modern medicine is basically a fragmented approach that ignores the whole in favor of looking at the parts.

"Of course we do have to keep in mind that there have been enormous advances in modern medicine in specific areas: surgical procedures, replacement therapy in cases of hormonal deficiencies, and the use of antibiotics to eradicate infectious disease. On the other hand, I'd have to admit that the widespread use of antibiotics is also fraught with problems. Today this approach is creating antibiotic-resistant organisms—germs—which are potentially a very great health problem. These organisms are resistant to the very drugs that we use to treat them.

"The basic problem is that our system today is disease-oriented rather than health-oriented. Doctors are always looking at individual diseases in isolation, but not at the solution to those diseases, which is holistic, which is to create health, wholeness. It's as if we're in a dark room, and we're spending all our time trying to diagnose darkness: how many kinds of darkness there are, how did it get here, and how do we get rid of it. In the midst of this focus, we'll miss the fact that all we have to do to get rid of darkness is to turn on the light. In fact, darkness in nothing other than the absence of light. All the different disorders that we find so fascinating in conventional medicine are really just an absence of one element, which is health. In a natural approach we focus our resources on enlivening health. It's a holistic approach that gets to the root of the problem of all diseases. It's an approach that can actually create a disease-free society."

Dr. Rothenberg says that interest in natural medicine is sure to grow as doctors all over the country continue to incorporate it in their practices and publish their research findings, and this will drive a change in public policy.

"Already, there's considerable interest in the mainstream medical community in complementary and natural medicine, something that wasn't there even a few years ago." He points to the announcement by the *Journal of the American Medical Association* that it will devote an entire issue to research on natural medicine in late 1998.[23]

"This approach can easily be integrated into our health care system," says Dr. Rothenberg. "The research shows it can help save hundreds of millions of dollars annually. Teaching doctors how to promote health from within will be more cost effective than trying to fight these innumerable diseases one by one, and it will be more humane."

Dr. Rothenberg walks with me out the door. I've got time before I have to catch a flight to the West Coast, so I skip the freeway and take the route through the city. In a few minutes—no surprise—I'm caught in traffic on Harry Hines Boulevard. Looming large to my left is the University of Texas-Southwestern Medical School and Hospital Center. Inside, I envision that people's lives are being saved— ER style—diseases are being treated, crises are being averted, and new crises are being created. It's a huge complex, an institution of fortresslike proportions. A sweeping change in the way we treat our sick and keep people healthy, at least on the scale of what Barry Charles and Stuart Rothenberg envision, would not come easily if the American people didn't want it. It is the people who are driving the reform. They are pushing the medical doctors, the men and women who took oaths when they became physicians to "heal or at least to do no harm," to take their oaths to heart. So now more and more medical doctors in this hospital and all over the country are working with other qualified health care professionals to identify new and better ways to care for our health.

How will that hospital look in five years? In ten years? It's exciting to think about because we can play a pivotal role. We can help those doctors make that decision and shape our future through the health care choices we make and through the people we elect to office.

9

Beyond Sustainable Agriculture: Going Organic

How damaging are chemical pesticides? Each square meter of healthy topsoil is home to as many as a million organisms, which maintain the fertility, drainage, and aeration of the land. A heavy reliance on chemical pesticides kills these naturally occurring soil organisms and interrupts the natural nitrogen cycle. By destroying the soil's ability to regenerate itself, these chemicals actually enable more pests to take over the soil, and an increase in pests produces the need for even larger doses of pesticides.[1,2] This vicious cycle, while profitable for the agrichemical industry in the short-term, destroys the long-term sustainability of agriculture. Worse, new evidence shows that the most heavily used agricultural chemicals are also hazardous. Farmers suffer from a high incidence of deadly diseases, including leukemia and cancers of the liver, prostate, stomach, skin, brain, and lip.[3] One herbicide, atrazine, which has been banned in many countries (including Germany, Italy, Sweden, Norway, and the Netherlands) but is still widely used in the United States, damages the liver, heart, and kidneys. In addition, many synthetic farm chemicals mimic estrogen and have been linked to reproductive disorders, including decreased sperm counts and sterility in males[4] and increased breast cancer in females.[5] These chemicals have even been linked to decreased intelligence in both males and females.[6,7]

November 10, 1997.   Given the choice, Patrick Piel would prefer that all the foods his family eats be grown without potentially hazardous chemicals. So would a lot of other people, when you consider that the organic market is the fastest-growing sector of the U.S. food market. Piel's preference comes from experience. He has been a farmer for thirty-four years. The first twenty-four years were spent growing food with commercial fertilizers; the past ten years growing it without them.

It's harvest time, and Piel is riding twenty feet up in the cab of his huge red combine. It is cold outside, maybe fifteen degrees Fahrenheit with wind chill, but the cab is toasty. I am sitting on a toolbox, squeezed in next to Piel, as he works the final fields of his 250 acres of land one hour west of the Mississippi. People say that Iowa is flat, but we are riding over farmland that keeps undulating like high, lazy ocean swells.

This is my first time on farming's front lines—at least since field trips in grade school—watching the first steps of my meal coming to market. At first glance it appears that the combine is scooping up nothing more valuable than an enormous mouthful of tall weeds, but a more careful look reveals thousands of soybean pods hidden amid the stalks. I am with Piel because he is a friend and because he is one of dozens of organic farmers across the United States who advise the Natural Law Party on agriculture policies.

"Other than the weather, the most serious problem for an organic farmer is weeds." Piel is shouting to me over the noise of the combine. "Foxtail can wipe you out. But as you can see, I have a clean field here." He looks at me for confirmation. I look ahead and nod, not knowing what I am nodding at. "I plowed this field early in the spring. I worked the soil down with a disk and let it sit until all the weeds sprouted. Then I ran my disk back over it again and chopped up all the weeds. Then I planted my soybeans with a soybean drill. I have a beautiful crop this year. No problem with weeds."

I ask Piel how what he does differs from the ritual of the farmers growing soybeans with chemicals all around him. He talks about a farmer a half mile up Highway 1.

"He prepares his field in the fall, and then, in early spring, he plants Roundup Ready soybeans, beans that have been genetically engineered to be resistant to the Roundup herbicide [the same herbicide that John Fagan talked to me about]. After the beans have grown about eight to ten inches tall, he sprays the crops with the herbicide. The weeds die, and plants live. A few days later the dead weeds—they're called dead carcasses—have withered away, and all that's left is a plain bean field."

Piel breaks away from his story for a moment to think. Two days before, he walked through that farmer's fields to look at his crops.

"It's scary in a way when you walk into one of those fields. You can actually feel the difference. I went into the fields right after they were sprayed, and I could see the tremendous amount of poison on the plants. The genetically engineered beans also look kind of plastic, not like real beans. Something had been altered in that bean. They were shiny in a weird way," he says.

Piel shuts down the combine and clambers down the metal ladder to my left. He has to knock some mud off the huge rotating blade that cuts the soybean plants. His produce will be used for human consumption, so it has to be delivered clean—no dirt. His neighbor's soybeans will be sold for animal feed or will be pressed into oils. They can be sold dirty.

We're rolling again, at about ten miles an hour, and now Piel is talking profits. He makes a lot more money growing organically than a conventional farmer does because his input is less and because the demand for what he grows, organic soybeans, is greater than that for beans for animal feed. Piel spends about $50 an acre on seeds and "green manure"—alfalfa, clover, or rye—whereas a conventional farmer spends about $135 to $150 an acre on seeds and commercial herbicides, pesticides, and fertilizers. Piel sells his soybeans for $20 a bushel, whereas a conventional farmer gets $7 a bushel.

"Bottom line: It costs me less than half as much to put plants in the ground, and I can make three times as much profit," he says.

Better yet, demand for organic is exceeding growers' capacities. "We are not keeping up by any means whatsoever. If I wanted to grow five thousand acres of this soybean, I could sell everything I grow and still have many, many buyers calling me. The organic market in the U.S. will buy. The Japanese will buy; the Chinese are importing," he says.

Piel's soybeans are first certified by the Organic Crop Improvement Association. He then delivers the beans to the nearby Reiff Grain Elevator, an operation that has serviced farmers throughout much of the Midwest for more than twenty-five years. Here is a sign of the changing times.

"For the first time Reiff has gotten himself certified organic so he can clean and bag our soybeans," Piel says, smiling. "There's a good profit in it for him. He makes over two thousand dollars a day cleaning the beans and loading them in containers that go to Japan [each bag is thirty kilos]. He'll do that many times in November, December, and probably January too. He could do many times that amount if the beans were there."

Piel has a kind, easy, weather-worn face and the rugged, leathery hands of a life spent working the soil. He has been farming, almost without interruption, since he was a ten-year-old boy helping his father work several hundred acres in Moscow Mills, Missouri (population 339), on a farm set off Highway 61, north of St. Louis.

He loves farming, but he is ready to make the shift from the fields to the classroom. He wants to take his thirty-plus years of experience and train farmers to "grow pure"—no commercial fertilizers, pesticides, herbicides—nothing that the Organic Crop Improvement Association wouldn't approve. "The future of farming is organic. Every year there are hundreds of people coming into organic from all over the country."

Piel's 250 acres are about average for organic. He talks to some farmers who do as little as 75, but there is a new trend toward large, up to 5,000 acres. Farming is hard work, and organic farming can be the toughest. So why does he do it?

"Somebody's got to; somebody's got to make the change."

Piel is surrounded by conventional farmers, men and women who just a few years ago looked at him with suspicion but who now approach him with genuine interest, often helping out during harvest time if he runs late, as he is this year.

"I get along with all the farmers around here. I do a lot of business with them. I have a great relationship with them. I don't preach organic, but they see what I am doing, and if they are interested, then they will change," he says.

I swivel clumsily on my toolbox and squint out back through a narrow window to see the glow of freshly threshed beans piling high in the combine's grain bin behind me. It takes about twenty seconds from the time the blade in the front severs the stalk for the beans to make their way through various screening processes and pour out into the bin. Piel tells me he can fill up a bin of 135 to 140 bushels in about thirty-five minutes. "They come out clean and pure," he says with pride, "just how the buyers want them."

I call Piel the next day to see how late he worked last night. He has been under tremendous pressure to finish the harvest in the next few days and has been out in the cold late to get the job done. He says he climbed out of the cab at 2:00 A.M.

"I love farming, I do. I also love to teach, to set an example for other farmers. I have a lot of experience. I have been through it all—every possible experience you can imagine, I've been through it. The future is organic."

Moving Public Policy Toward Organic

Francis Thicke knows agriculture. He received his Ph.D. in soil fertility from the University of Illinois and has spent four years working in Washington, D.C., at the U.S. Department of Agriculture Extension Service as the national program leader for soil science. He has also been farming his whole life.

Now forty-seven, Thicke grew up working on his father's dairy farm near the tiny town of La Crescent, Minnesota, across the river from La Crosse, Wisconsin. Even after he went away to college or worked with the USDA, when he came home for a visit, "I'd pick up like I never missed a beat." For fifteen of those farming years he has been doing organic agriculture. So Thicke knows agriculture from all directions—from the government and university sides, as a conventional and an organic farmer—and he has seen, firsthand, the impact of the agrichemical companies. In Thicke's view, it is time

110

for the U.S. Department of Agriculture to take a strong position in support of organic agriculture.

He is standing in the back of his pickup truck, stabbing big clumps of straw with a pitchfork and flinging the clumps ten yards away beneath a big, wide overhang, about the size of an Olympic swimming pool. He has jammed my microcassette recorder into the chest pocket of his red plaid shirt, and as he talks, I can see he is trying to remember to speak into his shirt pocket. I am standing beside the truck, shouting up questions. Thicke is trying to be helpful, but he has a lot going on. He checks his watch regularly, and he is constantly looking around to make sure his cows are where they should be. It's 3:00 P.M., it's getting near feeding time, and he has a schedule to keep.

Thicke and his wife, Susan, run this fifty-cow, 176-acre organic dairy, which sends milk products to HyVee, Easter's, and other local grocery store outlets in the southeast area of Iowa. Thicke's cows have a better life than cows in a conventional dairy, although, he says, "I don't have to work any harder to do it."

Thicke uses controlled grazing, which means that he has divided his farm into many paddocks and rotates his cows around the paddocks, letting them harvest their own food (forages) when the crops are at their peak of their nutritional value, for as many months a year as the weather allows. In contrast, most conventional dairy farms confine their cows. As a result, farmers must harvest the feed, store it, bring it to the cows, and then haul the manure back out.

"A waste of time and energy," Thicke says. He also feeds his cows only organic grain, avoids antibiotics, and doesn't use BST—bovine somatotropin—the controversial genetically engineered hormone that increases milk production in cows. As a result, he says, he doesn't have many of the problems conventional dairy farmers do.

"Cows develop foot problems from spending so much time on concrete, their immune systems are weakened from overuse of antibiotics, and their udders fail from being pushed to the limit of production. To get the most production, cows are fed highly concentrated rations and finely chopped forages, which can cause metabolic disorders. One common example is twisted stomach, which comes from not feeding a cow enough of what it was designed to eat: long-stemmed forage."

Thicke blames such poor treatment of the cows on "just too much emphasis on high production at any cost." He says that the average cow on a dairy farm lasts only about two lactations—about two years—in the milking herd before she is sold to be slaughtered. Then he points to several of his cows standing behind a fence. "We have a cow that's going to have a calf soon, and she'll be fourteen years old in a few weeks. We also have a couple of thirteen-year-old cows, and some ten years old. That would be unheard of in a conventional dairy."

The tone of Thicke's voice suddenly changes. "Careful of the bull behind you, Bob. He's okay, he just plays, but he plays rough, you know." I turn, and waist high is the face of a very curious, very formidable black bull, nuzzling at my shirt.

I continue with my questioning, trying to seem as casual around the big bull as I might around a mean-looking dog sniffing suspiciously at my feet.

The conversation shifts to organic farming as public policy. I am aware that the organic food market is booming. It grew 26 percent in 1997 and has been averaging about 20 percent a year growth for the past five years. But how is *organic* defined in the dairy industry? I ask.

"It means basically that the feed has been grown on land that hasn't had any chemicals on it for three years, at least," he answers, "although the biotech industry is trying to push genetically engineered food as organic. That has to stop."

Thicke contrasts organic agriculture with sustainable agriculture. "Sustainable doesn't mean the same thing as organic. It is an overused term that just means going in the direction of fewer chemicals and a little better stewardship of the land, but it's not well defined, and now everyone is using it, even the biotech companies. Whereas *organic* is well defined, it's concrete, and it's marketable," he says. "That's why the organic market is growing. Nobody sells anything that's 'sustainable.' "

Thicke (and I) are carrying buckets of feed to cows across the yard. He has, by his own description, a small farm. Today's commercial dairy operations are mammoth by comparison. Is organic destined to be sort of the "boutique shops" of agriculture, compared to the Wal-Marts of commercial farming?

"No," he says, shaking his head firmly. "Dairy farming could easily be changed over to organic. We already have the soil fertility taken care of through manure, and the weed and pest control are not really that difficult."

So why aren't more farmers using organic?

Ignorance of the facts and ignorance how to do it, he says. "People say, 'How can you feed the world with organic?' But they just haven't looked closely to see that it is viable, to see that farmers are making it work. When I hear doubts, I always think of solar energy, which many experts said wouldn't work in the northern U.S. Meanwhile there are a lot of people building solar houses that work just fine. It's the same thing with organic farming: Some people say it won't work, but there are a lot of people doing it just fine."

Thicke says the reasons organic farming can be viable today, more so than it might have been twenty years ago, are knowledge, technology, and expanding organic markets. Farmers know more about the cycles of pests and crops and have better equipment for controlling weeds.

"People think of organic farming as going back to their grandfather's way of farming, but it's not. It's using some sound knowledge from them, but also going much beyond that."

Thicke says more research is needed to move organic farming along faster, and that research, in principle, should be coming out of the land grant universities.* Instead the vast majority of the research is going toward chemical use in agriculture.

We are walking toward the barn, and I step gingerly over an electrically charged wire fence, put there to keep the cows in. Thicke is talking about changes that need to be made in three major areas: research, education, and conservation.

"First, the USDA needs more focused research on organic farming, not 'sustainable' but organic," he says. "That's mandatory." One promising sign of a shift in that direction, he says, came in the latest budget proposal for USDA, which included a section on research on organic farming.

"Second, we need to change the way we educate agricultural stu-

*Every state has one university funded by the government to do research on agriculture. These are the land grant universities.

dents. Right now we isolate them from the farms. Students spend four years in undergraduate school and little or no time on a farm. Then they go to graduate school and into research programs, and even then it's rare they get on a farm. When they are finished with school they are supposed to go out and teach farmers? It doesn't work that way. We need to integrate the farming experience into their education and professional experiences: internships for undergraduates and sabbaticals for researchers. We also need exchanges where farmers do some teaching and reinvigorate the land grant system."

Thicke stops his train of thought and tells the story of how, when he left the USDA to go back to farming, no one could believe his decision. " 'Why would anybody ever leave the USDA for a farm?' my colleagues wanted to know," he recalls.

Why did they respond that way? I ask.

"Probably because they didn't have the skills to farm," he says with a laugh. "There is a big gap between paper pushing and farming.

"As far as conservation goes, over the years the USDA has spent a lot of money for soil conservation, but what have we gotten for our efforts? Soil erosion may be a little less, but no-till farming, which requires chemical weed control, has increased dramatically, driven largely by USDA programs. This increased use of agrichemicals has put more pressure on our water resources, which has forced the USDA to spend many millions of dollars over the last decade on water quality programs.

"So it turns out that the USDA's prescription for good farming and soil conservation are, in fact, creating serious problems in a lot of other areas, such as water quality and animal and human health. We have to take a more holistic approach to protect our resources. When organic farming is done right, it helps protect everything—water, soil, air, plants, animals, and humans. We ought to give farmers in the U.S. incentives to farm organically, just as is being done in Europe right now."

Thicke puts in long hours on his farm. He works from 5:00 A.M. to 7:00 P.M., seven days a week, in sun, rain, or bone-chilling Iowa snow. He is trying to cut back, though, training someone to help out with milking and other chores.

Why are you doing this? I ask.

"A lot of reasons, but mainly conviction and challenge," he replies, sounding a lot like Patrick Piel. "My conviction is that I don't think we should be putting all these chemicals into the soil. My challenge is to find ways to do it and to work out systems so other farmers can do it too."

Thicke's conviction spills out in other ways. He heads a mentoring program that trains local farmers in southeastern Iowa who want to shift to organic agriculture; he is a member of the USDA's State Technical Committee, which advises USDA administrators on how to implement USDA programs; and he is a member of Iowa's Organic Certification Advisory Committee, which is developing guidelines to regulate certified organic production in Iowa.

We have to stop talking now because he is pouring buckets of grain into a grinder that is so deafeningly loud I can't hear myself think. Afterward he tells what he puts in the feed: corn as a base—"the energy for the cows"—then hay, which provides fiber and some protein, and lastly soybean meal, which provides more protein—all of it organic.

We have just tramped through mud and are now feeding more cows, pouring the grain into troughs. It doesn't look like much food, considering how big the cows are, and they seem to be inhaling it as if they could never stop. Are cows always this hungry? I ask. Will they always eat no matter when you put it out?

"Yes, they'd eat this grain until they got sick and died," Thicke says, chuckling to himself, as he carefully pulls away the bucket of grains.

Thicke says the move toward organic agriculture in public policy is sure to be discounted by many people, but it's a move that is environmentally mandated, market-driven, and already taking place across the country.

"For a long time researchers, in particular, thought organic was just too far out, they would simply discredit it as unnecessary," he says. "But times are changing, and there is definitely more interest now—especially with the booming organic market. Even the governor of Iowa is behind organic certification for the state. He's pushing it for economic reasons, but nevertheless he's pushing it."

Thicke shows me the barn where he and Susan milk the cows, the holding tank where the milk is cooled, a smaller tank where it is pasteurized (a legal requirement in Iowa) but not homogenized, and the machinery where the milk is bottled. His market has grown nearly 20 percent a year over the past five years, and he works hard to keep up with the demand.

He leads me upstairs to the apartment that he built for Susan and him—"temporary quarters," he tells me—until he can start work on a new house this spring. Susan is working on the books. She looks up and smiles. Francis tells her I am following him around for a book I am writing on the Natural Law Party. I look around at the apartment. Temporary nothing, I think. This place is beautiful, a dream farmhouse: huge wooden rafters cut across a high-beamed A-frame ceiling, thick carpets, antique furniture, a blazing wood-burning stove, needlepoint-covered pillows thrown on overstuffed sofas and chairs, and books and magazines piled up everywhere. There is a small television in the corner, but it looks as if it doesn't get much use.

Thicke loads me down with some of the magazines and articles on agriculture that I have requested. As he rifles through drawers, I scan what I have. On top of the stack is a proposal from the Illinois Stewardship Alliance calling for new government policies that promote safe, humane, and environmentally sound treatment of livestock. The problem with current policies, the alliance claims, is they allow "highly concentrated animal confinement systems—or factory farms—which can overload the environment with risky manure containment lagoons, cause surface and groundwater pollution through runoff and leaching of manure; generate offensive odors and overload air emissions; and saturate the soils with excess nutrients." Such factory farms also "push smaller farmers out of the market, disrupt rural communities, and use inhumane practices on animals."

Factory farms are a big problem here in Iowa, and the government is struggling for ways to deal with it. The proposal I have in my hand offers a sixteen-point action plan for enacting public policies to correct the problems, including far more stringent regulations, proper planning for manure management, more regularly held inspections, and a ban on large-scale facilities in environmentally sensitive areas. I fold the proposal and put it in my coat pocket. I will pass this along to the Natural Law Party's platform committee for further review.

I also have a copy of the newsletter from the National Campaign for Sustainable Agriculture, an organization headquartered in Pine Bush, New York. The newsletter reviews the campaign's achievements and setbacks in pushing for funding for sustainable (I imagine Thicke saying, "organic, organic") agriculture programs under the Clinton administration. "Peaks and valleys," the report concludes. I stuff that report into my pocket. In fact, everything Thicke gives me looks good.

I thank him and his wife for their time and hospitality. I have been moved by the work they are doing. It's people like them, I say, who make me realize even more strongly than before that the Natural Law Party can be a mainstream political voice for America. Clearly, no other party has so many people speaking up quite so loudly.

10

America's Energy Future: A Solid Basis for Optimism

More than 50 percent of the electricity in America is produced by coal-burning power plants, the dirtiest of fossil fuels. The dangers of burning coal are well documented. It produces acid rain, which has severely damaged our forests and waterways and costs society nearly twenty-five billion dollars each year.[1] It pumps into the air each year an estimated 150 tons of mercury, which can cause neurotoxicity in fetuses as well as enter the food chain. Research also shows that air pollution and other contaminants from burning fossil fuels kill sixty-four thousand Americans a year—more than those who die from auto accidents.[2]

These facts alone are enough cause to shift our energy system to clean, renewable energy technologies. However, a three-volume study by twenty-four hundred scientists on climate change resulting from global warming presented to the United Nations in December 1995 makes the shift even more imperative. The study projects a 1- to 3.5-degree centigrade increase in world temperatures by the year 2100 based on projected carbon emissions. The study also sees a fifteen- to ninety-five-centimeter rise in sea levels.[3]

While scientists continue to debate the impact of increased CO_2 emissions, global average surface temperatures during the past decade have been the highest in recorded history.[4] It appears clear that there is significant risk of climate change that could severely undermine standards of living for people in all countries and do so for hundreds of years to come.

August 23, 1996, Washington, D.C.   The backdrop is perfect. A spectacular photograph of the earth—that familiar NASA picture of an emerald green jewel hanging out there in empty space—stretches from stage floor to the high-beamed ceiling of the Grand Ballroom of the Mayflower Hotel. You can't miss the message during this mini-conference on renewable energy: Ours is a majestic birthplace, a magnificent home in the heavens, and we need to keep it that way.

That's the point the speaker is making right now. But he's also talking about how precarious our home has become. Christopher Flavin is senior vice-president of the Worldwatch Institute in Washington, D.C., and coauthor of *Power Surge: Guide to the Coming Energy Revolution*. He is also one of America's leading authorities on the hazards of global warming and the need to shift to renewable energy technologies. He is addressing four hundred Natural Law Party candidates and supporters assembled in Washington for the party's national nominating convention. The message Flavin gives is a nonpartisan one, the same he would give to the Republicans and Democrats.

It's summer 1996—less than eighteen months before the conference on global warming scheduled to be held in Kyoto, Japan—and the facts about the dangers of carbon dioxide emissions are starting to seep into the public awareness. And Christopher Flavin, with his books and lecture tours and research, is at the forefront of the education of America. This is what he tells us:

A direct consequence of an energy system that consumes fossil fuels is that we are dumping roughly six billion tons of carbon into the world's atmosphere each year. These are fossil fuels that took billions of years to pile up in the earth's crust, and they are now being consumed in a relatively short time. In fact, in the last century, since the fossil fuel age started, we've significantly altered the chemical composition of the atmosphere.

Scientists around the world are working hard to figure out exactly

119

what this increase in concentration of carbon dioxide and other greenhouse gases is going to give us—and our descendants.

"The changes in average global temperature that scientists are projecting may not seem all that extraordinary," Flavin says. "But when you work with computer models that are used to simulate the world's climate, and you look at all of the feedbacks that exist, it turns out that the changes will dramatically affect the various relationships that determine the climate we have in particular regions of the world today."

Areas that are relatively hot and dry today may become even hotter and drier and turn into desert. Areas that are warm, tropical, and wet will probably become wetter and subject to more frequent and more severe tropical storms. The strength of hurricanes and the length of hurricane season are likely to strengthen. In fact, a variety of changes that are likely to increase in the earth's weather systems would increase the number of natural disasters, increase the magnitude of those damages, and also seriously threaten food production in many countries as changing weather patterns undermine our ability to grow food.[5]

Flavin's not letting up. He notes that we might be able to cope with this change if we had a population of a billion or two billion on the planet and didn't have all of our preexisting environmental problems. "But in today's increasingly crowded world, it's clear that climate change could severely undermine standards of living for people in all countries, and do so over many centuries to come," he says.

"The problem is that once greenhouse gases are in the atmosphere, there's no easy way to remove them," he adds. "With a local air pollution problem, you can put in place new technologies or new policies and change the problem overnight. It's the same thing with solid waste; it's the same thing with a lot of environmental problems. But with global climate change it's going to be irreversible for centuries to come.[6]

"Basically, this is a problem that we're bestowing on our children and grandchildren and leaving it up to them to craft a solution—a solution that's going to be much more difficult in the future than it is now."

Actually, Flavin is optimistic about the future. He gives two reasons: energy conservation and new technologies.

"Technologies and policies are at hand to deliver a new kind of energy system relatively quickly," he says. "It may seem hard to imagine that we could replace our oil refineries, internal-combustion engines, and coal-fired power plants with solar-powered generators, wind turbines, fuel cells, and other new technologies. But remember, the energy system we have today was created about one hundred years ago. And look at the rapid pace of change that we've seen in computers and telecommunications—all in the past twenty years. With the energy technologies we have today we can certainly create a very different kind of energy system—a sustainable energy system—over the next twenty years."

How can we push for that change? someone asks. The market will drive it, Flavin answers, and it will be driven through cost savings. As an example, he ticks off a few facts showing the waste and inefficiency of the current energy system:

- A typical coal-fired or nuclear power plant turns two-thirds of the fuel into waste heat.
- An automobile effectively utilizes only about 15 percent of the energy of the gasoline that's in its tank.
- A typical lightbulb uses only about 10 percent of the electricity that's coming into it.

"The whole system can be made much more efficient, and that will cut energy use of all kinds," he says. "That means even if new energy technologies are a little more expensive at first, they will still be more economical in providing the lighting, transportation, computing power, and other services that we need."

It's also time to move away from an energy system based on digging up and transporting bulk fuels, consuming them rather inefficiently, and putting carbon dioxide into the atmosphere. "We need to shift to a system that is based on manufactured technologies that are efficient and that are decentralized and modular in nature," Flavin says. "Already there are economies of scale. For example, a power plant is on the market that you could hold in your hand, and it costs less per kilowatt than the coal-fired power plant that's probably providing power to your home. There are also newer technologies, such as gas turbines and fuel cells, and manufactured renewable energy technologies, such as wind turbines and solar cells.

"In many cases, the cost of these technologies is already very competitive with fossil fuels and will fall further as they go into mass production in the next few years," he says.

Another sign of change on the horizon is wind energy, the fastest-growing energy source in the world today, yet few people know about it, according to Flavin. Nuclear is growing at only 1 percent per year, coal has not grown since 1990, and natural gas is growing at only 2 to 3 percent per year. But the wind power industry has averaged a growth rate of 20 percent per year since 1990, and in 1995 it grew 32 percent.

Flavin is a compelling speaker, and everyone is silent, listening. He outlines what's ahead and what needs to be done to get there. "We're at the beginning of a new age. We have to change some energy policies to get new technologies into the market. We need to charge for pollution rather than let people pollute for free. We need to tear down the market barriers that currently prevent wind power and solar-powered generators from gaining access to the energy grid."

There are quite a few environmentalists among the four hundred candidates here at this convention, and there are many others—doctors, business leaders, lawyers, homemakers, retired people, etc.—who are working to change our energy and environmental policies. Looking out over the audience, Flavin says, "If politically motivated people like yourselves get involved and work at the state and national level to make these policy changes, we can and will have an energy revolution in the next twenty years. We will create a sustainable energy economy."

Green Energy

I am standing in a corn-stubbled farm field outside the tiny town of Cedar, Iowa. It is icy cold, and there are two inches of snow on the ground. In front of me Tom Factor stands ten rungs up on an aluminum ladder that is braced against a metal tower that rises another 160 feet in the air. Attached to the tower, every 50 feet or so, are wind vanes, solar and temperature sensors, and tiny cups that catch stiff winds, coming today from the north, and spin furiously around. Factor is working to program a logger box at the base of the tower that connects together all the cables from the instruments above. He is unscrewing things, jiggling wires, and screwing things back in.

Factor is director of the Iowa Wind Energy Institute, and this is a wind-monitoring station. The station, one of twenty that Factor patrols, collects data for the Iowa Energy Center, a state-mandated agency for conducting research and helping put in place programs that can reduce Iowa's dependence on fossil fuels. These stations measure the wind to help plan a utility-scale implementation. Such stations, found in windy areas all over the country, are a key link in the rapidly growing high-tech world of renewable energy technologies. These technologies represent the energy future of America.

It is a crystal-clear day. I walk to stay warm while Factor works. There is not a cloud in sight. I turn, and behind me, maybe fifteen miles away (this part of Iowa is very flat; you can see a long way), I spot huge billowing clouds erupting out of the horizon. "What is that?" I shout over to Factor.

He turns. "That's a coal plant. It supplies electricity to our whole region. That's the smokestack from the plant."

That represents the past. Coal is shipped by train from Wyoming to fuel Iowa. The coal is burned in plants that pump carbon dioxide and pollutants into the air, contributing heavily—most scientists now agree—to global warming and acid rain and posing a threat to the very health of the planet. This is an archaic technology compared with the one that stands quietly before me. The information from these wind-monitoring stations will be used to run huge wind turbines. Such turbines are economical, clean, and entirely renewable (it's going to be a long time before America runs out of wind). This is the present—and the future.

Factor is a member of the American Wind Energy Association, active in projects with the National Renewable Energy Laboratories, and an adviser to the Natural Law Party's energy platform committee.

We are far from telephones and power lines, so a cellular phone, attached to the data logger and powered by a solar panel, downloads the data at regular intervals to computers at the offices of the Iowa Wind Energy Institute. Factor then analyzes the data and reports to the Iowa Energy Center in Ames. His maps and reports are posted on the energy center's Web site. The National Renewable Energy Laboratories, a division of the U.S. Department of Energy, in Boulder, Colorado, as well as meteorologists, independent power producers, and energy planners will use Factor's data to help estimate what the output characteristics of different wind turbines would be in different locations—vital information for understanding the economics of implementing wind energy in America.[7]

I ask him why he needs to collect such detailed information.

"Very small differences in wind speed make huge differences in the electricity-generating potential of the wind," he replies. "If you have a site that has an annual average of twelve miles per hour and another site that has an annual average of fourteen miles per hour, the fourteen-mile-per-hour site will produce as much as forty to fifty percent more electricity, with the exact same equipment, as the twelve-mile-per-hour site. That may seem like a very small difference in wind speed—one that you probably wouldn't notice if the wind were blowing on your face—but the difference in electricity production and economics would be vastly different."

Factor folds up the ladder and slides it into the back of his station wagon. His work is done. We head home, an hour away, and I ask him questions about the future of renewables—wind, solar, and biomass; how America's energy portfolio is changing; why the change is happening so fast—yet why it's taking so long.

We turn off a muddy farm road and pick up Highway 210 heading south. Outside my window, in the distance, we can still see smoke pouring out of the coal smokestacks. Eighty-six percent of Iowa's energy comes from burning coal, and it has been that way for decades.[8] But times are changing, renewable energy technologies are proving their worth, and the U.S. Department of Energy predicts that within the next ten to twenty years, wind energy in particular will be a significant part of the U.S. energy portfolio. Experts estimate that Iowa alone has enough wind resources to supply 5 percent of the energy needs of the entire nation.

"There many advantages of wind energy," Factor says. "The construction of new wind power plants is now cost-competitive and often more cost-effective than fossil fuel alternatives, such as coal and diesel. Wind energy also keeps jobs and money in the state. A wind farm of one hundred turbines can be maintained by servicing turbines one at a time instead of closing down the whole plant for service, as is often the case with fossil fuel plants. You can also produce the electricity in incremental amounts. If you need a little more energy, you can put up a few more turbines instead of building another large-scale power plant."

Critics claim there are disadvantages to wind—in particular, the fact that wind is intermittent—but Factor says that's becoming less of an issue because of the deregulation of the electric utility industry. "Wind energy is now being sold on the open market, and like any commodity, it can be shipped anywhere in the country. If it's windy in the Midwest and we're producing excess power here, then that energy can be shipped across transmission wires to the East or to the South, and vice versa. There also are systems that hybridize wind and solar, or wind and hydroelectric power, giving you solar-generated electricity or hydro-generated electricity when the wind is not blowing."

I ask, If wind is so economical, abundant, and clean, why does it represent such a small portion of the energy pie? It's a loaded question, but I want to hear Factor's answer.

"One reason is that it's still cheaper to continue to fuel an old coal plant than to build a new renewable energy plant," he says. "In Iowa today, the cost of producing a kilowatt of electricity by fueling an existing coal plant is about one and a half cents. The cost of producing a kilowatt of electricity from a new wind power plant is four and a half cents. But if wind power had access to the low-cost financing options available to utilities and were being produced on the scale of fossil fuel plants, it would probably cost two and a half cents per kilowatt-hour. That would make it far more cost-competitive."

Even as Factor talks about the potential cost-effectiveness of wind energy, he knows that there are more advanced technologies than wind, such as hydrogen fuel cells, but their costs are high. "Fuel cells are probably the energy source of the future," he says. "They produce steam as a by-product—an energy source without pollution.

Fuel cells can store power from solar roof tiles and solar window coatings or a small wind turbine. A cell can be placed in the basement of a house, thereby completely eliminating costly transmission grids. People would have their own clean sources of electricity. But it's not currently financially viable to implement. This is one of many examples of innovative products being developed with a view toward solving our fossil fuel dependence."

I ask Factor how America ranks in the world for renewables.

"Europe is far ahead in renewables compared to the U.S. For example, Europe in 1996 has held down CO-two emissions to just one percent above the 1990 levels, while U.S. emissions rose nine percent during the same period.[9] Within the U.S., California has taken the lead in renewables, with Minnesota, Texas, and now Iowa supporting the greatest new growth. Here in Iowa contracts have been signed and the installation will take place in the next two years for close to two hundred fifty million dollars' worth of wind turbines. That represents a little more than one percent of Iowa's electricity generation."

What has the reaction been from the fossil-fueled utilities?

"They have been opposed from day one. In 1992 the Iowa legislature implemented an alternative energy production law which mandated that the utilities produce a tiny fraction—one-point-two percent—of their total electric output from alternative renewable energy sources. The utilities resisted it. They fought heated battles in the courts and in the media. They claimed the plan would cost taxpayers millions of dollars to install these new technologies. They also claimed renewables were not necessary, that they were already producing enough clean electricity. Independent power producers found themselves caught up in the courts for five years, spending hundreds of thousands of dollars, fighting batteries of utility lawyers who employed every kind of stalling tactic. Fortunately the state law was upheld, with a few alterations."

Have the fears of the utilities come true?

"It certainly doesn't appear that way," Factor says. "In fact, the utilities are starting to understand that developing wind energy is very smart. It's a hedge against the inflationary costs of fossil fuels, and it gives them hands-on experience with a new technology that is going to become an important part of their portfolio as the years progress."

The free market is also starting to show its force. "Many people are requesting and willing to pay more money on their utility bills to assist the installation of renewable energy sources," Factor points out. "There are many surveys that show there is a very large customer base that will pay more for green energy—renewable energy or energy from clean sources—and these surveys have been verified with contracts. Consumers are starting to understand that they can vote with their dollars; they can push forward the transition to a better world through their buying choices."

I ask Factor about the other renewables. Iowa has plenty of sunlight and plenty of crops. While he believes that wind energy holds the most promise, solar and biomass will also play an essential role in a renewable energy portfolio. He discusses their pros and cons: "Solar energy has many excellent applications and is very useful in certain parts of the country. Currently, photovoltaic solar panels cost five to eight times more per kilowatt than wind energy because the solar panel materials and their efficiency are not yet as cost-effective as wind energy. In sunny areas with little wind and modest energy requirements solar can make a big impact. And costs will drop significantly with increased demand and breakthroughs in technology. Also, passive solar heating and hot-water collectors can significantly reduce electricity usage."

Because there's so much cropland and crop residue in Iowa, Factor says, there's considerable research being done in the state on biomass. "Biomass generators burn a fuel source, such as crop residues, grass, or wood, that generates heat to drive a turbine." There are also biomass digesters that directly digest grains and produce methane, which is then burned. They can also produce methane from city waste, which reduces landfill and odors while recycling trash. But there are some potential problems with biomass. First, if you grow special crops for biomass, such as switchgrass, it can take precious farmland out of food crop production. Second, you may end up using a lot of energy to harvest and transport the fuel source. And third, you may have to use polluting pesticides or fertilizers to grow a monoculture type of plant. So it's debatable whether biomass will become a very major electricity-producing fuel source. However, biomass will definitely have some important applications in certain locations, particularly here in Iowa, where there's a lot of crop residue."

What will it take to shift America's energy consumption away from fossil fuels toward renewables?

"Government incentives are needed to support new energy sources," Factor says. "Because of our current utility and automotive corporate infrastructure, if we rely only on economic forces, the rate of change will be too slow. Look at federal tax incentives for the fossil fuel industry. This is a mature industry which needs no support, yet it receives over five billion dollars each year.[10] And this doesn't take into account the enormous costs of keeping our oil pipeline open to the Middle East or the health and environmental costs of fossil fuels."

Factor supports a wide range of policy changes, including overhauling fossil fuel subsidies, giving tax credits to energy producers using renewable technologies, and setting renewable portfolio standards that would require power producers to provide a minimum of 10 percent of their power from renewable sources by the year 2010. Basically he wants to level the playing field for independent power producers to deliver renewables.

But there's another reason to change our energy system. "China and the rest of the developing world are looking to the U.S. as an economic and technological model," he says. "They are poised to implement an energy infrastructure to support electricity and automobiles that is just like ours. If that happens, the impact on health and the environment could be catastrophic. We have to set an example for the world through our use of reasonable renewable technologies.[11]

"But it all comes down to education, because energy is market-driven," he says. "People have to want green energy, even at a slightly higher price initially at least, because they know it will save the environment now and for their children's children. We have to protect the future today."

The Principles

11

The Roots of Natural Law in American History

December 5, 1997. It is such a relief to get out of Washington, D.C. I am making the eight-hour drive south to the Blowing Rock region of northwestern North Carolina for a conference of Natural Law Party leaders and to spend a morning with Mike Tompkins to find out about the roots of natural law in American history. As I drive, the present disappears into the past, and nature slowly reclaims its domain. I sweep by the town of Manassas, thirty miles outside the District and the site of Bull Run, where Union soldiers were routed in the first major battle of the Civil War. I pass the turnoff for the Natural Bridge in western Virginia, where Thomas Jefferson rode to escape the pressures of government and seek spiritual renewal. I make my way up into the Blue Ridge Mountains, crossing the New River several times, as it winds its way northward through mountains cherished as sacred by the Cherokee.

It may be a half-day drive from Washington to the balcony where I am standing in the shadow of Grandfather Mountain, scanning the snow-covered vista of rolling mountains that stretch out southeastward ninety miles toward Charlotte, but I am in a different world. Above me, seven planets and the moon are strung out like pearls on a string across the evening sky. Astronomers say it will be a hundred years before anyone will see a sight like this again.

I should probably just kick back and enjoy the panorama. But I've just been in Washington, and I'm thinking politics. I can feel the sharp contrast with our nation's capital, where lawmakers enact laws that bear little resemblance to the natural laws that surround me now, and I'm feeling frustrated and angry instead of easy and relaxed. The laws coming out of Washington are not rooted in the eternity and balance of nature's laws; they are dangerous, misguided laws that are rooted in short-term economics. Regulations that govern our precious resources—energy, food, environmental, and human—can be bought and sold to the highest bidders.

The role of natural law in public policy has been the foundation of democracies dating back to the early Greeks, dominated the writings and speeches of America's founders, but today it's given a backseat by politicians and lawmakers. The Natural Law Party believes that this is dangerous for the nation and that it is not what most people want. Natural Law Party leaders are working hard to change it. I am here to find out what needs to be done.

What Is Natural Law?

I never understood, when I was in school studying American history, what the words *laws of nature* actually meant. I knew they showed up frequently in the writings and speeches of America's founders. They are, after all, carved in stone in the Jefferson Memorial, the same words that appear in the opening lines of the Declaration of Independence. Were they some religious term that has since grown irrelevant or politically incorrect? Or were they archaic scientific terminology? I never *got it*. I never realized that natural law was the driving force that shaped American democracy. I also never took the time to read in depth about the men who founded the nation: George Washington, Benjamin Franklin, John Adams, Thomas Jefferson, James Madison, and the others. What were the subtle forces that shaped them? What did they study in school? What so inflamed them against authoritarian British rule and inspired them to invoke the term *natural law* as they wrote the Declaration of Independence and the U.S. Constitution?

In a few minutes I'm going to find out. Mike Tompkins and I are off the beaten path but are searching for one. We are working our way down the side of a steep ravine, looking for a path through woods to a huge rock I've been told about that overlooks a hundred miles of mountains. There we're going to sit and talk about natural law. We find the path, if you can call it that, and we continue straight down a rocky cut through the woods, dodging and dipping through a thicket of brush and branches of hickory, oak, poplar, hemlock, and pine. The trees are grand and huge, even though the region was clear-cut in the 1930s. That happened about the same time that President Franklin Roosevelt launched a massive public works project to build the Blue Ridge Parkway. It has to be one of the most beautiful roads in America. No billboards, no gas stations, no fast foods. It's an elegant 469-mile two-lane ribbon that twists like a high-country river through these ancient mountains, starting in North Carolina and running dry not far from Washington. During the spring, summer, and autumn months, caravans of cars make their way along the parkway, their passengers stopping to picnic and to gape and gaze at the vistas. No one in a hurry takes the parkway. This is a pilgrimage with no destination in mind other than the natural spectacle around the next bend.

We find our rock. I sit, and Tompkins stands quietly for a moment. He is a healthy-looking forty-nine-year-old, over six feet tall, with handsome, well-chiseled features, thick black hair and not a hint of gray in sight. "He's very vice presidential," one television news anchor told me after an interview in Denver.

Politics runs in Tompkins's veins. He's a descendant of Presidents John Adams and John Quincy Adams and of Daniel Tompkins, who was governor of New York and vice president for eight years under President James Monroe. Tompkins graduated from the prep school Andover in upstate Massachusetts as a Presidential Scholar and National Merit Scholar, with a perfect 1600 on his SAT exam and a ticket to Harvard. At Harvard he studied philosophy, anthropology, and literature, participated in the political reform efforts of the late sixties, and graduated with honors.

Tompkins has spent nearly two decades studying, writing, and lecturing on natural law and promoting to government leaders in Washington, D.C., a natural law–based approach to education, health care, and crime prevention. He has also worked closely with John Hagelin at the Institute of Science, Technology and Public Policy.

It turns out I am not alone in my ignorance about natural law. Few people have any real understanding about what natural law is or what it meant to our founders. So people enjoy it when they hear Tompkins talk on the campaign trail about natural law. They also seem deeply satisfied when they hear him talk on how the ideas about natural law that were central to the founding of America are the same ideas that are central to the Natural Law Party today.

Tompkins sits down. I make an obvious statement: American democracy changed the world. I ask him to put it into context. What was happening in the world at the time?

Tompkins paints a picture of an exceptional time, of an America "imbued with an atmosphere of extraordinary optimism about human knowledge. A new world had been discovered and explored—new lands, new plants and animals, new languages, new cultures, all grist for the mill of the new scientific method. Sir Isaac Newton had discovered the laws of planetary motion binding all celestial bodies in a harmonious unity. Political thinkers asked, 'Aren't there universal laws that unite all moral and political phenomena in a similar way, and can't we design the state so government doesn't get in the way of those laws?'[1]

"That was the mood of the time. Franklin and Jefferson were scientists, among the greatest of their day, on the cutting edge of this spirit that there was nothing we could not know, that all that exists is perfect, that the best way to do things is nature's way. There's a delightful story about a resolution passed on the eve of the Declaration of Independence in a town meeting in Ashfield, a small town in western Massachusetts. In their resolution the citizens declared 'that we do not want any Goviner but the Goviner of the univarse and under him a States Ginaral to Consult with the Wrest of the united States for the Good of the Whole.'[2]

"The founders knew that what they were attempting in building this new federal republic was novel. They saw it as an experiment in self-government that would be watched by the rest of the world with skepticism and a touch of envy because never before had this type of government been attempted over so large a territory. They were practical men—lawyers, businessmen, farmers—who also knew they had to build carefully if their experiment was to stand the test of time. In every decision they made, in every action they took, they felt the guiding hand of Providence. Though most were not churchmen, most did believe in a divine intelligence, and their compass was the philosophy of natural law."

Tompkins pauses to take in the view. It's a spectacular panorama up here: waves of deep blue mountains. The sun pokes its way through a big tuft of clouds down low on the horizon, and I can feel its warmth on my face. I take off my bulky parka. It's so easy to think up here. I remember reading that Thomas Jefferson and others had the nation's capital moved out of New York to the then-remote swampland of Washington, D.C., to get it away from the stress of urban living. I'm not sure that lawmakers in D.C. would be willing to pack up their offices right now and move to a more pastoral setting, but regular trips to the Blue Ridge would serve the nation well. We all need reminders of the precious covenant we have with nature, but for lawmakers it shouldn't be considered a luxury; it should be part of their job description.

Tompkins talks about how the influence of natural law pervaded the thinking of our founders. They thought of natural law as the supreme government. "John Adams called natural law 'the Great Legislator of the Universe,' " he says.[3]

He adds that our founders located the source of all our rights in natural law. "They believed that our individual rights to life, liberty, and the pursuit of happiness don't come from man-made law or from the tradition of customs and practices known as common law but belong naturally to all individuals by virtue of their participation in a universe ruled by eternal principles of order.

"Our founders also derived our political rights from natural law: the right to form a government, to vote, to have a say in the running of the country. These all were radical ideas when America was founded. In the first sentence of the Declaration of Independence, Thomas Jefferson attributes to 'the Laws of Nature' the right of the American colonists to establish their own government, 'to assume among the powers of the earth a separate and equal station.' "

Finally, Tompkins says, the founders also saw in natural law a model for this government. "John Dickinson, a delegate from Delaware to the Federal Convention in Philadelphia that drafted the U.S. Constitution, told his fellow delegates, 'Let our government be like that of the solar system. Let the general government be like the sun and the states the planets, repelled yet attracted, and the whole moving regularly and harmoniously in their several orbits.'[4] This was more than a metaphor for federalism; it reflected a deep-seated belief among the founders in the order of the universe and our place in it."

Tompkins stands up to stretch. The rock is still cold, but the air is getting warm. Little patches of snow remain from a huge storm that dropped forty inches several weeks ago. We start climbing up a ravine, switching back and forth, back and forth. In a few minutes, with another panorama in sight, we find dry ground and sit down against some trees.

Probably I should know this already, but I wonder where the founders got their ideas about natural law.

Tompkins tells me they studied them in school and were very widely read throughout their lives. I'm sure he could talk for hours, but he gives me a five-minute history of natural law in the West.

"America's founders studied the classical literature of Greece and Rome and were schooled in the Judeo-Christian tradition," Tompkins begins. "One of the earliest ideas about natural law is found in Greek philosophy. The term used is *logos*.[5] It means the unity, order, and destiny of the universe. This idea was developed by later philosophers who believed that each individual has a nature and at the same time is part of the larger nature, that each individual is developing the full potential of his or her nature in harmony with everything else. The purpose of law in a society is to preserve order so the individual can develop fully. For this to succeed, man-made law must be in tune with natural law. This is what justice meant to Plato and Aristotle.[6]

"A century later the Stoics took the concept of natural law a step further. They coined the term *cosmopolis*, from which we have our word *cosmopolitan*. Their idea was that we don't belong just to a particular town, state, or country but are citizens of the cosmos. We live in the cosmic city-state, and in this state we're all equal. Male or female, rich or poor, we all have the same fundamental right to the full development of our potential as essentially cosmic beings. For the Stoics, happiness comes from living our full potential, which is the same thing as living in accord with natural law; the two are one and the same.

"Natural law was at the basis of the most pervasive and successful legal system of classical times, Roman law. The civil law of Rome as well as the law between Romans and foreigners was held up to the standard of the *jus naturale*, the natural law, which was eternal and universal. A Roman jurist would examine a case and ask, 'Is my judgment in accord with the universal principles of natural law?' If it wasn't, he knew that the man-made law he was applying needed adjustment.[7]

"This natural-law based system maintained the Pax Romana, the Roman peace, and it endured as the foundation of legal systems throughout Europe for more than fifteen hundred years."[8]

I marvel at Tompkins's words. How could it be that I never learned this in my unabashedly liberal arts education? Natural law pervaded the Western philosophical, legal, and political thought that led to the founding of our republic. I had no idea of its influence until Tompkins started stitching the whole thing together.

"Christianity brought a new layer of understanding about natural law," Tompkins continues. "Christian thinkers distinguished between the absolute, eternal natural law of God, which had prevailed in the Garden of Eden, and a more relative natural law of latter-day man. This was the law that the individual discovered when he tried to understand God's eternal law and lead a good life. This gave great dignity to the individual and was the seed of later ideas about the natural rights of man.[9]

"Throughout the Middle Ages, legal systems were based on natural law—on a combination of Roman law and Christian doctrine," he says.[10]

During the Renaissance, according to Tompkins, the church began to lose its hold on secular governments. So European political thinkers sought a new justification for state power in yet another set of ideas about natural law. One crucial idea was "the state of nature."

"The state of nature was somewhat like the Garden of Eden or the cosmopolis," says Tompkins. "In this abstract state all were free and equal in exercising their rights to pursue happiness. In order to protect these rights, individuals formed a community. Once they had formed that social compact, they made a contract with an authority—a prince or sovereign—whose job it was to protect their rights. They loaned that sovereign some of their rights, and thus the state gained legitimacy. None of this actually happened—it was a theoretical model—until the founding of America."

Tompkins says that natural law theory so dominated the thinking of the eighteenth century that many universities in Europe established professorships of natural law. Many scholars and political activists wrote about natural law and the natural rights of man and described how if those rights were not being protected, the social contract was void and citizens had the right to revolt and set up a new state.[11]

Clouds are gathering in the southeast. Thunder rumbles in the distance. Five minutes ago we could see the glint of sunlight reflecting off the office towers in Charlotte. Now we can't. In these mountains the weather changes quickly.

Tompkins brings the story of natural law home to America. He says that all these influences—from the ancient Greeks to the modern thinkers—came into focus in the Declaration of Independence and the U.S. Constitution. "These great works were not sudden eruptions of a radically new theme of government," he says. "They were prominences in a broad political culture that had been gradually evolving for thousands of years."

I ask him what the founders were trying to structure with the new government.

"They believed that the order inherent in the universe could in some measure exist in human society, as long as government was set up in the proper way. They recognized what Madison called 'faction'—the tendency of individuals and groups to pursue their selfish interests to the detriment of the common good. To limit faction, they innovated new forms of government, such as the separation of the powers of the state into executive, legislative, and judicial branches, as well as a system of elected representatives. They thought that these new features, along with the vastness of America, would dampen the ills and enhance the virtues of democracy. An improved democracy would turn conflicting private interests into a public order that would better reflect the order of the cosmos.[12]

"The American experiment succeeded," he says. "Most countries in the world have since copied our model. But today we face challenges the founders never dreamed of: incredibly powerful technologies, much greater population densities, vanished geographical frontiers that leave us nowhere to expand, and an interconnected yet volatile global community."

As a result, Tompkins says, the systems innovated by our founders are no longer operating effectively. He gives several examples. "With instant communications and rapid transportation systems, sheer size is no longer an impediment to faction. A letter sent across the country no longer takes two months; it goes in a keystroke. The two-party stranglehold on our democracy—something not even implied in the Constitution—has dangerously weakened the separation of powers. Almost all the people who now make up the legislative, executive, and judicial branches of our government are either Democrats or Republicans. If they are on the same side of an issue, such as access to the election process, then the separation of powers has broken down and no longer serves the public interest. And our elected leaders can't effectively represent the people. A member of Congress in the late seventeen hundreds represented ten thousand to fifteen thousand people. Today that same office 'represents' six hundred thousand people."

It's time to head back. Tompkins has to give a lecture on this subject in fifteen minutes. We jump across a snowy creek bed, push through some brush, and get on a paved road. We walk a few hundred yards before the road starts to drop downhill. The conference center is about a quarter of a mile off to the right.

Those are some of our problems, I say. So what are the solutions?

"Basically there's just one," Tompkins answers. "We have to become truly self-governing, and that means we have to learn how to live in accord with natural law. We can never turn back the clock. Our challenge is not to stop progress but to align it with natural law. For this we must do today what the founders did in their day. When they wanted a better government, they took an old model of democracy and improved it with the best science of their time. To meet our challenges, we have to do the same thing. We must look at the way nature governs in the light of new scientific knowledge and do a better job of harnessing natural law. If our geographical frontiers have vanished, we find there's a new frontier within us. When we start developing our inner potential, we become healthier, more creative, and more prosperous as a result. If our representatives no longer represent us effectively, we don't need an additional five hundred thirty-five members of Congress; instead each of us can become more self-governing. That means each of us can learn to live more in accord with natural law so we don't cause problems for ourselves and others. If the separation of the powers of government is not protecting our interests, then we need to elect new leaders from new political parties who will ensure that it does.

"Our founders established a structure of government that protected individual rights and allowed the individual to flourish. It's not enough just to maintain the structure they put in place. In our far more complex world we must take the next step. We must empower ourselves with knowledge of how to develop our full potential, how to wake up to the totality of natural law within ourselves."

Tompkins senses that I need a little more explanation. "Modern science tells us we are not just a part of natural law but are its totality, that all the laws of nature found throughout the universe are also found in us. When we experience this reality, when we realize that we are cosmic, we begin to live spontaneously in accord with all the laws of nature that govern our health, our environment, and the whole universe. We don't make costly mistakes that need a big government to clean up. Then our government will be just like the government of nature: efficient, effective, and automatic. It will have 'automation in administration.' "

Tompkins also says that nature's government is nourishing to all. "Everywhere in nature we see infinite diversity evolving in one harmonious whole. That's nature's government at work, and it's the ideal of democracy as well. Our government, if it's functioning in harmony with natural law, will keep the country unified, while, at the same time, it will strengthen diversity and bring satisfaction to everyone.

"The Stoics said we are citizens of the cosmopolis, cosmic individuals. When we awaken to this reality, our government will be on a par with what John Adams called the Great Legislator of the Universe. This is the vision of the Natural Law Party. The knowledge is available to realize this vision today; it's up to us to use it."

This is just the knowledge that John Hagelin has been talking about since he started running for president in 1992.

12

Science, Consciousness, and Public Policy

Developing consciousness is the cornerstone of the Natural Law Party's platform. This is because America's problems are human problems—crime, domestic violence, drug abuse, and declining health in the face of an epidemic of unhealthy habits. The way to uplift human behavior is not through legislation regulating details of people's lives. You can't have police in every home, playground, business, and classroom. Instead the way to elevate human behavior is through education that expands creativity and intelligence and brings broad comprehension; education that harnesses America's most precious resource—human consciousness—and brings life into harmony with natural law, empowering people to govern their own lives better, so they create fewer mistakes and fewer problems for themselves and others, and lead healthier, more productive, more satisfying lives.

—JOHN HAGELIN

I studied the social sciences and journalism as a university undergraduate in preparation for a career I imagined would be spent largely in politics. I never could have predicted at the time that when I went to work with a political party, I would have a fluency in quantum mechanics and an understanding of theories of consciousness as well. After more than six years with the Natural Law Party, following John Hagelin all over the country, I now have both.

We have a completely new worldview today that has overturned the Newtonian model that was in place at the time of the American Revolution. While, just as in Newton's time, exciting new worlds are opening up at a faster and faster pace, these worlds reveal not only the unfathomable diversity on the surface of life but also the unfathomable unity that lies within.

Physics began as a march inward to discover the ultimate building blocks of nature, the discrete, foundational, material cornerstones upon which everything rests. Instead physics found not concrete matter, not atomlike particles at the basis of everything, but underlying fields, whose wavelike excitations constitute all "matter," all energy, all life. Discoveries of these fundamental fields and their applications through technology have completely transformed society, giving rise to modern electronic, communications, laser, and nuclear technologies.

But such discoveries are also transforming our understanding of *who we are*—of our minds, of our consciousness, of our place in the cosmopolis. What is consciousness, and what does it have to do with a political party?

John Hagelin is certainly qualified to answer that question.

First some background: Hagelin was born on June 9, 1954, in Pittsburgh, Pennsylvania, and grew up in Fairfield, Connecticut. He was at the top of his class at the Taft School for Boys and tallied the highest possible score on the school's IQ test—a genius 165. His success at Taft propelled him to Dartmouth College and launched him into the life of a research scientist. After just three years he graduated with highest honors in physics and coauthored and published a highly praised independent study in physics. He won a fellowship for graduate study at Harvard, where he received his Ph.D. in particle physics. Predictions made by Hagelin in his doctoral research at Harvard continue to be verified today. He is widely recognized as one of the world's experts in the behavior of certain elementary particles, according to his doctoral adviser, Howard Georgi.

Hagelin pursued physics with a passion, winning postdoctoral positions at two of the world's most prestigious research institutions, the Stanford Linear Accelerator Center in Palo Alto, California, and the European Center for Particle Physics in Geneva, Switzerland. In 1984 he accepted a post as head of the physics department at Maharishi International University in Fairfield, Iowa.[1] He did this, he said, motivated by his deep interest in developing human consciousness and convinced that the most advanced unified field research could take place there. His physics career flourished. He was the principal investigator of a National Science Foundation research grant on unified field theories, and he codeveloped, with physicists at other universities, a highly successful theory that unifies the fundamental forces and particles of nature. His sixty published research articles (e.g., "Weak Symmetry Breaking by Radiative Corrections in Broken Symmetry") include some of the most cited references in the physical sciences, according to *Current Contents* magazine.[2] His long-standing concern over social problems also prompted him to found the Institute of Science, Technology and Public Policy, a think tank at the university for seeking out, researching, and implementing innovative, scientifically proven solutions to America's social, economic, and environmental problems.

He can talk with expertise about a vast range of issues, from nuclear power and genetic engineering to election law reform and weapons of mass destruction. But his real expertise is in the cutting edge knowledge of quantum physics, as well as in how it sheds light on the understanding of human consciousness—specifically, what consciousness is and why it is so central to the Natural Law Party's platform. Given the time, Hagelin will talk about it in depth on the campaign trail, even though it doesn't always fit neatly into a sound bite format, and from what I've seen, no one glazes over, no one gets lost—not even the press. That's because he makes the issue simple and straightforward and because, it turns out, the issue is highly relevant to public policy. In fact, the Natural Law Party believes that human consciousness is the most crucial issue in its platform because consciousness is the most valuable resource we have as a nation. It is the untapped creativity and intelligence of 260 million citizens. Hagelin believes that by better understanding that resource and by learning to harness it naturally, we can solve many, if not all, of our problems.

October 7, 1992. Hagelin is back at Harvard for a very important lecture date. He is here not as a physicist but as a presidential candidate in his first run for president, speaking at the John F. Kennedy

School of Government. He is a featured speaker in a series on American democracy. The hall—theater-style seats up a steep incline—is jammed with several hundred students, faculty, and staff. Hagelin stands behind a spare podium on a stark wooden stage with a dark blue curtain behind him. He opens his talk with a broad brushstroke, introducing the usual basic platform points of the Natural Law Party, e.g., what the party stands for in health care, crime, education, foreign policy, energy, etc. Then he suddenly shifts gears.

"The uniqueness of the Natural Law Party is that we are a party of deep scientific principles. Unfortunately we don't always have an opportunity to present this knowledge, especially in a two- or three-minute sound bite. Tonight, however, I want to explain some of the deepest principles that underlie this party, principles that inform all our various policy planks. Specifically, I want to talk about the central role of human consciousness in public policy."

Hagelin knows that *consciousness* is a confusing term, in academic circles as well as for the general public. Say the word to some people, and they'll think you're talking about "consciousness raising" on an issue debated in the news. Others will think you mean someone was unconscious and now is awake. Others will assume you mean developing your inner creative potential.

The reason there's no clear consensus on consciousness is that most of us, including most scientists, have been using the wrong model, Hagelin says. "For three hundred years scientists studied inert matter as the ultimate reality—the building of blocks of life. On this material basis they constructed models of consciousness. Human intelligence or consciousness was, and in most circles still is, perceived as entirely a by-product, or epiphenomenon, of brain functioning, the macroscopic outcome of numerous microscopic electrochemical processes in the brain."

This means that consciousness has been seen essentially as *nothing*. You can't develop consciousness because there is nothing there to develop. This material, mechanistic model concludes that an individual's intelligence is basically fixed by genetics, fixed at birth.

"This purely materialistic view is woefully out-of-date," Hagelin says. "As lay scientists we are trained to see atoms and molecules as matter—miniature solar systems with electrons orbiting the nucleus. But that picture doesn't work. It was abandoned in the early

1900s because it failed to explain anything about atoms. Quantum mechanics took its place and has proven to be highly successful. But quantum mechanics has something rather radical to tell us about the foundation of the universe: *There is no matter down there.* Instead of a material electron, you have an electron wave function. But a wave function is just a concept. It's the potentiality for an electron to exist, and that's all there is at the quantum mechanical level: pure potentiality. The deeper you go in the exploration of nature, the more tenuous nature becomes. The more you try to grab on to the substance of what's down there, the more it slips through your fingers. Because it is not a 'thing' at all; it is a notion."

According to Hagelin, those notions constitute the four fundamental fields: gravity, electromagnetism, the weak force, and the strong force. Underlying those four fields is the unified field of natural law, the source of all forms and phenomena in the universe, including you and me.

"We have learned that the unified field pervades everything, gives rise to everything—not just the nature that we see outside of us but our innermost nature as well. We're not separate from nature, we're part of nature, and we share, if we go deeply enough, that same universal field that pervades everything."[3]

Hagelin says that our material body contains the same fundamental atoms and molecules, and is governed by the same fundamental laws, that govern the universe. In the same way, our intelligence, or consciousness, shares the same unified field of intelligence that governs the whole of nature. Our individual consciousness is like a wave in the ocean of nature's intelligence.

Hagelin has been on the cutting edge of this research for twenty years. He has brought together some of the best minds in physics to analyze these parallels. He has written many scientific papers on the connections between consciousness and the unified field, addressed critical audiences at hundreds of university physics departments internationally, and has written a book for government leaders and their science advisers, entitled *Manual for a Perfect Government: How to Harness the Laws of Nature to Bring Maximum Success to Governmental Administration.*

As novel as it may seem at first, this understanding of consciousness is not a new one among many scientists and physicists who share a deep grasp of nature's functioning. In fact, in the early 1900s Sir Arthur Eddington, the great English physicist, one of the fathers of quantum physics, was among the first to appreciate the inherently subjective nature of the deepest levels of nature's functioning when he said, "All through the physical world runs that unknown content which must surely be the stuff of our own consciousness."

Hagelin says that it's striking how the deeper structure of intelligence reflected in the human mind and consciousness precisely mirrors the deeper, quantum mechanical levels of intelligence seen in nature.

"Scientists have long been amazed at how the logical structure of the mind, which takes its most concrete shape in the various mathematical formalisms and theories developed over the past several centuries, precisely mirrors the intelligence displayed throughout nature," he says. "These logical, mathematical structures, spawned by the human mind, seem to fit nature like a glove."

Physicist Eugene Wigner, honored as the father of the atomic age, marveled at what he called the "unreasonable effectiveness of mathematics in the physical sciences." For Einstein, "the eternal mystery of the universe is its comprehensibility" by the mind. For Hagelin, the fundamental connection between consciousness and the unified field can best be understood through the integration of ancient and modern science.

"There are profound traditions of knowledge, dating back thousands of years, that offer an expanded physical framework for consciousness. Until the advent of quantum mechanics, this ancient knowledge remained virtually indecipherable. But now, in light of recent scientific discoveries, these ancient descriptions make sense. They describe consciousness as a universal field of intelligence underlying the whole of material creation.

"You can look with great mathematical precision and find that the deepest structure of human intelligence—as codified in modern mathematics and described in great detail in the ancient Vedic texts,[4] for example—exactly mirrors the structure of nature's intelligence displayed in the laws governing the physical universe—especially at the quantum mechanical level. One is drawn to conclude that the unified field of physics and the field of consciousness are one."[5]

For Hagelin this is more than an abstract academic exercise. He points out that these ancient traditions offer procedures that access and apply this field of consciousness in daily life. Some of these procedures are being used today in the workplace to improve productivity and in schools to boost creativity and being prescribed by doctors to reduce stress. He says that the Natural Law Party supports any procedure that has been proven through extensive research to develop human consciousness.

A student asks for specifics.

"Many programs aim to do this—different techniques of meditation and self-development—and we are looking carefully at everything," Hagelin says. "Right now the program with the most research is the Transcendental Meditation program,* a nonreligious, nonphilosophical procedure for reducing stress, promoting health, and increasing creativity and intelligence."

I look around the room. Meditation is quite mainstream in America today, and most everyone is familiar with the TM technique, but nonetheless there are a few surprised looks. You don't find meditation in too many political platforms. Hagelin has seen these looks before. He explains. "More than six hundred studies have been conducted on the effects of the TM technique at over two hundred independent universities and research institutions during the past thirty years, including Harvard, Stanford, and UCLA Medical School. The National Institutes of Health have given several million dollars to research the technique's effects on reducing high blood pressure and preventing heart disease. It's been used in schools, businesses, hospitals, drug rehabilitation centers, and prisons to help solve problems that nothing else has been able to solve. These are the kinds of applications, and that is the kind of scientific track record, that merit consideration for public policy. As research on other programs demonstrates their effectiveness, those programs will be incorporated into the platform as well."

Since John Hagelin spoke at Harvard back in 1992, he has given this talk many hundreds of times. Just as very few people know much about the role third parties can play in a democracy, so too

---

*Introduced by Maharishi Mahesh Yogi forty years ago, and now prescribed widely by doctors, used in some of America's largest corporations, and practiced by more than five million people of all ages, religions, and educational backgrounds.

few people know how programs that develop consciousness—our most precious resource—can be used, for example, in highly stressed, violence-scarred communities to improve health, learning ability, self-esteem, relationships, and society as a whole. So when reporters ask why such programs are in the platform, as they inevitably do, I tell them stories about their use in our inner cities. Those stories answer their questions better than I ever could.

The Applications

13

Quiet Time at the Fletcher-Johnson School

The drive from one end of America to the other took me one hour and fifteen minutes in my rented Chevy Lumina. I started the journey in Potomac, Maryland, a serene and beautiful bedroom community north of Washington, D.C., where I spent the night at the home of a friend, and I reached my destination in southeast Washington, the hard-core drug- and gang-infested world that is a fifteen-dollar cab ride from the White House, but a million miles away from the American dream. America works for people in Potomac. Nothing much works for the people in southeast Washington.

It's January 14, 1998, 10:15 A.M., and I am driving up a hill and turning into the parking lot at the Fletcher-Johnson Learning Center, just off Benning Road at Forty-sixth Street, a place whose back streets are so harsh, so destitute, so crime-ridden that it is considered one of the worst areas in the country. The Fletcher-Johnson Learning Center is a public school, grades K through nine. It is a huge, imposing concrete building; out of context, it almost looks like a castle without turrets—a fortress without windows—sitting at the top of this hill. I am fifteen minutes late for an appointment with George Rutherford, Ph.D., the principal of the Fletcher-Johnson Learning Center. There are two security guards at the top of the stairs, where I sign in. But there is no metal detector. In fact, I had been told that Rutherford's school is the only public school out of twenty-five in Washington with no metal detectors.

I write my name and am escorted to Rutherford's office, where I wait. Rutherford is out but will be back shortly. A young boy walks in and takes a seat one chair over from me. Within minutes we are old friends, telling each other secrets. Howard is seven and is waiting for someone to come take him home. He has ringworm. He shows me his spelling and arithmetic tests. Only one mistake on all of it. He is a Washington Redskins football fan but likes Jerry Rice of the San Francisco Forty-niners (my team, I tell him). An older child pushes open the door and talks to Howard. It is Keith, his eleven-year-old brother, coming to look out for him. Keith leaves, and we resume our conversation. I ask Howard about Dr. Rutherford. Do your friends like him? I ask. Big smile and a nod. "Yes. A lot! We all call him Doc."

Howard tells me that he has three brothers and eight sisters. His oldest brother is in jail.

You're not going to go to jail when you grow up, are you? I ask. "No," he says, shaking his head firmly. "I'm gonna get a good job when I grow up. I'm gonna be a taxi driver and make lots of money and buy a big, fancy house."

A few more minutes of chitchat pass before Keith comes to gather up Howard and take him downstairs to their aunt, who will take him home. Howard and I are pals. He sticks out his hand for a final shake, and then he's off.

I sit there thinking about how Howard eagerly voiced his aspirations for his life, and it bothers me. How naive I am to think he would want to be a doctor or a teacher or an investment banker! Who is his role model? I was to hear later in the day that any child in southeast D.C. who has a father with a job has a hero in his life and is the envy of his classmates. In fact, when many kids are asked what they want to be when they grow up, they often admit, "What difference does it make? I'll probably be dead." Or else, "I'm going to jail where you get two squares [meals] and TV."

I've got a *Washington Post* in my lap. Front page: Sixteen-year-old girl is shot and killed at a gas station. I look for the address. It's on Benning, just four blocks away. It seems that a sixteen-year-old boy, a classmate, was trying to make conversation. She ignored him. He pulled a pistol out from his belt and fired several shots into her chest. That was yesterday. Across the top of the metro section is a story of the city manager from Austin, Texas, a white woman, who has been hired to manage the cash-strapped, no-morale District of Columbia. There is a big outcry over why a white woman from out of the District has been chosen over a local black person. I make a mental note to ask Rutherford about that.

There's another article, a column by Courtland Malloy, an elegant and poignant writer, talking about how black males have a dispro-portionately high risk of getting prostate cancer, AIDS, high blood pressure—basically, of dying an early death.

Before I can find anything else to uplift me, George Rutherford pokes his head in the door, offers a big, open smile, and motions me out into the hallway. We shake hands and say how good it is to see each other. I follow him through some double doors and down concrete steps across a hall and into an anonymous, unmarked base-ment office. This must be where George Rutherford gets away from it all. A cellular phone that he carries in his hand at all times and a walkie-talkie stuffed in his back pocket never stop ringing, never stop demanding his attention. It is here that we spend the next ninety minutes as he talks about education, race, stress, building a community, and developing consciousness.

George Rutherford stands about six feet one inch, is fit and trim, with hair that is closely cropped and a hairline that is receding. He doesn't have a line of worry in his face. In fact, he has a seamless, almost boyish face and looks ten or fifteen years younger than his fifty-nine years.

Rutherford was born in Charles Town, West Virginia, and attended nearby Bluefield State College for one year. He transferred to Shepherd College, where he was the only black to play on the college's all-white basketball team. That was in the mid-fifties, and it is clear in his retelling that he felt the cruel brunt of racism. After one year he transferred to Still-man College in Alabama, from which he graduated with a teaching cre-dential. He and his wife, Sandra, moved to the D.C. area, where he taught in the public schools for ten years. Then, in 1973, with four children to look out for, Rutherford and his wife agreed that he should go back to school, this time to the University of Pittsburgh, and get a Ph.D. in counseling psychology. In 1978 *Dr.* George Rutherford took over as principal of the Fletcher-Johnson Learning Center.

Rutherford has turned Fletcher-Johnson into a safe haven for his 700 students—699 African-American and 1 white, ages four through sixteen. It's a refuge from the mean streets—from the drugs and filth and violence—and from the absence of discipline and love of many of their parents who are crack addicts or in jail. Rutherford is deeply loved and admired by his teachers and staff—you can see that in the way they greet him as he walks through the halls—but more than that, he is adored by his students, both past and present. He is a real-life *Stand and Deliver* movie. He can even walk up to gangs on the streets—shooters and druggers—and talk without fear.

His suit coat is off, and he's got on big yellow suspenders. He clasps his hands behind his head and waits for my first question. Before I can speak, he eyes the *Post*. He is annoyed by the people in his community who would divide the city over race. He points to the headline about the white city manager from Austin. "Racism cuts both ways," he says. "Here is a woman who seems to be very qualified, who could help the District, who wants to come and make a difference, and we've got people here who bring up race. Will we not let her come because she's white? My only question is, Is the woman qualified to do the job? It's so deep, this racism thing, and it's both ways. The only hope, the only solution is more, and better, education that changes people from the *inside*."

Rutherford is a churchgoing Baptist. He is an intelligent, energetic, caring family man and an involved pillar of his community. He tells me the part of his life story that got me here. He was invited to hear John Hagelin speak in October 1992 at the Natural Law Party's national nominating convention at the Grand Hyatt Hotel in Washington. Rutherford says he was "awestruck" by Hagelin—by his intelligence and how he articulated the issues, the problems and solutions. More than that, he was struck by Hagelin's honesty. (This is from an educator who has weathered thirty-five years of turbulent political firestorms in D.C.'s public school system.)

"John Hagelin is an honest man, I could tell right away," Rutherford told me. "He cares about the common people; he is compassionate. If he wasn't so honest, he might do better in politics—but only in the short term, not in the long run."

Rutherford read through the platform and saw research on the Transcendental Meditation program cited in the health section. Intrigued, he looked into the technique, and he started it as a way to help reduce the stress load on his heart. He couldn't believe the deep rest and peaceful repose the technique provided him, easily and at will. There was nothing foreign about the experience. It was all very familiar and very comfortable, a simple technique that he learned easily. He thought of his students, of his school, of the vise grip of tension that each child must cope with every day. It's a stress that can cripple, that can crush, that can demoralize a youngster's dreams and aspirations. It can make him crazy, make him unable to concentrate or focus in school, make him turn to drugs, to crime, to violence. You think of the suburbs, and maybe you don't think stress is an issue that needs to be part of a political platform. But, Rutherford says, when you think of southeast Washington, you think, What could be more important?

He saw immediately the benefits of the technique in his own life, and he wanted to give the same to his students and teachers at Fletcher-Johnson. Why not, he thought, structure a "Quiet Time" into the school's daily routine, twenty minutes twice a day, once before class began at eight-fifty in the morning and once before school was out at three-ten in the afternoon? No talking, no goofing. Students could draw quietly, they could rest their heads on the desk, or they could practice TM. Basically they could do whatever they wanted, but they had to do it quietly. Rutherford was serious about it. He decided that anyone who caused a problem during Quiet Time could be suspended.

He broached the idea to his teachers, and he got a go. The consensus was, the stress is overwhelming, we have to do something. So four years ago they started Quiet Time.

"We get the students down first thing in the morning and again at the end of the day. They are calmer, and as a result, the whole school feels better. Otherwise they come to school crazy—and stay that way all day," Rutherford tells me.

A nonprofit organization in the D.C. community raised funds to pay a qualified TM teacher to teach any student, parent, or faculty member who wanted to learn the technique (a student was required to bring a signed letter of permission from a parent or guardian) and to provide regular follow-up. Since Quiet Time began, several hundred students have learned the program. Nothing compulsory. It's just available to anyone who is interested. Rose Phillips is teaching TM to students who want to learn. She is a grandmother who was raised in Harlem and, like Rutherford, is a Baptist. She has taught TM in the inner cities for decades. She says the most noticeable benefits from TM are that the kids are more eager to learn: They read better; they have less of an "attitude" or edge about them. They are more polite to their teachers and get along better with their classmates. They learn faster and remember things better.

While the structure of the program has not been as ideal as Rutherford might have wanted—students at Fletcher-Johnson frequently get transferred to other schools, so the kids practicing the technique who move are left without follow-up—the improvements in the meditating students both academically and socially have been so dramatic, so heartening, so real that he "can see the light at the end of the tunnel" for schools in his community.[1] He is planning to retire soon, and his dream is to open a charter school where TM would be at the core of an otherwise standard academic curriculum.

I ask Rutherford to show me around Fletcher-Johnson. The school is big. There used to be 1,450 students here just a few years ago, but a large housing project nearby was condemned, and the families and the students from there were relocated elsewhere. We walk along a hall that suddenly opens up into a huge, open space, with clusters of desks—twenty desks in this corner, fifteen desks in that corner—filling up the void. These are classrooms. It's so odd, I tell Rutherford, because basically there are no classrooms. He shrugs and nods. He's been here for twenty years, is used to it, has no reason to complain, can't do anything about it anyway. But why the layout? I ask. He tells me that for some reason the architects figured that several big open spaces, almost like miniauditoriums, would be a better learning environment than closed-off rooms. So that's what he's got. Standing partitions with charts and maps and poster pictures do their best to separate one "class" from the next.

Noise can be combustible in a building like this, I think, so I can see another reason for Quiet Time to start the day off right.

We are walking through yet another hall that is completely empty. It looks as if it's Sunday, and no one is here, not even the janitors. I ask what's going on. Rutherford runs a very tight ship. If it is class time, students had better be in class. We turn a corner and run across a few stragglers, and Rutherford is on their backsides fast: *"James! What are you doing out of class? Where should you be?"* James smiles and scurries down the hall, turns the corner, and slips through a door into his "classroom."

It's what is called tough love. And Rutherford is nothing if not tough and loved at this school. As we walk through class areas, every student who sees him—I am not exaggerating here—lights up, young and old, boys and girls alike. It is overwhelming. I've never seen anything like it. "Hi, Doc!"; "Howya doin', Doc!"; "What's happening, Doc?" they say. Then they see me trailing a few steps behind, just watching the whole thing unfold, and fleeting puzzled looks cross their faces, as in "Who's *that* guy?" But then they are back looking at Rutherford, eager for his glance, his approval, his love. He is their father, grandfather, uncle, big brother. He is as devoted to them as they are to him. In fact, he hires as many former students as he can to work at Fletcher-Johnson after they finish school—as teachers or administrators, if they graduate from college, or as maintenance staff, if that is their qualification.

We're back from our walk. It's noon, and Rutherford has more to say, but he has to excuse himself to help out the faculty with lunch duty. Fletcher-Johnson is cash-strapped. The stoves and ovens once used for home economics are cold because there was no money to hire someone to teach that course. There is not even money for substitute teachers. If a teacher is out, someone has to take the class, even if that someone is the already overworked George Rutherford.

He leaves me in the office with my thoughts. I am surprised at how strong Rutherford is on TM. Is he pushing for it too hard? But then I catch myself. What can I possibly know? In an hour I will leave here, drive back across the Anacostia River, past the White House, up Massachusetts Avenue, and head out to Potomac, Maryland. My stress will be coping with sluggish rush hour traffic. George Rutherford will stay right here in this awful, unrelenting pressure cooker with the ever-present specter of violence and death hanging over everyone. He is cloistered here with his seven hundred kids, and their parents and grandparents, and the thousands of other kids he has had as teacher and principal during the past thirty-five years who have never left the southeast. Rutherford's students and their families—whatever remains of them—thrive, not on money or material comforts that 99 percent of Americans take for granted but on the love and support for one another that Rutherford tries to foster at his school. I decide that he isn't pushing too hard.

Rutherford bursts suddenly through the door, both phones ringing, followed by two men from custodial services. He signs some papers for them and then takes a call from his secretary. The pace is quickening; our window of leisurely chat is closing fast. On top of everything, in a few minutes Fletcher-Johnson has a big basketball game, and there's a lot he has to do before the first tip-off. He looks at his watch and says we've got a few more minutes.

I ask about his own children. They are grown with their own families, he says. Two of them are teachers in the D.C. school district, one is a biochemist, and one helps manage a Washington law firm.

I ask him about the state of the Union and about politics. I ask him if America's economic boom is reaching his community.

"None of it," he says.

I ask him about Republican and Democratic policies. Do they make an impact in his community?

"No, not really," he says.

What do you get from them? I ask.

"The same old stuff, warmed over," he says.

What's that? I ask.

"Welfare reform," he says dismissively. Rutherford says he's not interested in welfare reform. He wants his students—and his community—to be more creative, intelligent, dynamic, determined, and resilient. To have more self-esteem. To be more successful. He wants his kids to be as happy, healthy, and fulfilled as the kids in the suburbs. Why not? Why can't they be? He wants this from the depths of his soul, and it cuts him deeply that they're not.

Rutherford's not a finger pointer, but he does say that the Democrats and Republicans share much of the blame "because they offer nothing new and because they keep out anything that is new.

"The two-party control of the system is terrible. Blacks have been forced to choose between the Republicans and Democrats. And because there's nowhere else to go, they have to take what the Democratic Party offers them, which isn't much of anything."

He supports the Natural Law Party, is interested in how it's growing, wants to see it do well, wants to see Natural Law Party candidates at least win some congressional seats in the coming elections.

"The Natural Law Party offers a very real choice for black people. As the party gets better known, I predict it will get a lot of votes from a lot of people, including African-Americans. African-Americans survive on hope. That's what keeps us going. The Natural Law Party has a platform that gives us reason to hope."

Epilogue: On my way home I scan the radio dial. A commercial catches my ear. A woman is asking listeners to support a child overseas who, for just a few dollars a month, will get food, books, and a new chance at life. The irony! I remember Rutherford telling me how Fletcher-Johnson arranges Thanksgiving and Christmas dinners for families who have no money for such festivities, even housing for those who have none or who live in squalor. I think, as the woman gives out the address, Save your money, America. You can help youngsters in desperate need right here in your nation's very own capital city.

F A C T S

- Students carry 270,000 handguns to school each year; 22 percent of inner-city male youths own guns; 9 percent of eighth graders carry a gun, knife, or club to school at least once a month.
- The death rate of U.S. children is fifteen times higher than the death rate of children in Northern Ireland at the height of the troubles.
- In the last twelve years, suicide rates in the United States have doubled for ten- to fourteen-year-olds and increased 28 percent for fifteen- to nineteen-year-olds.
- Nationwide 11 percent of teachers have been assaulted in school.
- Nearly 30 percent of high school students drop out.
- SAT scores are declining, illiteracy has reached epidemic proportions, and American students fall far behind students from other industrialized countries in mathematics and the sciences.

14

An Opportunity to Meditate

STUDY LINKS DRUGS TO 80% OF INCARCERATIONS—ALCOHOL HAS HIGHEST CONNECTION TO VIOLENCE. That headline in *USA Today* on January 9, 1998, says it all. It's yet another study on the tie-in between alcohol, drugs, and crime, this time from the National Center on Addiction and Substance Abuse at Columbia University in New York. Despite billions of dollars spent on conventional rehabilitation measures, things aren't getting better. In fact, they're getting worse. Experts say that we need to be bold, that we need to do something new to stop this vicious cycle. My mind rolls back to a meeting I had sixteen months ago with Judge David Mason of Missouri's Twenty-second Circuit Court in St. Louis.

October 7, 1996, 10:00 A.M., Washington, D.C.   Judge Mason is here to address a conference on crime prevention in the China Room of the Mayflower Hotel. The event is being sponsored by the Natural Law Party. Other speakers include Dr. Ann Hughes, professor of sociology at the University of the District of Columbia and an expert on youth crime; Rudy DeLeon, former member of the California State Board of Prison Terms and deputy secretary of the California

Youth and Adult Correctional Agency; and Jay Marcus, author of *The Crime Vaccine*,[1] a critically acclaimed book on new approaches to crime prevention. This is another in a series of public forums put on by the Natural Law Party to investigate new solutions to America's problems, in this case crime. It's not a partisan event; participants are here from all political parties.

The consensus among conference participants is that rehabilitation in America is failing badly. It is failing because our approach is palliative; it is superficial. It doesn't address the underlying cause, which is stress—usually inner-city stress, which is several orders of magnitude greater than most of us in America have ever experienced.

The stress-crime connection is gaining considerable weight among scientists and criminologists. Scientists now have a better understanding of the biochemistry of stress and the biochemistry of violence. It turns out they are not distant cousins; they are, in fact, cause and effect.[2]

It also turns out that the usual risk factors for crime—growing up in the inner cities, living in an abusive home environment, a lack of educational opportunities, a lack of employment opportunities, etc.—alone are not the immediate causes of crime. (There are kids who grow up in the inner cities who don't commit crimes, and there are kids who grow up in the suburbs who commit very violent crimes.)

Missing from this old diagnosis has been the understanding that each of these risk factors adds up to make one big risk factor: stress. For some reason some people are not resilient enough or healthy enough to overcome these individual risk factors, and they get very, very stressed, and that, it turns out, is very, very dangerous.

Stress is something real. It's toxic and deadly. It's in the body, not just in the mind. It manifests itself as biochemical and neurological imbalances—low serotonin, high cortisol, EEG brain abnormalities—that have been linked to violent, criminal, or addictive behavior.[3]

The problem with our current rehabilitation approaches is this: Psychological strategies alone, such as counseling, therapy, and mentoring, don't adequately affect the blood cells and brain neurons

161

where stress does its damage. To be truly effective, rehabilitation strategies must significantly reduce stress, and then, as a natural by-product, there should be increased serotonin levels, reduced cortisol levels, increased coherence in EEG brain functioning, and normal cortisol responses to stress.[4]

The good news is that research shows that such strategies exist[5,6]. This is what Judge Mason has come to Washington to talk about, the reason why he interrupted his crowded court docket and traveled halfway across the country.

Judge Mason is a big man. He must be six feet five inches tall, and he weighs well over four hundred pounds. He has accomplished much in his life already, so I figure that he is probably in his early forties, but he doesn't look it. He has a soft, kind, open face. But don't be fooled by appearances. He has a reputation in St. Louis as being one tough judge.

He talks to us about his own upbringing. He grew up on the hard-scrabble streets of Brooklyn in the sixties. He never knew his father, his mother was a drug addict, so he was raised by his grandmother ("a small woman, and if she was mad at me when I was a teenager, she would stand up on a chair and slap my face, hard"). He finished high school, put himself through college, and earned a scholarship to Washington University Law School in St. Louis, where he graduated near the top of his class. He won the National Collegiate Debate Championships in 1983 (no surprise there: he is a gifted, commanding speaker). After passing his bar exam, he served five years as a trial counsel and general counsel for the Missouri Department of Corrections, and as a trial lawyer in a distinguished St. Louis law firm. He is now in his sixth year as a circuit judge.

The men and women Judge Mason sees every day in his courtroom are just the type of people that George Rutherford is scared to death his boys and girls will grow up to become. They are drug dealers, thieves, muggers, and murderers.

Judge Mason says that if he's going to send a drug addict back out on the streets, as he must do at some point—you can't keep everyone you arrest locked up forever—then he must ask himself what tools he has given the kid to help him stay clean every moment of every day, to keep him from sliding back down into the murky depths from which he came. The kid's counselor can't be there on the street corner whispering in his ear at every moment, Stay away from crack, stay away from alcohol. What can Judge Mason give these men and women, who stand before him with their lives in his hands, to help them get strong from within? He tells the conference that he's decided to give them TM. He wants them to meditate. I look around the room. Most people seem to take his pronouncement in stride, but there are a few raised eyebrows, a few double takes. A reporter from the *St. Louis Post-Dispatch* is scribbling down notes, racing to keep up. The judge continues. He says that personally he doesn't meditate and that his decision is not a casual one. He has spent more than a year carefully examining all the research on the technique—including studies showing a 35 to 40 percent reduction in recidivism rates among meditating inmates[7,8]—and on that basis alone he is convinced that it will help his probationers a lot. He wants to give them a fighting chance back on the streets.

September 19, 1997, 1:30 P.M., St. Louis.   It's been almost a year since I saw Judge Mason at the conference, and now he's done what he set out to do. He is presiding over a special graduation ceremony in an office building on the south side of St. Louis. Forty people stuff themselves into chairs, theater style, in a cramped conference room. They are the mothers and fathers, spouses, children, and friends of a handful of probationers who have just completed a unique three-month training course. The probationers are guilty of assault, drug trafficking, and robbery. They are here because they learned to meditate: twenty minutes, twice a day, and twenty-two follow-up classes. He has given them something he hopes will make them more resilient to stress, better able to resist the ever-present lure of drugs and crime, and able to feel better about themselves from the inside out.[9]

None of the thirty men and women who learned the TM technique had ever heard of it before. They had no clue what it was about and were not, you might say, "prone" to meditating. But now they are experienced meditators, and from what they say, it's working.

One by one, several of the graduates get up to say a few words.*

- Ric Sculley, thirty-two, arrested for assault and battery, says that he feels calmed and relaxed for the first time in his life. "I haven't felt any rage at any time since the start of TM, and you could count the times on one hand I've been angry. I've even walked away, laughing, from verbal confrontations that would have led to anger bursts or physical confrontations. I've also found no conflict with my practice of TM and with Christianity."

- Willie Benton speaks on the "value-added" benefit of meditating behind bars. "If it wasn't for TM, I don't think I could have done the seven months in jail like I did, without having one fight or serious argument. Even the people who know me from the streets noticed my behavior after I got out and asked me how I stayed so calm and settled. Meditation has made me an all-around better person, and I plan to stick with it."

- Charles Wilson, thirty-eight, recalls: "I still remember my first day after I learned to meditate. I felt a freshness—or better yet, like I've shed my old skin," he says. Then, Wilson, a Muslim, draws from an analogy in the Koran. "It's almost like a quiet within oneself, like the *Khalifah*—water which always returns to its natural state—peace."

Judge Mason listens closely. It's clear that he's satisfied.

"I know that I have a reputation in the community, particularly among defense attorneys, of being very tough," he says to the graduates. "And it is true that I can be tough. But for a judge to say that he or she is going to be tough on crime and not, at the same time, look for every possible way to help the offender to avoid reoffending is to me the lowest level of hypocrisy that a judge can have. So I

---

*The names of the probationers have been changed, but their ages, sex, reasons for arrest, and comments have not.

constantly search for anything I can find that will help the people coming into my courtroom avoid coming back.

"Our court system operates like a McDonald's. Guys come in, they give a five-minute plea, and then I send them to a probation officer. When they violate the law again—bam!—they are back in court. In and out. In and out. Over and over. But nobody says, 'Let's stop a minute. Let's think about the individual. Let's think about how we can help that person make better decisions.[10]

"Quite frankly when I first heard about TM, I thought it was weird. But I listened. Thank God I did. Because I have heard nothing but good stuff. I am looking forward to seeing the successful completion of your probation. I am looking forward to running into you on the street and we can talk and laugh about all this. I am looking forward to all of your great successes," he says, a smile spreading across his face, as he makes eye contact with each probationer. "Thanks for increasing my hope."

15

The Forgotten Victims of Inner-City Stress

West Oakland, California, was *Miami Vice* in the mid-1980s, caught, as were so many other impoverished inner cities, in an epidemic of drugs, alcohol, and violent crime. Murder rates soared as whole families were destroyed.

Who took the brunt of it? "Everyone was a victim," says Frank Staggers, Jr., M.D., who at the time was the director of alcohol, drug, and methadone programs at the West Oakland Health Center, one of the largest health centers in the United States to provide health care to an urban black population. But the forgotten victims, he says, were the elderly, the grandparents who had to absorb the loss, bury the pain, and then shoulder the enormous responsibility of raising a family all over again when their sons or daughters, grandchildren, or friends had been killed.

Dr. Staggers also carried a heavy patient load in general medicine at the health center. Many of the people he saw were elderly, and most of them had serious high blood pressure. In the inner city, high blood pressure can be like a death warrant. It strikes blacks twice as often as whites. It's the leading cause of death among older African-Americans. But because conventional wisdom among doctors at the time discounted any significant link between stress and hypertension, modern medicine offered little in the way of effective stress management to patients. Treatment then—and it's still true today—was through medication. Dr. Staggers believed otherwise. He saw that his patients' blood pressures were highest when they were under the most stress. He tried something. He would ask his patients to sit quietly in a chair in his office for a few minutes after he had taken their blood pressure. A few minutes later he would check again. Down. Not much, but down. A good sign.

Despite an almost backbreaking caseload, he felt compelled to venture in a new direction: research. What would happen, he wondered, if his patients were practicing something that really gave the body a deep rest? There was an urgency to find out the answer.

"Hypertension among black Americans is a much more malignant disease than in white Americans," he says. "It tends to come on earlier, tends to be more severe, and tends to create more organ complications: more strokes, more heart complications. It requires much more potent approaches to treat it."

First Dr. Staggers looked for techniques to study. "We looked for techniques that were standardized, which meant that they were taught the same way every time, everywhere. If it's taught a thousand different ways, then the study can't be replicated by another researcher. We also looked for techniques with a track record, something that had research to back it up. Finally, we wanted to answer a very simple question: Is it better to have the mind relax and have the body follow suit?" After careful investigation of scores of procedures they settled on two, one of each type: the Transcendental Meditation technique and Progressive Muscle Relaxation (PMR), a widely practiced, well-researched physiological approach to relaxing the mind and body.

Next Dr. Staggers looked for funding. He contacted scientists at Maharishi University of Management for help in the search. Together the researchers spent several months in early 1987 applying for grants and being refused for a "faulty hypothesis." No one linked stress to hypertension; it was a very controversial idea. They finally received two hundred thousand dollars from the Retirement Research Foundation in Chicago. Dr. Staggers recruited two hundred older African-Americans who suffered from mild high blood pressure, and the study was under way.

The experiment was set up like this: Participants would be randomly selected either to learn TM or PMR or to join a control group. Each participant would be matched with one from the control group for age, sex, weight, etc. Each participant would be involved in the program for three months. Blood pressure would be monitored regularly and compared before and after the three-month study. The entire project took Dr. Staggers and his colleagues almost eighteen months to complete.

The results were striking. The TM program group did the best—the technique proved to be about twice as effective as PMR—while the control group was the least effective. But perhaps even more significantly, the TM reduction was as deep as that of high blood pressure medication, but without the often harmful side effects of such drugs.

Dr. Staggers and his colleagues wrote up two studies based on the experiment. Both studies were accepted for publication in the American Heart Association's journal *Hypertension*—the first in March 1995, the second in August 1996.[1,2] Both studies received considerable national and international publicity in the medical and public press. But even before the publicity had kicked in, the mainstream scientific community was catching on: Stress was finally being recognized as a risk factor in hypertension, and stress reduction was seen to be an viable potential antidote. In fact, the results have proved so promising that the National Institutes of Health have given more than five million dollars to continue the TM research on African-Americans, to look at its effects over a full year, not just three months, and to evaluate its influence on other risk factors for heart disease.

Today Dr. Staggers, forty-six, is the medical director of the Haight-Ashbury Free Clinic Drug Detoxification Center in San Francisco and the medical director of a methadone program at Successful Alternative for Addiction and Counseling Services (SAACS) in Hayward, California. He also continues to see patients at the West Oakland Health Center.

For Dr. Staggers, the implications of these findings go far beyond a twelve-point drop in systolic blood pressure. "Most Americans can't comprehend the amount of stress in these poorer inner-city communities," he says. "Most of my younger patients are either stressing themselves to death, drinking themselves to death, or drugging themselves to death. They need something to break the vicious cycle."

He would like to see many such proven preventive approaches made widely available, and reimbursable, by Medicare and other third-party providers. "There are two types of medicine: restorative and preventive. Why do we wait for Johnny to overdose on drugs, have a heart attack or a stroke, or get shot and then come up with all these high-tech mechanisms to restore him to life? It makes more sense to put the money into preventive medicine. Why not prevent the pathology from occurring in the first place?"

16

Creating a True Peacekeeping Force

We are all caught in an epidemic of stress of global proportions. Stress manifests as a deadly plague that cripples the individual—heart disease, drug addiction, domestic violence, etc.—and whole societies. From the inner-city violence of southeast Washington, D.C., to the rampant bloodshed of Bosnia, to the explosive tensions of the West Bank, to the threat of all-out war with Iraq, one fundamental component is deeply rooted social stress, tension, hatred, fear. The primary difference is degree. Just as modern medical science offers no cure for individual stress, modern social science offers no cure for social stress. In both cases, however, there are approaches that have proved effective. And, it turns out, the approaches are basically one and the same.

January 20, 1998. I am talking with Greg Spitzfaden in an office that is a testimony to the heaven and hell of human nature. In the middle of the room, on a light gray pedestal with wheels, is an incubator that will sustain the life of a newborn infant. Next to it, in a partially opened cheerful yellow box the size of a computer monitor, is an autopsy kit. Both units are headed to Sarajevo this week.

There are papers everywhere, citations everywhere for jobs well done, photos of Spitzfaden's wife, Linda, and their two girls. There are orders for sixty tons of powdered milk to go to North Korea, for truckloads of vegetable seeds and agricultural tools to Angola, for cases of medicines to Rwanda and Haiti. The office is a mess. It looks like what it is: an office that directs disaster relief efforts.

Spitzfaden, fifty, heads a company in Peterborough, New Hampshire, that provides humanitarian relief to disaster areas, both manmade and natural. His is a commercial venture, a business, but his clients are all nonprofit relief and development agencies. The agencies raise millions of dollars, and his company helps them by supplying goods and services at the best possible prices and shipping them overseas, and it often goes on-site to coordinate their use. For short-term relief Spitzfaden's company provides medical supplies, food and shelter, and emergency aid. For the long term it provides health programs and agricultural goods and organizes the rebuilding of the physical structure of blighted areas—anything that can help a country or a people get back on their feet.

I am talking with Spitzfaden today to get his response to President Clinton's announcement before Christmas last year that he will keep U.S. troops in Bosnia beyond June 1998, the return date he promised last year. The president admitted it was a mistake to have set such a hard-and-fast date. Now he won't speculate when they will return. Peacekeeping forces have stabilized the peace, the killing has stopped, and if they leave, it will flare up again, the president said. He asked the American people for their support for the troops. The appeal worked. Only a few months earlier polls showed voters wanted American troops out of Bosnia. But new polls show a 20 percent swing in the president's favor. The possibility of a return to the wholesale slaughter of human life among the Bosnian Serbs, Croats, and Muslims is too much for Americans to bear. The troops should stay.

No one in the United States wants American troops to be the world's policemen, but what are the choices? Nothing else works. Right now two hundred thousand American soldiers—one-sixth of our standing military—are deployed in hot spots, or potential hot spots, around the world. Trained to fight and kill, our men and women in uniform must now play a strange new role: global peacekeeper. According to U.S. Defense Secretary William Cohen, we should get used to the role because it may be ours for a long time.

Beginning in January 1996, shortly after the Dayton Peace Accords were signed, Spitzfaden traveled for several weeks throughout Bosnia and the former Yugoslavia to evaluate the needs for relief and rehabilitation. He says that he was relieved when President Clinton sent troops, and he supports their presence in Bosnia today. "If we had not gone, the accords would have meant nothing. And if we leave now, the accords will mean nothing," he says.

But two years have passed since Spitzfaden left Bosnia, and he is still trying to make sense of "the senseless death and destruction and the limited long-term influence of our relief and peacekeeping efforts."

Even though he has traveled on similar assignments to the Sudan, Angola, Rwanda, and Ethiopia—ushering in medical supplies and construction materials—for some reason the Bosnia experience hit him the hardest. It made him realize most clearly that "the U.S. is doomed to be the world's cop unless we can do something to intervene on a level that scales back the white-hot stress and tension that have a grip on these regions."

Spitzfaden's wife, Linda, president of a publishing firm in Peterborough, was a candidate for the U.S. Congress with the Natural Law Party in 1994. So Greg Spitzfaden is aware that the only political party even to consider such an intervention is the Natural Law Party. This is one of the reasons that Spitzfaden, a conservative New England businessman, supports the party.

I am here to talk to him about that and also to hear more about his experiences in Bosnia. Spitzfaden begins with the memories. He talks about Bosnia with immediacy, as if he had returned home only yesterday.

"I had seen television news reports coming from Sarajevo in which a reporter would be standing in front of a building which had been blown up in a section of the city that had been ruined. When I drove into Sarajevo, I saw that the whole city was like that. The town of Mostar was even worse; it looked like Godzilla had stepped on it: half the town was completely flattened. There were makeshift cemeteries everywhere. After a few days it became the norm to see destruction. I had gone into the heart of darkness."

172

The arrival of U.S. troops saved the day. "The people were so grateful. I was never prouder to be an American," Spitzfaden says, then recounts two stories.

"I sat down for lunch at a café in Sarajevo. On the wall behind me were shells and pockmarks from gunfire. Opposite that wall, on the wall in front of me, there was nothing but a small framed American flag."

Spitzfaden caught the eye of a waiter and gestured at the flag. "Without the Americans we would still be fighting," the waiter told him.

Another time he had tea with an elderly couple in their apartment in Zenica, a small town forty miles outside Sarajevo. The fighting had passed by the town, but nevertheless thousands in it had starved to death.

"This elderly couple—the husband was a Muslim, the wife a Croat—had survived by eating grass and by selling their furniture to buy drinking water," he says. "The woman started crying when she saw me. She gave me a big hug, rocked me in her arms, and said that she loved me because I was an American.

" 'Without Americans we'd be still fighting and killing each other,' she said. 'Please never leave.' "

The phone rings and blasts us both out of the nightmare. Spitzfaden takes the call and then turns back to our conversation.

We have to leave sometime. What will happen? I ask.

"No one knows," he replies. "No one in government, in the military, in international relief. It's frightening.

"We are good at keeping people from getting killed. And we are good at getting buildings rebuilt and taking steps to begin normalizing people's lives. But we don't know how to reduce the deeply rooted stress—the hatred, the hurt, the anger, and the bad blood that seem to go on from generation to generation. There's no relief agency, there's no UN that can do anything about that. The problem runs so deep. There were people I met who were very forgiving, who said, 'Let's just forget it and move ahead.' But there were others who said, 'Wait till we get our weapons, we'll do the same thing to them.' "

Spitzfaden recalls a comment from a colleague in the relief effort, Boris, who had been an officer in the Croatian Army and lived

173

through the worst of the battles. "Boris said that there was just too much negativity, too much negative energy, and people had to fight."

Spitzfaden says it's a simple yet telling analysis of what sparked the war, and it also provides a glimpse of where we should look for answers. "I believe the UNESCO charter had it right when it said: 'Wars begin in the minds of men.' And it is in the minds of men where we'll find the solution. We'll never find it anywhere else."

Preventive Defense

Over the past three thousand years there have been more than five thousand peace treaties, each of which has lasted an average of nine years. History shows that paper agreements among nations are not a foundation for lasting peace.

—JOHN HAGELIN

February 8, 1998. It's been less than a month since I spoke with Greg Spitzfaden. Bosnia has gone from the front pages to a scant mention in the press. Focus has shifted from the peacekeeping forces in Europe to the massive military buildup in the Persian Gulf and the specter of war with Iraq. Saddam Hussein's brinkmanship with the United States, which, as of this writing, has been put on hold by an agreement hammered out by UN Secretary Kofi Annan, has revealed—at least to the public mind—the changing balance of power in the world. So-called rogue regimes, such as Iraq, Iran, and Libya, can hold the world hostage. Such countries have already developed, or are working hard to develop, chemical, biological, and nuclear weapons, and the missiles to deliver them, that will forever alter defense strategies—both international and domestic. Now any well-financed and determined group can build a nuclear bomb using instructions off the Internet and carry it in a suitcase. How do you defend against that? It's the same with chemical weapons. Anyone can build one of those deadly weapons using equipment that makes agricultural chemicals. U.S. air strikes in Iraq could blow up much of the country, but they wouldn't eliminate all biological or chemical weapons–manufacturing plants. Besides, if it's not Iraq, it can just as easily be some other country or terrorist group. The strategy in defense must shift to prevention: prevention of tensions, prevention of hostilities, prevention of conflict. Those who are responsible for maintaining the peace know this all too well.

William Perry made the point clearly during a speech at Harvard University, on June 3, 1996, when he was U.S. secretary of defense. He said, "Preventive medicine creates the conditions which support health, making disease less likely and surgery unnecessary. Preventive defense creates the conditions which support peace, making war less likely and deterrence unnecessary."

What constitutes prevention? According to military experts, the best ways to prevent the spread of weapons of mass destruction are export controls and nonproliferation regimes; diplomatic initiatives; confidence-building measures, such as educational and military exchange programs; the seizure of proscribed materials necessary to the manufacture of weapons of mass destruction; and the threat of economic sanctions or diplomatic isolation. Other analysts, less optimistic, talk of providing everyone in, say, Manhattan, with a gas mask, in case terrorists explode canisters filled with deadly anthrax.

Such efforts are sure to help, but most experts agree they are also likely to fail, at least once—and that one time could be catastrophic. John Hagelin spoke often about these problems during the 1992 and 1996 campaigns. He also spoke about a unique, but scientifically proven, solution. One press conference stands out in my mind.

December 6, 1995. Washington, D.C., is awash with press conferences on the Dayton Peace Accords. I know this because this week the Associated Press's "Day Book"—a daily and weekly calendar of media events in Washington—is packed with news events that offer reporters ample opportunity to hear the Republican and Democratic reaction to President Clinton's decision to send U.S. troops to Bosnia. Most of those press conferences will feature politicians arguing the merits of the peace accords and the wisdom of putting American lives on the line. Is this another Vietnam? those in opposition are demanding to know. Are we getting in over our heads?

At about the same time that Greg Spitzfaden is preparing to fly to Sarajevo to organize aid for that war-ravaged country, John Hagelin is at the National Press Club for a news conference to discuss a proposal that he says would help bring peace to the region. It's a good press turnout that includes several wire services, the *Chicago Tribune*, and CNN.

Hagelin opens the news conference by commenting on the impact of sophisticated new weapons systems and a rapidly changing balance of power. He says that the United States is more vulnerable than ever to attack, and for that reason we must explore all possible avenues for preventing hostilities and conflict.

"There is no viable defense against today's high-tech weaponry," Hagelin says. "Once a single MIRVed ICBM is launched, there is no missile defense system in place that can prevent the wide-scale destruction of cities. Even after substantial reductions in global arsenals, thousands of nuclear weapons remain. At least forty-six weapons are known to be missing from the former Soviet arsenal, and recent nuclear tests in China have stirred fears in the international community of runaway nuclear proliferation.

"Furthermore, regional and ethnic conflicts in the Middle East and Eastern Europe have shown that even small nations can imperil world peace and stability, holding other nations hostage through terrorism, biological warfare, and weapons of mass destruction.

"In light of the wholesale destruction threatened by such weapons, the role of diplomacy and other means to prevent the outbreak of war has become especially crucial," Hagelin continues. "Unfortunately history shows that neither treaties nor threat of arms can ensure lasting peace and security. When stress builds up in collective consciousness, inevitably it erupts as violence, conflict, and war among nations. Then it doesn't matter what treaty has been signed. Over the past three thousand years there have been more than five thousand peace treaties, each of which has lasted an average of nine years. History shows that paper agreements among nations are not a foundation for lasting peace."

Hagelin then levels a blast at Congress for making America second only to Russia as the world's leading arms merchant.[1] "In 1998 U.S. taxpayers will underwrite six billion dollars in subsidies for the purchase of U.S. weapons and services by foreign governments,[2] and many of these governments are unstable and undemocratic. This global arms peddling has tarnished America's reputation as a pro-

176

moter of peace, fostered deep-seated international ill will, and led to an increasingly dangerous world in which American soldiers are forced to confront our own weapons on the battlefield.[3] Heavy lobbying by the defense industry, including large financial contributions to congressional and presidential campaigns,[4] has perpetuated America's enormous peacetime military budget which exceeds the combined military expenditures of every other nation in the world."[5]

Hagelin pauses. He is about to introduce a pivotal idea in the Natural Law Party's platform that he knows will stir some controversy. It will be taken seriously by some members of the press and not by others. But he knows the first step in making public policy is public debate, and he is confident that his idea has the backing of a growing number of researchers, sociologists, and criminologists.

What is it? The effects of stress-reducing meditation on society. Specifically, Hagelin wants to talk about research showing that collective practice of Transcendental Meditation has been used to reduce stress and conflict in violence-ridden and war-torn areas. He takes an objective, science-based position. We live in a scientific age, he says, and no matter how unusual something may sound, if there is enough scientific evidence to support that it works, we should try it.

The principle is this: Wherever there are large numbers of meditators, violence and crime in the entire population are reduced. "War breaks out when the escalation of tensions among rival peoples and nations leads to a catastrophic breakdown in negotiations," he says. "Look at Bosnia. Look at the West Bank. Look at Iraq. Until recently there has been no reliable means to diffuse such escalations of stress and to avert diplomatic breakdowns. This situation has changed dramatically. During the last twenty years there has been more scientific evidence on the effects of collective meditation for diffusing social stress and resolving international conflict than any previous approach in the history of the social sciences."

Hagelin brings reporters up to speed. "We already know from research sponsored by the National Institutes of Health that Transcendental Meditation dramatically reduces stress in the individual. Now, on the basis of more than forty studies, we know that collective practice of this technique produces the same effects throughout society."

Hagelin refers the reporters to several studies in their press kits that show crime rates, sickness, violence, conflict all fall sharply. "For example, seven consecutive interventions by such coherence-creating groups during the peak of the Lebanon conflict each brought highly significant reductions in the level of conflict—in war deaths and war-related injuries—and brought significant progress toward peace. Specifically, war deaths fell an average of more than seventy percent during these interventions, and the decreased tension and significantly more peaceful atmosphere allowed diplomatic initiatives to succeed where they had previously failed."[6]

The findings may sound unusual, Hagelin says, but research on collective meditation has been published in some of America's most respected peer-reviewed scientific journals, including the *Journal of Conflict Resolution, Social Indicators Research, Journal of Mind and Behavior*, and the *Journal of Crime and Justice*.[7] "The research has employed the most sophisticated statistical methodologies and has been subjected to rigorous examination through peer review. It comprehensively controlled for alternative explanations and other confounding variables."

I look around the room, and I can almost hear reporters thinking: Renewable energy, yes; natural medicine, yes; meditation to lower high blood pressure, yes; but group meditation to reduce violence and conflict?

There is ample research to confirm that this approach works, Hagelin points out. However, what's been missing is an understanding—a model—of *how* it works. That's what he wants to discuss now.

"The idea that the coherent influence of meditation could transform society is one that has many precedents in nature," he says. "There are natural amplification mechanics that are found throughout society and in nature that can leverage even small influences into a striking transformation."

He takes the microphone out of the podium stand and walks across the stage to an easel. He points to a chart with drawings of two blocks of iron. Each block is filled with tiny circles that represent iron atoms. The block on the left has atoms with their north-south poles pointing in random directions. The block on the right has atoms with their north-south poles aligned with each other. The block on the left is an ordinary piece of iron. The block on the right is a powerful magnet. The only difference between the two—and it's a big one—is the alignment, or coherence, of the atoms.

"A block of iron with many atoms is an example of what is a many-body system. A many-body system displays different phases of collective behavior. In this case"—Hagelin points to the chart—"the block of iron can be in a magnetized phase or a demagnetized phase. Depending upon even minor changes in environmental conditions, the behavior of the iron may be completely transformed. And at a certain temperature, through natural amplification mechanisms, as few as one percent of the atoms in the iron block, when they are aligned with each other, will create a transformation throughout the entire piece of iron, causing all the atoms to line up and produce a very strong magnet.

"A society is a more complex many-body system than a magnet," Hagelin continues with a smile. "It follows that even minor variations in temperature, climate, natural resources, and environmental influences give rise to totally different societies—with different languages, mores, cultures, and traditions.

"Research similarly shows that even very minor increases in temperature can significantly impact crime rates," he says.

"So it is not surprising that when you lower the social stress level—or lower the social temperature—and increase the coherence of society even slightly by a group of individuals practicing these technologies of consciousness, this would produce broad transformations throughout society."[8]

As Hagelin speaks, I recall my own experiences talking to reporters about this research. Either it fits into their picture of the universe or it doesn't. One science writer at a large metropolitan newspaper read through the research and told me he thought the whole idea "made good sense." But another reporter told me, "I don't care how many studies you show me published in how many reputable journals. I don't believe it, and I never will believe it."

For many people the idea that collective meditation influences anything other than the meditators themselves runs counter to everything our senses tell us. We don't see the connection. The music coming from the broadcast station across town that reaches our car radios is carried by radio waves—ripples in the invisible but very real electromagnetic field. But a question I heard a lot was, What connects *people* together? What is the mechanism, what is the field, that allows people meditating in one place to create an influence on people everywhere else?

Hagelin is a quantum physicist. He is talking about how nature functions. He says that while our senses may tell us one thing—that we are separate individuals—the underlying reality is different. Nature may appear in discrete units, but just beneath the surface, nature is seamless, interconnected. In fact, according to modern physics, everything in the universe is more than closely correlated; everything is one.

"At the most obvious and concrete levels of human existence, we are distinctly individual in character—our body, appearance, personality, et cetera. But deeper levels of human nature are more universal," Hagelin says. "At the level of quantum mechanics the body is just a localized excitation of the electron, quark, electromagnetic, and gluon fields—universal fields which we have in common with every other individual. At the very deepest level the individual is just a fluctuation of the unified field, the field of consciousness. It is at this deepest, most universal level of natural law that the technology of collective meditation works."[9]

And that is why the influence is so powerful.

Hagelin is asked how scientists react to the research. "It depends upon how carefully they have studied it," he replies. He refers the reporter to a statement from one researcher, David Edwards, Ph.D., a professor of government at the University of Texas at Austin, who has followed the research closely for the past twenty years.

Dr. Edwards, who does not practice Transcendental Meditation technique, said: "I think that the claim can be plausibly made that the potential impact of this research exceeds that of any other ongoing social or psychological research program. The research has survived a broader array of statistical tests than has most research in the field of conflict resolution. I think this work, and the theory that informs it, deserve the most serious consideration by academics and policy-makers alike."

Hagelin is asked if what he is proposing is prayer. No, he answers. It doesn't involve prayer or any religious attitude, nor does it require belief or coaxing or cajoling of people to be kind or forgiving or open-minded. It is a scientific approach that produces a *physical influence of peace*. It reduces built-up social stress and tension in the collective consciousness.

For these reasons, says Hagelin, he would support the establishment of a "coherence-creating group" of one or two thousand experts in Transcendental Meditation and its advanced techniques* in Bosnia to help reduce stress, violence, and conflict. He calls it a Group for a Government.

A reporters asks for specifics. Who would constitute these groups?

Hagelin says that anyone could be trained—students, the unemployed, refugees—"but the most practical implementation would be to establish a prevention wing of the military.

"Already two hundred thousand men and women in our armed forces are on dangerous peacekeeping missions around the globe," he says. "They have already been dispatched to trouble spots throughout the world to prevent the escalation of tensions and the outbreak of armed conflict. They are often under tremendous stress themselves. To reduce their own stress, while simultaneously helping to create a tangible influence of peace in their environment, a small percentage of these troops could be easily trained in these peace-promoting technologies.[11] This would make their efforts even more effective. Local citizens could then be trained to take over once the violence had been significantly reduced and peace had been created."

February 8, 1998. I am driving Hagelin to the airport in Charlotte, North Carolina. We are in a fierce rainstorm that has the traffic on I-77 moving at a crawl. On the radio the newscaster is talking in surprisingly matter-of-fact, almost blasé terms about the prospect of war with Iraq. In the car Hagelin is dictating quotes into a tape

---

*It didn't come up in this news conference, but reporters sometimes asked about an advanced technique known as Yogic Flying. "It's an exotic name for a very simple procedure derived from the classical texts on yoga that dates back three thousand years," John Hagelin would say. "These ancient texts maintain that the long-term practice develops the ability to levitate—thus the name—but it's widely practiced today for its scientifically proven effects in creating EEG brain wave coherence, increasing mind-body coordination, and producing a profound influence of reduced stress and increased coherence that extends into the social environment."[10]

recorder for a press release on the Iraq crisis that will go out to four hundred newspaper editors and radio and television news desks across the country. In a week the release will be outdated—at least in the short term—because of a UN-brokered peace agreement. But the problem will really never go away. It will erupt again and again in other parts of the world.

I ask Hagelin how he would explain to the American people the decision to establish a coherence-creating group in Iraq—or any other potential hot spot in the world.

He pauses for a moment. "I would say that before we commence with the horror of exposing our servicemen and women to bodily risk, and before we rain terror from the skies and kill tens of thousands of civilians, we're first going to try a peaceful approach. We do it out of a sense of human conscience in our effort to leave no stone unturned and to pursue all peaceful alternatives. This approach has proven effective in multiple replications involving the Middle East. Its total implementation would cost less than a single B-one bomber."

What about criticism from some members of the scientific community?

"We are living in a scientific age, in which the truth or falsehood of any hypothesis stands or falls on the basis of scientific evidence," he replies. "And the evidence overwhelmingly supports that we try such an approach first. So we will proceed on with full scientific confidence and with the backing of criminologists, sociologists, and experts in conflict resolution who are familiar with the research and endorse its efficacy."

What would he foresee happening if such a group were established? I ask.

"If the results of previous applications are any indication, we would see a softening of the tensions, followed by an openness to negotiate in a constructive atmosphere, one not governed by intransigence and brinkmanship. And out of this we would hope to see an agreement that's satisfactory to the U.S. and our allies, to the international community, and to Iraq itself, a solution that would be in everyone's long-term best interests."

Hagelin is interrupted by a call on his cell phone. I think back on conversations I've had with reporters on the idea. This is what I say:

Nothing else has worked to prevent violence and conflict, at least over the long term: not treaties, not coercion, not a "credible threat of war," not economic sanctions. If group meditation can work, it makes sense to try it out. If it fails, then it will be just another thing that has failed in the long history of failed peace efforts. But if it works, if it succeeds, we have something powerful that can help us create a safer, more peaceful world during this very precarious time.

Hagelin is off the phone. He says basically the same thing. "William Perry [the former U.S. defense secretary] was right when he said that we need a preventive approach to defense that creates conditions that support peace. Reducing built-up social stress is key. If this approach can do that—and the research shows that it can—then it's worth a try. It's the humane thing to do."

We're at the airport. The crashing thunderstorm has passed, leaving a hard rain, but nothing that will keep the jets on the ground. Hagelin grabs his overnight bag from the backseat and heads into the terminal to catch a U.S. Airways flight to Kansas City, where he'll hold a series of party-building meetings with local organizers. I turn on the radio, and now the news is about violent flare-ups tearing apart the Serbs and Kosovo Albanians in Yugoslavia, fanning fears of a new Balkan war. It's the same with the Israelis and Palestinians. I think of Greg Spitzfaden, working under relentless pressure in his office in Peterborough, New Hampshire, to send emergency supplies to war-ravaged lands throughout the globe. I think he would agree with John Hagelin: It's worth a try.

The Campaign Trail

17

What's So Funny about the Campaign Trail?

October 1, 1996. Mimi Hall is looking for humor. She wants funny stories from the third-party campaign trail. She has already spoken to the Libertarians and the Greens and hasn't gotten much to work with. Now she has John Hagelin and me racking our memories for something humorous and newsworthy on this Saturday afternoon as we sit on stools in an almost empty newsroom at *USA Today*'s national office in Arlington, Virginia, just across the Potomac River from Washington, D.C.

Hall covers politics for *USA Today*, and she is doing a feature story on third-party presidential candidates.

The fact is, Hagelin tells her, it's really not that funny on the campaign trail. You do wait long hours in airports to take bargain basement flights (now, that's a riot), and you do stay in the homes of supporters rather than in hotels as often as possible to save on expenses (awkward? Sometimes. Funny? Not really).

It may not be particularly funny, but during the final weeks of the 1996 campaign it was a blast. I had three cellular phones ringing nonstop; I was scheduling interviews for John Hagelin and Mike Tompkins around the clock. There was interest, interest, interest everywhere. Hagelin claims to this day that if the same media attention that the Natural Law Party rode for the last month of the 1996 campaign (a drop in the bucket compared with the Republicans and Democrats) could have been sustained for another month, Natural Law Party candidates would have received ten million votes, not two and a half million.

Hall is waiting patiently for her funny anecdote, and Hagelin doesn't want to disappoint, so he confides a true story. During his acceptance speech at the national nominating convention, broadcast live via C-SPAN, Hagelin knocked over a tall glass of ice water on the podium shelf. The water submerged his notes and poured off the lip of the podium, soaking his shirt and pants. Hagelin vowed to himself to speak for as long as it took for his pants to dry. And he did. He went seventy minutes—twenty-five minutes over his scheduled time, adding details that didn't appear anywhere in the original draft. When he walked off the stage, as dry as if he just came from the cleaners, no one was the wiser. After telling this story to Hall, Hagelin rethought the wisdom of it and asked her not to reprint it. She agreed. But now time has healed all, and the story can be told. I'm afraid that's about as funny as it gets.

January 14, 1998.   Traveling the country now in a "party-building" mode is entirely different from traveling when the election is four weeks away. The buzz is off. On the other hand, you really get a chance to talk to people. That's what John Hagelin, Mike Tompkins, and Kingsley Brooks are doing as the early months of 1998 roll by. In two days they go to California for a series of intimate living room meetings. This is how the party is built. I decide to go with them. There are two people I have been eager to meet with: Harold Bloomfield, M.D., and Rashi Glazer, Ph.D. They represent the cutting edge of key Natural Law Party policies.

I grew up in California, and though I moved away twenty years ago, whenever I come back, the state amazes me. There are health food stores the size of huge Safeway supermarkets, both the *Los Angeles Times* and the *San Francisco Chronicle* have written major editorials calling for the banning of genetically engineered ingredients from organic foods, and billboard advertisements offer consumers "green energy" to fuel their homes. In California you can choose the energy company you want just the way you choose a long-distance phone service. For a few dollars more each month you can have an energy package to run your appliances that includes renewable energy, such as wind or solar. The rest of the country seems to be catching on. I recently saw a news story on how the Ford Motor Company is moving 250 of its top executives from Dearborn, Michigan, to Irvine, in southern California, to live and work. Ford wants its most creative minds to absorb the state's "style of thinking" and put it into their design plans for cars in the next century.

California is a nation unto itself. One in nine Americans lives in the state. It also boasts the fifth-largest economy in the world. When the Natural Law Party qualified for the 1996 ballot in October 1995, the news received national and international publicity. Today the party is the fourth-largest active party in the state, after the Democrats and Republicans—and just behind the Reform Party. In one city, Compton, just outside Los Angeles, the Natural Law Party is even larger than the Republican Party.

I'm heading out the door. It's forty degrees and pouring rain here in Washington, D.C. The Weather Channel says it's sunny and seventy in San Diego. This is the kind of campaigning I like.

18

New Leadership for California

As governor I would make a fundamental shift from a costly crisis management approach to a cost-effective, prevention-oriented government. Our dollars would be invested in developing the health and creative genius of each one of our citizens using scientifically proven solutions.

—HAROLD H. BLOOMFIELD, M.D.,

NATURAL LAW PARTY CANDIDATE

FOR GOVERNOR OF CALIFORNIA

Harold Bloomfield figured he had a genuine reason not to run for governor of California in 1998: time—or rather a shortage of it. The much-in-demand psychiatrist-author-lecturer was putting the finishing touches on his sixteenth book, *Healing Anxiety with Herbs.* He was then to crisscross America on a book tour that was to take him to more than a dozen cities in two months. He has a packed schedule of speaking engagements around the world *not* related to the book launch. He also has a busy private psychiatric medicine practice in Del Mar, California, twenty miles north of San Diego. How would he find the time to run an aggressive campaign?

So when John Hagelin broached the subject to him during a meeting at his home in mid-January, he was all ready to say, "Thank you very much for the offer, but no thank you—not this time." Instead, given a day to think it over, he said, "Yes, absolutely."

Dr. Bloomfield will make an excellent candidate. He is a Yale-trained psychiatrist, a leader in the fields of integrative psychiatry and natural medicine, respected and trusted for his common sense, down-to-earth, forward-looking views on life, relationships, and health care. His recent best-seller, *Hypericum* [St. John's Wort] *and*

Depression, put him in the national spotlight for the umpteenth time. He was featured on *20/20, Good Morning America, CBS This Morning*, as well as in *Time, Newsweek*, the *New York Times, People*, and *USA Today*. He has also appeared on *Oprah, Larry King Live*, and ABC News.

Harold Bloomfield has been a prolific author and coauthor. His books have sold more than six and a half million copies, have been translated into twenty-six languages, and include *How to Survive the Loss of a Love, How to Heal Depression, The Holistic Way to Health and Happiness, Making Peace with Your Parents*, and *Making Peace with Yourself*.

Dr. Bloomfield, fifty-three, is wearing baggy blue shorts and a baggy color-splashed Hawaiian shirt when he greets me with a huge smile at the side gate to his house, which sits up on a gentle hillside a long stone's throw from the Pacific Ocean, in Del Mar. He gives me a bear hug. I am not singled out. This is how he greets everyone. He has been called "the psychiatrist everyone trusts," and it's easy to see why. He is a genuinely warm, wise, happy, easygoing person. He has a beautiful home, but not in the slightest ostentatious. I get a quick tour of the premises. This is a family with fine taste, I think, but California casual is the byword. His wife, Sirah, a therapist herself, is out of town; his fourteen-year-old daughter, Shazara, has yet to awaken. We settle into separate sofas in his living room. It is a gorgeous sunny January day, but a bit brisk for my tastes. Dr. Bloomfield is comfortable in his summer attire; I am muffling a shiver in my long pants and sweater.

Time is short; he has a patient in forty-five minutes. So I plunge in with the questions. Why did he decide to run for governor with the Natural Law Party?

"I was extremely impressed with this independent, fresh voice in politics, a voice that was talking about, first and foremost, prevention programs and natural medicines. We all know that 'An ounce of prevention is worth a pound of cure.' And that's how I read the Natural Law Party platform in every area. So when I looked at what the Natural Law Party stood for and found that it resonated with the deepest levels of my own experience, I knew I had to run. I like the idea of people listening to new ideas. People can agree, they can disagree, but the point is that we have a dialogue."

Why not just run as a Republican or a Democrat? I ask. The structure is already there; the system is in place.

"Sclerosis," Dr. Bloomfield says, smiling. "There's so much structure in the Democratic and Republican parties that there has been a tendency for sclerosis to set in. *Sclerosis* in medicine means 'hardening,' as in *arteriosclerosis*, which is hardening of the arteries. There has been a codifying and rigidifying of the Republican and Democratic parties that often do not make room for new ideas and new solutions, and this creates frustration among voters. What I like about the Natural Law Party is that it's 'highest first.' It focuses first and foremost on prevention, which is in clear contrast with the crisis management approach of the Republicans and Democrats. The Natural Law Party has the fresh creative energy, freedom, and determination to bring reliable new programs and solutions to create a better world."

I describe to Dr. Bloomfield the book that I am writing. I say that one of my hopes is to awaken voters from a false sense of security that all is well under the leadership of the two main parties. Because the economy is strong, inflation is down, and crime is starting to go down, everyone thinks that everything is fine. So why bother about politics; why bother about what goes on in Washington or in our state capitals? I point out that because of the unholy alliance between big business and government, there are dangerous precedents being set in our agricultural policies, health care policies, energy policies, and foreign policies that bode ill for generations to come. So my conclusion is "We'd better wake up. We'd better care."

Dr. Bloomfield nods and agrees with me that such an approach is necessary to awaken many people from a slumber, but he likes the Natural Law Party's other tactic as well, one that emphasizes unfolding and actualizing our full potential.

"What I like about this party is that it not only uses sharp words, when appropriate, to get a point across, such as the potential dangers of genetically engineered foods, but also takes an approach that is unique in politics—and that is a positive one. The Natural Law Party says, 'Look what we can be.' That's what I resonate with most strongly. It's that fresh 'Let's step back from the chaos and rigidity of life as it has been in the past, and let's take a look at what realistically we can be. Let's find ways of educating ourselves and our children to grow up to be healthy, creative, sharing, cooperative human beings.' I am convinced this will bring the second American revolution, but this time it will be creative evolution, not revolution."

Dr. Bloomfield turns the discussion back to his area of expertise, health, a theme that surfaces regularly among Natural Law Party candidates and one that is a metaphor for every area of society.

"We spend ninety-nine percent of our almost one trillion dollars annually in the United States on what is called health care, but it is really disease care," he says, echoing Barry Charles's words. "And half of that amount is spent on end-stage illness, on extending the lives of people by few months or a year at best. We only spend one percent of that trillion dollars on anything that can be called health education or teaching people preventative skills. Our health care system has to shift its emphasis to prevention; otherwise we will be buried in illness and bankrupted by health costs."

Now he focuses in on emotional health, an area he believes is clearly not being properly addressed by the current health care system. "We have seen in our lifetime epidemic levels of anxiety, depression, insomnia, and stress. Over sixty million people suffer from anxiety: thirty million of them have anxiety disorders, which is severe anxiety, and the other thirty million have persistent symptoms of mild to moderate anxiety. It's not severe, but it still gets in the way of living life. Another seventy million Americans suffer from insomnia on a regular basis, which interferes with their work lives, causing them to make more mistakes and have more car accidents. Seventeen million Americans suffer from depressive illnesses, and another fifteen or sixteen million have what we call minor depression.

"Despite the fact that so many millions of people suffer from anxiety and depression, fewer than twenty-five percent receive adequate help. This means that tens of millions of people continue to suffer unnecessarily, and that creates a tremendous burden in society as well. We are also seeing an increase in stress-related disorders. According to a 1997 Gallup Poll, as much as twenty-five percent of our U.S. workforce suffers from chronic stress, which is estimated to cost U.S. business sixty to seventy-five billion dollars a year. Stress is excessive wear and tear on the mind and body, and it takes its toll both in the short term and over a twenty- or thirty-year period. Depending on where the weak spot is in your psycho-physiological makeup, that's where disease and disorder show up. For example, if you have a genetic vulnerability to depression, and you are under severe stress, there is a higher chance of your developing depressive illness."

Dr. Bloomfield says health care needs to look at new ways to strengthen the individual. "If we teach people cost-effective strategies to promote health and reduce stress, then individuals can avoid these vulnerabilities and, more important, develop a strong nervous system that allows them to unfold their full potential," he says. "The more the individuals in a society are living up to their full potentials, the less vulnerable we are going to be to problems, both individually and in society as a whole."

I ask Dr. Bloomfield, a psychiatrist, his opinion about research on group meditation positively influencing society. He responds that it's a matter of perspective.

"If you come from the old paradigm which is 'I am not a part of nature, I am an individual, and I don't pay attention to nature,' then the whole idea would sound ridiculous, because how can other individuals influence you? If, however, you come from the emerging new paradigm, not only in physics but also in social psychology, then it makes perfectly good sense. And that paradigm is that our individuality, on one level, is an illusion. That in truth we are part of a whole, and even though we're not attached skin to skin, each of us is a member of a larger social being, a larger collective consciousness. So the greater the number of individuals who are, as if, a conduit for that level of pure consciousness—that wholeness that underlies all individuality—the greater will be that positive influence on all the individual members in society."

I'm interested in Dr. Bloomfield's vision of California under his leadership. Pick a few areas, I tell him, and comment.

"As governor I want to make a fundamental shift in where we place our emphasis in government. For example, we should have the best prenatal care in the world, where any pregnancy is protected and provided for. We must provide Head Start programs—with private sector support—that ensure that every child is raised in an atmosphere of acceptance and nurturance. When that child goes to school, we want to make sure that we have the best public school system possible, where kids love to go to school because they are creative and inspiring places to go. And there should be great extracurricular activities that help each individual develop his or her full potential.

"In health care, as I said, the first order of business will be primary prevention. I would reverse priorities so that our health care system profits when it keeps people well, so that the less medical care people need, the more profitable the system becomes.

"I would build more emphasis on developing the creativity of our citizens. We can foster more think tanks to look at scientific solutions to specific problems, such as drug abuse, for example. What is it that we can teach those of our citizenry who have looked for pleasure in all the wrong places? What kinds of programs really work? As a physician working in government, I would come back to John Dewey's definition of science, which is 'a systematic means of gaining reliable knowledge.' That means we have to transcend bipartisan or multipartisan politics and take a look at the programs that can really make a difference in promoting health and developing creativity and potential.

"I would create committees of independent scientists to conduct research into the best programs for human development. I want the great state of California to lead the way—to have the healthiest, most productive, and most creative people on earth."

I ask him if he sees a sizable voter base for the Natural Law Party.

"Absolutely. I'm amazed at how rapidly the Natural Law Party has taken root and the good people the party is drawing to itself. There are tens of millions of people who, in their personal lives and in their work, support programs the Natural Law Party supports. I think that in the '98 campaign and in the 2000 presidential campaign, we are going to see these people coming to the Natural Law Party. Then the party will move away from a 'Gee, isn't that interesting, isn't that nice' response from the press and public and be taken even more seriously as a platform for the people who want to see a healthier, more prevention-oriented approach to government. This is exactly what we need for the twenty-first century."

It's time to wrap up the interview. We part company on a cautionary note, with Dr. Bloomfield saying that in order to have an impact on the political system, we have to get big money out of politics. "Corporations have been allowed to buy up the two main parties through lobbying efforts and other fund-raising schemes. We are in danger of creating a Disneyland-like political landscape where the really crucial ideas for creating a new society—natural medicines, renewable energy, organic agriculture, and real educational reform—never see the light of day because of the old, entrenched ways of doing things. We have to get away from the idea that we only have two choices at the polls, which, in reality, is one choice with a little variation. We need to support new parties as a way of reawakening democracy."

19

The Most Valuable Asset in the Global Information Economy

My lesson on the emerging global information economy starts, and then abruptly stops, during halftime of the Green Bay Packers–Denver Broncos Super Bowl. My teacher is Rashi Glazer, Ph.D., a Stanford-trained marketing expert who is now a UC Berkeley business professor and one of the world's leading experts on the marketing end of the information revolution. I pull him away from the television commercials and corner him on a sofa in the living room of Joe and Valerie JanLois, a Danville couple who are organizers of the Natural Law Party in northern California. I have joined John Hagelin, Mike Tompkins, Kingsley Brooks, and about thirty other party organizers and supporters for an afternoon away from party building to watch the AFC finally put one over on the NFC.

I hope to talk with Glazer about the booming U.S. economy, the onset of the knowledge and information age, tax reform, and the role of government in fostering a better educated, more enlightened workforce. Instead he gives me five minutes of polite but slightly distracted conversation as he keeps one ear and one eye turned to the television at his left, until I realize I am taking him away from his work. Glazer is, after all, a marketing consultant, and the $2.6-million-per-minute TV commercials being aired on the Super Bowl will be the subject of a lecture in the M.B.A. class he'll teach next week. He really can't talk to me now; he needs to watch television. We arrange to meet tomorrow after class, and then we happily return to our potato chips and the game.

It's been almost thirty years since I first walked across Sproul Plaza at the University of California at Berkeley. Back then the issues were clear-cut, polarizing, and proper nouns: Vietnam, Civil Rights, the Cold War. The campus was a seething cauldron of political opinions and activism. Today the issues are abstract, subtle, confusing, and all lowercase, but just as crucial and worthy of debate: the makeover and takeover of the world's food supply by a handful of biotech companies; the crisis over the content of health care, not just the delivery of it; and the massive sales of U.S. weapons all over the world. But today, as I head toward Rashi Glazer's class in the new fifty-million-dollar Haas School of Business, all is quiet on Sproul Plaza.

Compared with the drab old classrooms in which I sat through lectures on political science and journalism back in the late sixties and early seventies, Glazer's classroom feels like a executive meeting room in a business conference center. Brand-new, clean, smartly painted, the room is tiered and horseshoe-shaped. It comfortably holds fifty people—about twenty too few for this class, so students are jammed into corners for today's session, an optional review for M.B.A. students who want to bone up on some basics.

Glazer is a good teacher. Every few minutes he ends his thought with a question, pulling students into the discussion. It's a class on marketing accounting, and he's talking about fixed costs, variable costs, contribution margins, and break-even points ("but we're not in business to break even"). The hourlong session slides by quickly, and before I know it, I am spilling out into the hallway with a bunch of twenty-year-olds. I spot Glazer, and together we begin our climb up five flights of stairs and through an endless maze of corridors before we finally arrive at his office. I like it. Tidy but not obsessively so. One wall is covered with books. For a desk he's got three rectangular tables pushed together in a U shape and stacked high with papers. On the table against the far wall is a Mac computer ("Old and slow," he confides. "I need a new one").

Not only is Glazer very smart (one of his advisers at Stanford called him the most intelligent student he ever taught), but his students say he's very accessible and very likable. He's about five feet eight inches, weighs a solid 150 pounds, has thinning blond hair and deep-set, penetrating blue eyes. I'm way overdressed. He's wearing khaki slacks, a white dress shirt with light blue stripes, open at the collar, and Rockport casuals. I'm in a suit.

Before we get into the information revolution, I want to ask him some basic questions. I know he is a supporter of the Natural Law Party, but I am curious to know—as I am with just about everyone I meet—did he once consider himself a Republican or a Democrat?

Leaning way back in his chair, one leg crossed over the other, Glazer admits that he was neither. "I've voted over the years, but I had no party affiliation one way or the other. I looked at politics as not very relevant," he says. "I felt that the two main parties didn't really differ in their approaches, and anyway, I tended to look at economic and social factors as driving the nation's fortunes, not political factors."

Glazer says that one of the reasons he doesn't put too much trust in the political system is that the solutions promoted by the two main parties don't work. He is sounding a familiar Natural Law Party theme. "They're kind of phony solutions. Most money is spent on bandaging up problems that already exist, rather than solving or preventing them. But worse than that, many solutions are anti-ecological—they have toxic by-products—and I don't mean just environmental, but also social, economic, and political. They create another problem, which then demands another solution, which then creates another problem. So many products exist that are designed to clean up other problems created by someone else. Health care is an obvious example. So many health care products and services lead to other problems, which then create a demand for new products and services. It's a vicious cycle that doesn't end."

Glazer leans forward to make a point. He says it's hard to comprehend the extent to which problems are an economic engine. "Entire industries are devoted to helping people overcome something that shouldn't exist in the first place. It's an enormous waste of knowledge and intelligence. For example, our most talented accountants spend their time helping people understand and fill out tax forms that basically cause more problems than they solve. In our legal system consider the amount of time, money, and talent that goes to cleaning up problems that were created elsewhere. Our whole economy has a vested interest in problems. If problems went away suddenly, the economy and our social infrastructure would probably collapse."

But we're talking about a political party, the Natural Law Party, with programs to solve problems at their root and prevent new ones from arising. What's going to happen to the economy?

"It's a political process, it's not a revolution, so change won't happen overnight," he says, smiling. "As a more prevention-oriented approach begins to be phased in, there might be some dislocations, but nothing dramatic."

Rashi Glazer is recognized in the tight-knit circle of academia as one of a number of leaders in the field of business marketing. But in the emerging field of the information-based or knowledge-based economy, he is virtually in a class by himself. He is among the most knowledgeable and most sought-after speakers at academic conferences worldwide and is a top consultant to Hewlett-Packard, Intel, Motorola, and large phone companies, such as AT&T, Southwestern Bell, and Pacific Bell. His book *The Marketing Information Revolution*, published by McGraw-Hill, offers a definitive treatment of marketing changes coming with the global information economy.

I say to Glazer, Imagine for a moment that you're a consultant to the president of the United States. Where is the economy headed?

"We're obviously moving into a new era of economics," he replies. "We are moving out of the industrial revolution into a kind of a postindustrial revolution, where the real assets of the economy are no longer matter- or energy-based assets, such as steel and oil, but information- or knowledge-based assets, such as computer software and consulting. Early thinkers talked about this thirty or forty years ago, but now it's apparent to everyone that more and more of our gross national product, and the world's gross product, are information- or knowledge-based assets, such as a software company using a ten-cent computer disk to sell a five-hundred-dollar computer program."

The real impact of this change can already be seen in seismic shifts in the job market. "The industrial revolution has been about machines gradually replacing human beings as labor, until now the idea of human beings as labor is becoming obsolete," Glazer says. "Companies just don't need as many people as labor in the workforce, and that's why we see so many dislocations across the board. In the information revolution, however, companies will see the value of human beings not as labor but as intellectual capital. In the new economy the real assets will be people who can process information and create new knowledge.

"And as knowledge and information become the real asset of the economy, it's clear that there are going to be massive transitions that will require individuals to learn new skills. For this reason, education must be our number one priority.

"But when most people talk about education, they talk about training workers in a new set of skills, such as how to use a computer. The Natural Law Party takes it a step further when it suggests that it's not a matter of simply educating people in specific skills, but of educating a person in such a way that he or she is a perpetual learner. The real value of an individual as an economic asset is not just the ability to have a particular skill but the ability to learn *any* skill. This is going to be the key for individual survival, corporate survival, and national survival. Individuals who think that whatever they know today is going to be relevant five years from now are deluding themselves. If you think that, you're probably going to be out of a job. On the other hand, if you assume that what you know today is going to be obsolete five years from now, you redefine your job in life to be a constant learner. To the extent that you see yourself that way, then you'll always be employed because you'll always be learning and you'll always be of value. To the extent that government has a role to play in making individuals wealthy, making companies wealthy, and making society wealthy, then that government has a role to play in fostering, through education, individuals' capacity constantly to renew themselves. If you read the Natural Law Party's platform, particularly its section on consciousness-based education, you see that the party articulates this better than any other political party."

It's almost five o'clock, and Glazer has to meet his wife, Margaret, in ten minutes. The afternoon has turned dismal: overcast, foggy, and drizzly. I am enjoying this conversation and am not at all eager to leave the warm and dry of the office for the cold and wet outside.

I have just a couple more questions. I shift gears to America's booming economy. Who should get the credit? Clinton? Reagan's tax cuts in the eighties?

Glazer shakes his head no. He attributes the boom less to government policies and more to wealth-generating companies, such as Intel and Microsoft.

Will it last? I ask. Are we headed for a crash?

He shakes his head no again. He is bullish on the future. "We are just at the start of a tremendous growth period in world prosperity, and the microprocessor is the engine of growth. The microprocessor is a knowledge- or information-based technology that is making older industrial-based businesses much more efficient. As businesses become more efficient, prices drop and the economy expands. More wealth has been created in the last fifteen or twenty years, particularly in California, particularly here in Silicon Valley, than in the last twenty thousand years. I believe we're at the very beginning of a huge prosperity curve."

I ask him about the current budget surplus and the decision not to cut taxes. Glazer says that despite political posturing, taxes will come down dramatically in the United States "no matter what," and the reason is simple: competition.

"Because of the emergence of one global financial marketplace and because of the Internet, governments are going to be competing with one another for money. Right now, if you're a U.S. citizen, your money is here in this country. But the truth is, everyone wants your money; the whole world wants your money. What are they going to give you to get it? They'll have to give you something, such as less taxes, or else you can put it somewhere else."

In another country? I suggest.

"Yes, in another country," he replies. "And the minute that starts, the first thing to go down is taxes. This is already beginning to happen in the U.S., where states are competing with each other to give favorable tax breaks to companies. That's only going to accelerate to the point where entire countries are going to be competing for our tax dollars. It's inevitable."

With a trend toward lower tax revenues, how will we pay for skyrocketing cost of prisons, health care, environmental cleanup costs?

"It forces us either to live with the problem or to find a solution.

Inevitably government will be forced to ask, 'Are there new ways of doing things, new solutions out there that work better than what we've got?' Is there some way we can prevent a problem now, so we don't have to deal with it, and spend more money on it, later? That's where the Natural Law Party comes in. It is the only party with a platform that is prevention-oriented, with programs that are more effective and cost-effective than whatever the government is trying today."

Suddenly it's time to go. Glazer ends with a final look to where we are headed. "Buckminster Fuller said that in the emerging knowledge-based society, the world will always get wealthier because by definition, it's impossible to know less. You can only know more, so wealth will always be increasing. Another point that goes along with this is that there's no business that complains about having too much computer power. There's no company that says, 'Gee, I wish we had less power.' Every company wants more and more computer power. What they're saying is they want more information-processing capability. So if we look at human beings as capable of becoming the ultimate information processors—as lifelong creative learners—then no company would want fewer people. They would just want more people. This is the kind of education that government should invest in because this is the real wealth generator. The Natural Law Party talks about this a lot, and business is getting on to the notion. It's the next thing in the information revolution."

I leave this interview with Rashi Glazer very upbeat, very inspired. Glazer's insights—highly sought after by top business leaders—dovetail perfectly with what John Hagelin, Mike Tompkins, and other Natural Law Party candidates are talking about:

- America has a problem-based economy fueled by toxic solutions that create costly new problems. However, the marketplace is driving the nation toward nontoxic, natural law–based solutions that prevent problems before they arise.
- The global information economy demands employees who not only know new skills but are prepared to learn new information continually and are capable of creating

new knowledge continually. The marketplace is starting to drive educators to find new ways to develop the inner genius of everyone, no matter what his or her age.

- Competition is inevitably going to drive down taxes, leaving states and the nation with less revenue to address social problems. Again, the marketplace is forcing government leaders to find new, cost-effective, scientifically proven solutions that can solve existing problems and prevent new ones from surfacing.

In the heat of the campaign, when we're battling ballot access laws, arguing in court for our rightful place in public debates, and being refused fair coverage by the national press, sometimes I would see the Natural Law Party as a newcomer on the political road, hurrying, hurrying, hurrying to catch up with the Republican and Democratic parties. On one level that may be the case. But the reality is, the Natural Law Party platform is ahead of its time—and, fortunately, not by much anymore. Change is largely market-driven, and the market is driving America toward a prevention-oriented government that values human intelligence and creativity above all else. That realization is very energizing to me and somehow lifts the pressure of trying to "catch up" off my shoulders. I am smiling about all this as I snatch a twenty-dollar parking ticket off my windshield and head out for the next meeting.

The Future

20

This Is What Third Parties Do Best

I received a press release from the office of U.S. Representative Jim Moran (D-Virginia) about the launch of a new congressional coalition dedicated to shifting America's health policies away from a disease care system toward prevention. The wording sounded familiar, and it was. It echoes the Natural Law Party platform and the efforts of two leaders of the Natural Law Party in the Washington area, who have worked closely with Moran and other members of Congress during the past eighteen months to promote change in America's health care system.

I look at the date for the launch; it's in one week, on February 3. Too bad. Right now the Washington press corps is choked by stories of scandals and consumed with the brinkmanship between the United States and Iraq. I doubt there will be much press coverage of the news conference. Prevention lacks the glitz and glamour of scandal and the urgency of the specter of war. But in this case press coverage doesn't matter. There is substance in this story, and it doesn't require the media to give it life. There is also something else significant about this story: It showcases democracy at its best, it demonstrates the power of a good third-party idea when it is allowed entry into the national political arena.

February 3, 1998, 10:00 A.M. The room looks like a cross between a health fair and a birthday party. There are balloons everywhere and long rectangular tables are lined up throughout the room. Each table is piled high with flyers, handouts, and brochures on how to reduce high blood pressure, how to stop smoking, how to lose weight. There's a station for testing your cholesterol, one for testing your blood for diabetes, and a booth with a special camera that will project a "morphed" image of what you would look like if you weighed twenty pounds more or ten pounds less. Bright, colorful banners hang from the walls and across the edges of tables, revealing the presence of a veritable who's who of public health associations—organizations that have worked tirelessly for years to see this day: the American Heart Association, the American Cancer Society, the American Diabetes Association, Partnership for Prevention, and Shape Up America! People wander from booth to booth, sampling, looking, reading.

But this isn't a typical health fair. Actually it's a press conference at the Dirksen Senate Office Building of the U.S. Capitol. It's a festive event that signals—celebrates, actually—a long-overdue shift in America's health care policies. Today, for the first time in our history, a bipartisan, bicameral (both the House and the Senate) coalition will be launched to promote disease prevention and health promotion in America. This is the Congressional Prevention Coalition. It's being chaired by two Republican lawmakers and two Democratic lawmakers and endorsed by a long list of senators and representatives from both sides of the aisle.

Representative Moran is a driving force on Capitol Hill behind the coalition. He is sitting at the center of a long conference table and is joined by the three other founding cochairs of the Congressional Prevention Coalition: U.S. Senator John Chafee (R-Rhode Island), U.S. Senator Bob Graham (D-Florida), and U.S. Representative Jim Leach (R-Iowa). C. Everett Koop, the former U.S. surgeon general, and Denise Austin, a fitness expert, are also here to speak.

The goals of the coalition are threefold:

- To communicate to Congress science-based information about prevention-related issues

- To serve as a forum for discussion and education about prevention initiatives in social and economic policy
- To focus on ways to integrate disease prevention and health promotion into our health care system

Representative Moran tells the press that members of the coalition believe it's time to adopt "a more forward-looking approach to problems in the health system.

"Without micromanaging," he says, "government can do much to encourage private sector innovation, support community initiatives and public health activities, foster important research to ensure that the latest information is available to patients and practitioners, and modernize federal programs to reflect what we know about the advantages of prevention strategies."

Dr. Sarina Grosswald and Elizabeth Rice Arnold are sitting in the front row, "listening intently to every word," according to Grosswald. She is a nationally respected medical education consultant who ran as the Natural Law Party's candidate for the U.S. House of Representatives in Virginia's Eighth District in 1996. One of her opponents was Representative Moran. Rice Arnold is the director of Natural Law Party activities in the Washington area and a longtime activist for educational reforms and international peace initiatives.

Since the campaign Grosswald and Rice Arnold have worked with Moran and his staff—as well as with other members of Congress—to bring prevention to the forefront of the nation's legislative agenda. Moran credits the two women for the idea, and they acknowledge the efforts of other nonprofit organizations that have worked to push the idea of prevention forward. But in my mind, a lion's share of the credit has to go not to an individual or a group but to the people who are politically active in Virginia's Eighth Congressional District. This district, which includes Alexandria, Arlington, Falls Church, and much of Fairfax County, remains a rare bastion of real democracy in America. It is here, unlike most other districts in the country, that third-party and independent candidates are welcome to participate in candidate debates and other forums with Republicans and Democrats. Without such an open door, no new ideas—and no new coalition.

Specifically, Representative Moran participated in more than thirty candidate debates and forums with four other candidates running for office. That meant he was exposed to ideas other than those of his Republican opponent, John Otey. That also meant that he heard Grosswald, an intelligent and articulate woman, speak in depth about the importance of prevention—not just in health care but in crime, education, and environmental issues as well. Moran must have appreciated the ideas because in those rare instances when Grosswald was not allowed to participate, he made a point of introducing her as she sat in the audience.

"Representative Moran could see during the debates that my message of prevention was receiving a very good response from the audience," says Grosswald, who was associate director of education at the American College of Obstetricians and Gynecologists for eleven years and is now president of her own consulting company. "After a few weeks he would nod and say during the debates, 'Yes, I agree with that.' "

Grosswald recalls a debate held at the Jewish Community Center in Fairfax County, with about five hundred people in the audience and several television cameras covering the event. When Grosswald spoke on the issue of prevention, Moran publicly agreed with her. She recalls: "After that debate, the chairperson of the Northern Virginia Republican Committee came up to congratulate me, and said, 'You did an excellent job, Sarina. I wish you were running for us.' But then she said, 'The amazing thing was that Moran agreed with you. He has never agreed in public with an opponent. This was historic.' "

Immediately after the election, Moran met with Grosswald and Rice Arnold and said that he planned to establish a prevention coalition in Congress. He asked for their help. The two women canvassed the House, meeting with representatives and senators, senior legislative assistants, and health specialists and found strong support from both Republicans and Democrats.

"The idea seemed so obvious," Grosswald says. "The staff would say, 'Why haven't we done this before?' "

Grosswald and Rice Arnold also found that many lawmakers were already familiar with the Natural Law Party and its prevention-oriented approach. "There were four hundred Natural Law Party candidates running against Democratic and Republican candidates in 1996," says Rice Arnold. "If those candidates were allowed to participate in debates, then Republicans and Democrats heard our message, and they saw the positive response from the public."

Now, as the two women listen to the lawmakers speak at the press conference, they hear many of their own words come back to them.

Senator Chafee describes the coalition as "an idea whose time has come. As lawmakers from both parties join forces to tackle the challenges of health care this year, we must focus on the ways in which we can prevent Americans from getting sick, rather than just rely on the tried-and-true methods of treating illness once it occurs."

Dr. Koop calls on Congress not to lose sight of those issues that will most directly affect death and disease rates in the United States. "While proposals to reform the health care system are clearly important, what is equally necessary is a clear set of legislative policies that will reduce preventable death and disease. This is not a problem requiring additional fact-finding before action is taken. Developing a national prevention agenda clearly deserves the attention of policy makers and the medical community alike."

The launch is a success, and the news conference, while not drawing a huge press turnout, nevertheless is also a success. Representative Moran joins Grosswald and Rice Arnold as the news conference breaks up and people mill around and walk through the booths. He tells the two women that their work has been key to the start of the coalition. "You put the idea in our heads and you pushed our office to follow through with it," he tells them.

If you work for a third party, you know the history of third parties in America. You know, as I said earlier, that they have brought into national debate—often against considerable resistance—new ideas that have transformed the face of the nation, including abolition of slavery, a woman's right to vote, and child labor laws, to name just a few. In addition, if you work for a third party—or one of the two major parties for that matter—perhaps you can point to foundational ideas, policies, programs, and solutions that have made their way, through your party's efforts, into public policy and reshaped society for the betterment of all. The Natural Law Party, although just a youngster in years compared with America's other political parties, has already made a sizable impact on the nation. It makes up a long list that includes court challenges to overturn unfair ballot access laws, break down barriers to the public debates, and remove obstacles to equal access to the airwaves. It also includes bringing the dangers of genetic engineering into national awareness and mobilizing scientists and consumers to demand the labeling of such foods; working to shift America's fuel supply from polluting fossil fuels to clean renewables; lobbying to maintain the integrity of the organic food market; and highlighting for the first time in the political arena the effectiveness of scientifically documented programs for developing human potential that rehabilitate offenders, boost test scores, reduce high blood pressure, and lower stress, crime, and violence throughout society.

Look closely at this list. Some ideas you may agree with, some you may not, but that's okay. That's the value of spirited political debate; that's the basis of healthy democracy. Now consider for a moment how much better off the whole country would be if people didn't have to work so hard to get those ideas out there, if new parties were not largely outlawed from the democratic process.

America is on a roll. Business is booming, interest rates are down, and crime is on the decline. But there are a lot of very troubling trends that lie just beneath the surface, trends that bode ill for the future. Much needs to be done to change all this. But none of it will happen unless we change the laws that keep new ideas out of the political mainstream. As I reflect back on the launch of the Congressional Prevention Coalition, I think that the American people were fortunate that the light of democracy still burns in Virginia's Eighth Congressional District. Consider how many other good ideas are out there that never see the light of day.

21

Final Thoughts

The past six years on the campaign trail have been a remarkable journey for me: learning about issues that matter so much for the future of the world, finding out about solutions to problems that don't damage any part of life but nourish the whole of life, and meeting so many good people doing so many good things. What I remember most are the people. It's the people who are taking these new solutions as their own and giving them life—and giving us hope.

Third parties traditionally push the nation in new directions. But sometimes a new party is destined to do much more. Abraham Lincoln's Republican Party embodied the voice of a new America and transformed the nation. Now, nearly 140 years later, America is primed for another transformation, and Americans are searching for another new voice. The pendulum is swinging back in favor of natural law, and with it, the Natural Law Party is rising up to be that new voice for America.

**Natural Law Party of the
United States**
National Headquarters
Post Office Box 1900
Fairfield, Iowa 52556
Tel: 515-472-2040 • Fax: 515-472-2011
www.natural-law.org.
email: info@natural-law.org.

Appendices

The Natural Law Party's
Fifty-Point Action Plan
to Revitalize America

Platform Summary

GOVERNMENT

PREVENTION-ORIENTED GOVERNMENT. End crisis management through prevention-oriented programs that will both solve existing problems and prevent future ones from arising.

CONFLICT-FREE POLITICS. The Natural Law Party supports "all-party government"—bringing together the best ideas, programs, and leaders from all political parties and the private sector to solve and prevent problems. The Natural Law Party advocates an end to negative campaigning and partisan politics, and supports essential campaign finance reform to eliminate special interest control of government.

PROVEN SOLUTIONS. Government should be based on what works—not what is politically expedient or bought and paid for by special interest groups. There are simple, humane, cost-effective, scientifically proven solutions to all of America's problems. The Natural Law Party was founded to implement these solutions immediately in government.

GOVERNMENT IN ACCORD WITH NATURAL LAW. Solve problems at their bases by bringing individual life, and our national policies, into greater harmony with natural law through proven educational programs; natural, preventive health care; renewable energy; sustainable agriculture; and other forward-looking, prevention-oriented programs.

REVERSE THE CURRENT EPIDEMIC of individual and social stress by establishing groups professionally engaged in creating coherence throughout society. Scientific research verifies that such groups promote social harmony, reduce collective stress, and improve efficiency in governmental administration.

STREAMLINE THE FEDERAL GOVERNMENT by reducing government waste and mismanagement, cutting pork barrel spending, simplifying redundant bureaucracies, and encouraging decentralization and privatization wherever possible.

STRENGTHENING DEMOCRACY

SUPPORT LONG-OVERDUE REFORMS to ensure (1) equal access to the ballot, the media, and the public for all qualified candidates, (2) the elimination of PAC and soft-money funding of campaigns, and (3) a shift toward public sponsorship of campaigns in order to reduce the undue influence of special interest groups on election outcomes. Such reforms will fulfill every American's right to complete information about all candidates and their platforms while freeing elected officials to focus on serving their country rather than seeking campaign contributions.

ENCOURAGE VOTER PARTICIPATION in the election process by shortening the campaign season to two months, making election day a national holiday, and abolishing the electoral college. Restrict lobbying and limit congressional privileges.

ECONOMY

IMPLEMENT A PROGROWTH ECONOMIC POLICY, with a balanced budget by 1999 and a low flat tax of 10 percent by 2003. Only the Natural Law Party can cut taxes deeply—and responsibly—while protecting the integrity of our important social programs through the hundreds of billions of dollars saved annually by our cost-effective solutions to crime, spiraling health care costs, and other costly social problems. Simultaneously, by propelling the economy into a growth phase, our policy will create new jobs, reduce unemployment, and strengthen job security.

FULLY HARNESS AMERICA'S MOST PRECIOUS RESOURCE—the unlimited intelligence and creativity of America's 260 million citizens. In today's information-based economy, intelligence and creativity, innovation and ideas drive economic growth. The Natural Law Party strongly supports proven educational, job training, and apprenticeship programs that develop intelligence and creativity and prevent school dropouts. Only the full utilization of our human resource through the Natural Law Party's fundamental commitment to education will ensure America's competitiveness and future leadership in the family of nations.

EDUCATION

SUPPORT PROVEN EDUCATIONAL INITIATIVES and curriculum innovations, including:

- The Head Start program, to help children excel from an early age
- Proven developmental technologies, such as the Transcendental Meditation program, to increase intelligence and boost educational outcomes directly
- School vouchers to increase school choice, foster competition, and improve educational outcomes
- Federally guaranteed student loans and Pell grants for higher education
- Higher national standards and the practical means to achieve them
- National apprenticeship programs for students who are not college bound
- Computer-aided instruction, including Internet instruction

- Sound approaches to school nutrition and preventive health education
- Effective drug prevention
- Policies and programs to upgrade the status and skills of teachers

HEALTH

SUPPORT HEALTH STRATEGIES that focus on prevention and strengthen the general health of the nation, thereby shifting our national focus from disease care to health care. Recent research shows that 50 percent of deaths and 70 percent of disease in America are "self-inflicted"—caused by an epidemic of unhealthy habits. The vast majority of disease is therefore preventable.

SUPPORT THE INTRODUCTION OF FINANCIAL INCENTIVES that will help prevent abuse of the health care system and ensure high-quality care, including (1) medical savings accounts for Medicare and Medicaid subscribers, which will provide financial rewards for good health; and (2) vouchers enabling Medicare and Medicaid enrollees to choose any insurance plan or health care provider they desire, thereby promoting competitive costs and quality of care among medical providers.

The implementation of verifiable, cost-effective prevention together with the above financial incentives will rescue Medicare and Medicaid from bankruptcy, save the nation up to five hundred billion dollars a year in health care costs, and prevent untold pain and suffering.

PROMOTE LIFE IN ACCORD WITH NATURAL LAW through the reduction of individual and social stress, thereby achieving a lasting social transformation toward more life-supporting, health-promoting behavior among our citizens.

ENERGY AND ENVIRONMENT

SUPPORT THE DEVELOPMENT AND USE of new, environmentally clean energy sources, such as solar, wind, and biomass by (1) removing federal subsidies for fossil fuels and nuclear energy and (2) taxing fossil fuels to reflect their real cost to the nation.

IMPROVE ENERGY EFFICIENCY AND SELF-SUFFICIENCY by (1) supporting basic research on energy efficiency, energy storage, and fuel cells, in addition to electric, hydrogen, and highly energy-efficient vehicles; (2) providing financial incentives for homeowners and industry to use available energy efficiency measures; and (3) setting performance standards for energy-consuming and pollutant-emitting products.

LEAD THE GLOBAL EFFORT to prevent the destruction of the earth's forests, the decimation of the diversity of species, and the potential damage from ozone depletion and the greenhouse effect.

CLEAN UP AMERICA'S POLLUTED AIR, rivers, wetlands, and oceans by eliminating industrial pollution at its source and using waste products productively.

CREATE NEW JOBS AND NEW INDUSTRIES in energy conservation and renewable energy sources that will simultaneously benefit the environment and save the nation hundreds of billions of dollars.

AGRICULTURE

SUPPORT LEGISLATION that will ensure true social, economic, and environmental sustainability of agriculture while balancing the following goals: (1) ensuring high-quality, healthy food for consumers; (2) promoting health and longevity in farmers and in the population as a whole; (3) protecting natural resources and the environment; (4) cushioning farmers from the natural and financial instability unique to agriculture; (5) enabling farmers to better pursue financial profitability; and (6) restoring the vitality of family farms and rural communities.

MANDATE THE LABELING OF GENETICALLY ENGINEERED FOODS, and declare a moratorium on the release of genetically engineered organisms until the ecological impact of such organisms is established.

SHIFT THE U.S. POLICY FOCUS from "cheap food for the consumer" to "quality food for the consumer on a sustainable basis." Agrichemical use could be reduced 50 percent by the year 2000, and farm profits could increase through field-tested methods, such as integrated pest management, integrated crop management, and organic methods.

CRIME AND REHABILITATION

SUPPORT SYSTEMATIC, SCIENTIFICALLY PROVEN PROGRAMS to reduce stress in the individual and throughout society, thus eliminating the root cause of crime.

TARGET INDIVIDUALS at the highest risk for crime—the current prison inmate population—through proven rehabilitation programs and advanced scientific methods to assess rehabilitation and eligibility for parole.

IMPLEMENT COMMUNITY POLICING. Such programs have been credited with reducing crime by 40 percent during the last two years in New York City. In this approach, police are assigned to high-crime neighborhoods identified by computer tracking, work closely with these neighborhoods, and are rewarded for preventing crime.

REVITALIZE OUR OVERCROWDED URBAN CENTERS, breeding grounds for violence and crime.

INTRODUCE PROGRAMS proven to reduce drug dependency and promote mental and physical health.

SUPPORT EFFECTIVE EDUCATIONAL PROGRAMS to keep children in school, off the streets, and out of the reach of crime. The Natural Law Party's strong educational focus is the true, long-term solution to the pervasive problem of crime.

DRUG ABUSE

IMPLEMENT EDUCATIONAL PROGRAMS that directly unfold intelligence and creativity, build self-confidence, eliminate stress, and raise life to be in harmony with natural law, thereby eliminating the tendency toward drug dependence and helping prevent school dropouts—the principal targets for drugs and drug-related crimes.

PROMOTE PROGRAMS that have been shown to reduce drug dependency dramatically and to eliminate stress and restore balance in an individual's physiology and psychology (see the Health and Crime and Rehabilitation platforms).

SUPPORT PROCEDURES that will promote cooperation and coordination among the various law enforcement agencies responsible for interdicting, apprehending, and prosecuting individuals and organizations engaged in illegal drug and narcotics activities.

REVITALIZING OUR INNER CITIES

APPLY PROVEN EDUCATIONAL, health, economic, and crime reduction programs to improve the inner-city environment.

Use federally guaranteed loans to stimulate capital investment for start-up industries in urban enterprise zones. By targeting economically deprived urban areas, we can stimulate economic growth where it is most needed, thereby creating more jobs, a stronger sense of community, and the revitalization of our inner cities.

HELP PLAN URBAN INFRASTRUCTURE and housing that improve quality of life and restore a sense of community to the inner city. Promote the development of nonpolluting automobiles and public transportation, human-scale housing that discourages crime and supports neighborhoods in which families can grow and prosper, and the development of more parks and green spaces.

UPHOLDING THE RIGHTS OF WOMEN AND MINORITIES

SUPPORT ANY LEGISLATION DEEMED NECESSARY to uphold the guaranteed constitutional rights of women and of minorities.

DISSOLVE PREJUDICE AND BIGOTRY in society through educational programs that develop broad comprehension, increased intelligence, and improved moral reasoning and by reducing social stress that leads to fear and divisiveness.

INCREASE PARTICIPATION IN GOVERNMENT by women and by minorities to bring greater strength and balance to the administration.

ABORTION

OFFER PREVENTION OF ABORTION on a realistic basis through proven educational programs to bring individual and national life into harmony with natural law. The Natural Law Party believes that we can reduce abortions more effectively through education than through legislation—education that develops intelligence, improves moral reasoning, and promotes farsighted thinking and actions that do not create problems. Our nation's history shows that it is difficult to legislate morality, and the Natural Law Party believes that it is counterproductive for the federal government to outlaw abortion.

ENCOURAGE A SHIFT from public to private funding of abortion—specifically, private charity by those who wish to make abortion accessible for women who cannot afford it. Over time the government should eliminate the use of taxpayer dollars to fund abortion as a method of birth control. (The Natural Law Party would support public funding of abortions in cases of rape, incest, or medical necessity.)

SATISFY BOTH THOSE WHO ARE PROLIFE and those who are prochoice by (1) decreasing the number of unwanted pregnancies more effectively than legislation and (2) leaving moral responsibility in the hands of those whose lives are affected most.

FAMILY VALUES

IMPLEMENT PROGRAMS that resolve the root cause of the breakdown of family life today: epidemic stress levels throughout society, especially in urban centers. With the rise of greater social harmony, all individuals, and especially parents, will be able to make the most life-supporting decisions in their personal lives and the most nourishing decisions for the lives of their children.

CREATE JOBS, STIMULATE GROWTH, and ease the financial strain experienced by so many American families through our low-tax, progrowth economic policy.

FOREIGN POLICY

CREATE AN IMMEDIATE SHIFT in U.S. foreign policy away from military aid toward a more life-supporting policy based on the exportation of U.S. know-how—American expertise and technical assistance in business administration, entrepreneurship, education, sustainable (organic) agriculture and environmental technologies—supplemented where necessary with economic support. This new type of life-supporting assistance will allow many developing countries to become financially self-sufficient and thereby help eliminate global hunger and poverty.

Ensure that our foreign aid resources are applied effectively—not wasted through inefficiency, mishandling, or inappropriate allocation—by making foreign aid decisions in consultation with the government and citizens of recipient countries. Through this cooperative focus, promote unity and respect within the global diversity of cultures, religions, races, and economic and political systems.

DEFENSE

Support the creation of a prevention wing within the military, a group whose primary purpose is to prevent the outbreak of war and to strengthen and preserve national and international peace. Train as few as 1 to 2 percent of military personnel, constituting one or several groups of five to ten thousand, in the proven peace-promoting technology of the TM-Sidhi program. In addition, "inoculate" participating troops against the debilitating effects of combat stress, this prevention wing would help relieve stress in the nation as a whole, prevent incoherence within the government, and protect the nation from negative influences both inside and outside the country, including terrorism and war.

Responsibly reduce defense expenditures over time by creating a smaller, more flexible force that, when coupled with greater economic and security cooperation, can most effectively serve the nation's security interests and provide the basis for a more stable world. Encourage incentives to help defense industries diversify into nondefense markets and reinvest private sector funds and expertise.

IMMIGRATION

Support balanced immigration by allocating immigration quotas to each nation, thereby preventing dominance of any one nationality or ethnic subculture in America's melting pot tradition. The concentration of uninational subcultures in urban centers precludes acculturation, slows economic integration, and could lead to the birth of a permanent underclass.

REMOVE THE INCENTIVES FOR ILLEGAL IMMIGRATION by (1) increasing border defense through reassignment of selected military personnel and resources (see our Defense platform), and (2) improving economic conditions in neighboring countries through a foreign policy emphasizing technical assistance and U.S. know-how (see our Foreign Policy platform).

GUN CONTROL

ELIMINATE THE CLIMATE OF FEAR AND TENSION pervading America's cities and towns, which is largely responsible for the proliferation of guns and their use in acts of violent crime, through effective crime prevention programs (see the Crime and Rehabilitation platform).

UPHOLD EXISTING GUN CONTROL LEGISLATION as an appropriate balance between public safety and the constitutional right to bear arms.

The Natural Law Party Platform

Introduction
Government Supported by Natural Law:
A New Approach to National Administration

The Natural Law Party holds that natural law is the solution to problems. Government can solve problems at their basis through scientifically proven programs to bring every citizen, and the entire nation, into accord with natural law. By accessing the full range of nature's intelligence and harnessing its power, individuals and nations can govern themselves with the same perfection in administration displayed throughout nature.

THE PROBLEM

The federal government is besieged by problems, and legislation has proven inadequate to eliminate them. The American pandemic of crime, random violence, and drug abuse, disintegrating families, poverty, and staggering health costs has not responded to even the toughest legislation. Why?

Recent congressional initiatives to improve the quality of life in America have focused primarily on financial approaches—for example, shifting fiscal responsibility for the social safety net from the federal government to the states. But balancing the budget, reforming the tax structure, and addressing economic inequities will not stop Americans from falling ill, abusing drugs, or committing crimes (see the Health and Crime and Rehabilitation sections).

The debates over these bills have raised questions about the underlying cause of problems. In the search for answers, one theme increasingly heard is that the problem lies within, that all our problems are symptomatic of a deeper crisis of moral and spiritual values.[1] Yet no clear path to addressing this crisis has emerged.

To strengthen the moral and ethical fabric of our society, we need to look even deeper than the family structure and address the underlying cause of both family and social breakdown. We need to identify the fundamental cause of our problems and attack the problem at its source. Otherwise, more stringent welfare and child support rules will not by themselves instill stronger family values, eliminate teen pregnancy, restore a thriving work ethic, and encourage charity and volunteerism.

NATIONAL LAW AND NATURAL LAW

From the deepest perspective, our national problems have one underlying cause: violation of natural law.[2]

Natural law is the orderly principles—the laws of nature—that govern the functioning of nature everywhere, from atoms to ecosystems to galaxies. Over the past several centuries, modern science has identified many of these laws governing physical, biological, ecological, and social systems. Natural law is inherently "life-supporting"; it supports the life and evolution of innumerable species.[3]

Natural law is not a new idea in American government. Our Founding Fathers believed that the rights of every American citizen to life, liberty, and the pursuit of happiness are based on immutable laws of nature. They believed that through knowledge of natural law, both science and government would promote the goals of freedom and happiness of the people.[4]

Human behaviors that promote life, liberty, and happiness are in harmony with natural law. When people live in harmony with natural law, they don't make mistakes; they spontaneously uphold higher values, and they enjoy naturally good health and a life free from problems.[5] However, the knowledge of natural law uncovered by modern science, and disseminated through our educational system, has been insufficient to enable citizens to live and act in accord with the laws of nature. Thus, the whole population is constantly violating natural law, causing problems for itself and its communities.

"Violation of natural law" is action that fails to take natural advantage of the laws of nature or that stimulates them in ways that cause negative repercussions. Smoking is an example of behavior that runs counter to the natural laws that support good physical health.

Violation of natural law causes stress. Stress has consequences for both mental and physical health; the majority of all disease is said to be stress-related.[6] Stress causes a complex psychophysiolog-ical chain reaction in the human body. Chronic, acute stress leads to an out-of-balance biochemistry that has also been linked with anxiety, fear, anger, impulsive violent behavior, and substance abuse.[7]

Moreover, the combined stress of all the individuals in society builds up and creates a dangerous, criminal atmosphere in the whole community. This epidemic of stress has rent our social fabric and threatens the lives of Americans everywhere.

The government reflects this social disorder. Government is a mir-ror of the nation. When the country is full of stress and crime, this chaotic atmosphere has a debilitating effect on the performance of government.[8]

To deal with all the problems engendered by social stress, gov-ernment responds with laws, regulations, and costly social programs designed to protect us from ourselves. Most of the activities of our government—and most of our tax dollars—are spent compensating for the violations of natural law by the population. The laws and programs, however, can't solve the problems.

We can have a smaller, more efficient and effective government, one that is capable of solving problems. Such a government would function in alliance with natural law.

THE SOLUTION

The best government is "nature's government"—natural law, which governs the universe with perfect order and without a problem. Nations can govern themselves with this same perfection in admin-istration.

The most effective way governments can deal with problems is to prevent them in the first place—by enabling people to stop vio-lating natural law. How? Not through legislation but through edu-cation that brings the life of every citizen, and the nation as a whole, into harmony with natural law.

How does one learn to think and act in accord with natural law? Understanding specific laws of nature (for example, learning about the health risks of smoking) is helpful. But the laws of nature are too vast and complex to be fully comprehended intellectually. Intellectual understanding alone is also not enough to guarantee life in accord with natural law. A new kind of education is needed that will enable every citizen to live, and every government to function, spontaneously in harmony with natural law.

The most modern and most ancient understandings of natural law describe a universal level of nature's intelligence underlying all forms and phenomena in the universe, including the human mind and body. Modern physics has glimpsed this unified source of all the laws of nature. The oldest tradition of knowledge of natural law, the Vedic tradition of India, describes this universal level of nature's intelligence and states that it can be located, and accessed, at the deepest level of the human mind, at the level of pure consciousness.[9]

For thought and action to be in tune with natural law, it is necessary to experience and develop pure consciousness. This is not the commonly understood idea of consciousness raising: becoming more sensitive to or knowledgeable about issues. Pure consciousness is the fundamental level of awareness, the basis of all thinking and behavior. It is the deepest level of natural law in the individual, which is identical with the deepest level of natural law that administers the entire universe. Developing consciousness means connecting individual life with this holistic value of natural law—with nature's government.

> **1.** To bring the life of individuals into accord with natural law, education must provide a technique to give them direct access to the holistic value of natural law in pure consciousness.
>
> One such technique identified by science is the Transcendental Meditation program of Maharishi Mahesh Yogi. The Transcendental Meditation technique (which originates in the Vedic tradition) is a simple, natural, effortless procedure that allows the conscious mind to settle down and directly experience pure consciousness, the simplest form of human awareness, where consciousness is open to itself. This experience creates a unique state of restful alertness in mind and body, which dissolves accumulated stress and fatigue

while developing the individual's latent creative potential and ability to think and act in tune with natural law.

Extensive scientific research has documented the many positive effects of bringing individual consciousness into harmony with natural law. More than six hundred studies, conducted at more than two hundred independent universities and research institutions, have shown that these techniques increase individual intelligence and creativity, reduce such stress and stress-related behavior as anxiety, hostility, and aggression, and improve mental and physical health.[10]

The research shows that as individuals practice this technique and gain intimate familiarity with the holistic value of natural law in their own consciousness, they spontaneously begin to think and act more in harmony with the laws of nature that support health and well-being for themselves and their social environment. They are less inclined to violate these natural laws. Relevant findings include improved health and reduced health care costs,[11] decreased drug, alcohol, and tobacco abuse,[12] decreased criminal recidivism,[13] and improved psychological and moral development.[14]

The Natural Law Party strongly recommends that this program for developing consciousness be made available to students in our educational system, so that students learn from an early age how to live in accord with natural law. In addition, rehabilitation and law enforcement agencies should immediately adopt this successful approach to reducing crime and substance abuse.

2. To address social problems fully, governments must reduce social stress by bringing the whole society into accord with natural law.

Society as a whole has a collective consciousness, which is the sum of the consciousness of all its individual members. Individual consciousness influences collective consciousness, and in turn is influenced by it.[15,16]

If collective consciousness can be brought in tune with natural law, the whole population will cease to violate the laws of nature. Social stress will be reduced, and problems such as crime and violence will automatically decrease.

Research verifies that one powerful and successful program to reduce stress in collective consciousness and promote social harmony and well-being is practice of the TM-Sidhi program by groups together in one location. The TM-Sidhi program is an advanced meditation program to release stress, which leads to improved cognitive ability,[17] intelligence,[18] health,[19] and psychological and moral development.[20] The TM-Sidhi program includes the technique of Yogic Flying. Research has found that EEG brain wave coherence increases dramatically during TM-Sidhi Yogic Flying,[21] accompanied by the subjective experience of deep happiness and exhilaration.

The TM-Sidhi program is not, however, practiced solely for its beneficial effects on the individual. Its chief purpose is to produce profoundly positive effects in collective consciousness. When groups practice the TM-Sidhi program together, they enliven the deepest level of natural law throughout the whole population. Forty-two scientific studies have shown that such coherence-creating groups (constituting as little as the square root of 1 percent of the population) promote highly significant decreases in violent crime and other negative tendencies and increases in positive social and economic trends.[22]

3. Government should function with the efficiency and effectiveness of nature's government.

The Natural Law Party promotes a new definition of government: Government should be able to prevent problems. A government without the ability to prevent problems is not a sovereign government. It becomes crisis-driven, a victim of situations and circumstances. Moreover, such a government itself becomes an unwieldy and costly problem for the nation. To fulfill its highest goals, every government should create and maintain one or more groups of seven thousand experts trained in the TM-Sidhi program professionally engaged in creating coherence throughout society. (The group could be established from the military or from among students, the unemployed, etc.) Such a group would quietly bring the support of natural law to national law, solve problems at their basis in individual and collective consciousness, and promote the highest level of efficiency in governmental administration.

This is a practical, highly cost-effective, fundamental solution to our nation's problems, one that will bring both immediate and long-term results. As our government runs low on funds, our federal officials have been wrangling over short-term, essentially reactive solutions. But without bringing national law in tune with natural law, no legislative initiatives will ever succeed in eliminating social and economic problems and developing a strong moral core at the heart of our nation. For this reason, the Natural Law Party supports the use of programs to reduce societal stress and bring national life into accord with natural law.

Economy

The Natural Law Party envisions a flourishing national economy in which no citizen suffers from unemployment, recession, runaway inflation, or any other economic hardship; in which America's businesses are highly competitive in the international marketplace; in which the crippling national debt is reduced and eventually eliminated; and in which the tax burden is significantly decreased, enabling everyone to enjoy greater prosperity and a higher standard of living.

THE PROBLEM

A healthy economy is the key to America's domestic strength and international leadership. Without industrial and corporate might, the United States cannot remain competitive in world markets, satisfy domestic needs, or continue to play a major role in world events. America has enjoyed exceptional economic growth in 1997 and thus far in 1998, but our economy still faces serious challenges.

For example, President Clinton and Congress have taken credit for the recent U.S. budget "surpluses," but in reality they have created an economic illusion through deceptive federal accounting practices. They have not cut spending at all; instead they have borrowed surplus Social Security revenues to pay for excessive federal spending in other areas. This action jeopardizes the future of the Social Security program, effectively turning Social Security payroll taxes into a 15 percent flat tax on income rather than an investment vehicle for employee retirement. America is already over five trillion dollars in debt—about twenty thousand dollars per citizen—and in fiscal years 1998 and 1999, despite Congressional Budget Office projections of budget surpluses, the national debt will increase by more than one hundred billion dollars annually. Any credit for recent U.S. economic growth should rightly go not to government but to the hardworking Americans whose creativity has led to increased productivity.

In addition, the increasing income disparity between the wealthiest 20 percent and the other 80 percent of Americans indicates a great imbalance in our economy. Although profits and productivity have increased during the past two decades, the purchasing power of the average American has declined significantly. For example, in 1993 the average American worker had to spend twenty-six weeks' worth of wages to buy a car, compared with seventeen weeks in 1973. Many wage earners—especially those in lower-income brackets—have limited resources, no opportunity to save, little job security, and no way to cope with emergency medical needs.

Excessive taxes and a burdensome, overly complex, and punitive tax code stifle economic growth. The seven-million-word tax code is so convoluted that the Internal Revenue Service itself has trouble understanding it, and corporations spend four times as much on tax compliance as they do on taxes.[1] In addition, special interest groups have successfully manipulated the tax code by creating loopholes to benefit specific businesses, a practice that results in corporate welfare and creates disincentives to economic growth.

In the words of the Kemp commission, the present tax code "is beyond repair—it is impossibly complex, outrageously expensive, overly intrusive, economically destructive, and manifestly unfair. . . . We believe [it] cannot be revised, should not be reinvented, and must not be retained."[2] Yet despite strong popular pressure to change the tax code, Republicans and Democrats, controlled by special interests, have thwarted any meaningful improvement.

American businesses are saddled by the highest health costs in the world. Health benefits have become the third-largest expense after raw materials and straight-time pay for most manufacturers and the second-largest expense for most service businesses. For many employers, the cost of corporate health benefits precludes real salary increases for employees, and many otherwise profitable businesses are driven into bankruptcy by these spiraling expenses.

Finally, to maintain our technological edge in the competitive international marketplace, American businesses require highly skilled workers. Alarmingly, our high school students score near the bottom in international comparisons of industrialized nations: 28 percent of youths entering the U.S. job market are high school dropouts,[3] and the number of Americans earning doctoral degrees has declined in recent years, yet Congress has cut funding for student loans. America therefore faces a creativity challenge that must be solved for our country to maintain its domestic and economic strength.

THE SOLUTION

BOOSTING NATIONAL CREATIVITY. In today's information-based economy, intelligence and creativity (i.e., innovation and ideas) drive economic growth. Clearly, America's most precious natural resource is our human resource, the unlimited creative potential of our 260 million citizens. Given today's low test scores and high dropout rates, the most crucial economic strategy that government can adopt is to harness America's untapped creativity. The Natural Law Party strongly advocates proven educational, job training, and apprenticeship programs that develop intelligence and creativity, prevent school dropouts, and bring life into accord with natural law. Only the full utilization of our human resource through the Natural Law Party's fundamental commitment to education will ensure America's competitiveness and future leadership in the family of nations. (For a complete discussion of the Natural Law Party's educational programs, see the Education section.)

LOWERING TAXES. The most powerful *fiscal* action our government can take to stimulate the economy is to lower taxes. The Natural

Law Party can cut taxes deeply, and responsibly, without adding to the deficit or cutting essential services. Many parties have promised lower taxes but have been unable to fulfill these promises because of the depth and complexity of problems faced by government. The Natural Law Party, through its cost-effective solutions to crime, spiraling health costs, and other costly social problems, will save the nation hundreds of billions of dollars annually. On this basis the Natural Law Party can offer a realistic strategy for significant tax reduction that protects the integrity of our important social programs.

One simple and viable way to implement across-the-board tax cuts is through a low flat tax. The Natural Law Party has designed a low flat tax that includes an exemption for America's poor and lower-income families. Beginning in 1998 at 18 percent, our tax rate would fall to 10 percent by 2003 as the Natural Law Party's cost-effective solutions to the nation's problems began to bear fruit.[4] The Natural Law Party's low flat tax would stimulate and sustain strong economic growth. This strong economic growth, with its associated increase in government revenues, combined with the savings from our cost-effective solutions, would ensure a balanced budget and gradual repayment of the national debt without borrowing from the Social Security trust fund. This proposal would also reduce the size and scope of the IRS, eliminate loopholes for the wealthy, and put an end to corporate welfare.

In addition to our flat tax proposal, the Natural Law Party is continuing to study alternative tax options, such as a consumption tax, that might decrease the tax burden for Americans. We concur with the Kemp commission's fundamental requirements for a new tax code: fairness, simplicity, neutrality, visibility, and stability.[5]

ENTERPRISE ZONES. The Natural Law Party supports the use of federally guaranteed loans to stimulate capital investment for start-up industries in urban enterprise zones. By targeting economically deprived urban areas, we can stimulate economic growth where it is most needed, thereby creating more jobs, a stronger sense of community, and the revitalization of our inner cities.

CUTTING CORPORATE HEALTH COSTS. The enormous burden of corporate health care expenditures can best be reduced by improving employee health. Research shows that appropriate preventive health care programs can significantly improve health and reduce health care costs,[6] thereby freeing financial resources for greater productivity, profit, and investment. Therefore, a Natural Law Party government would encourage businesses to implement such programs to improve corporate health and productivity and to reduce employee stress and substance abuse.[7]

CREATING MACROECONOMIC STABILITY THROUGH INCREASED SOCIAL COHERENCE. The Natural Law Party also supports programs that have been shown to dissolve social stress and conflict, thereby providing a more positive and stable environment for economic growth and prosperity. Most analysts are aware of how businesses are influenced by such macroeconomic factors as inflation, unemployment, economic cycles, and the threat of international conflict. However, businesses are also in a position to change macroeconomic trends in a positive direction for the benefit of the organization and society as a whole. For example, research has found that even a single group of seven thousand to ten thousand practitioners of Transcendental Meditation and its advanced programs can produce a significant decrease in inflation and unemployment rates, as well as improvements in other economic indicators.[8] Businesses that incorporate such programs into their employee benefits packages help ensure economic stability by creating a more coherent and stable society. The recent meltdown of the Asian financial markets underscores the need to insulate the U.S. economy from global economic uncertainties, and the establishment of such coherence-creating groups will help protect our nation's current economic strength.

SHARING THE BENEFIT. As the economy continues to improve, we anticipate higher pay, better working conditions, shorter work hours, and a shorter workweek. We believe that the American workforce should reap the benefits of a powerful economy through a higher standard of living.

Through cost-effective solutions to the nation's problems, responsible tax reduction, and proven programs to boost national intelligence and creativity, the Natural Law Party will propel the economy into a sustained growth phase. This progrowth policy will simultaneously create jobs, reduce unemployment, balance the budget through increased government revenues, and retire the national debt. Only the Natural Law Party offers a comprehensive, viable strategy to accomplish these goals.

Health

The Natural Law Party is committed to ensuring a long and healthy life for every American. By bringing life into accord with natural law, the prevention-oriented health programs proposed by the Natural Law Party will significantly reduce disease and promote the health and vitality of all Americans. As our nation's health improves, we can lift the massive burden of health care costs, thus freeing our nation's resources for greater progress and prosperity.

THE PROBLEM

Too many Americans suffer from poor health.[1] The United States has some of the worst health statistics of all industrialized countries, yet America has the highest per capita health care costs of any nation.[2]

Why is the U.S. medical system such a cost-effectiveness disaster? The answer is that our health care system is really a disease care system—it focuses on the management of illnesses rather than on the prevention of disease and the promotion of health—but the vast majority of our national health is influenced by factors over which this disease-based approach has little control, such as nutrition, stress, societal problems, and environmental toxins. Consequently, in the absence of effective prevention, our present disease care system can never create a truly healthy society.

Recent research shows that 50 percent of deaths and 70 percent of disease in America are *self-inflicted*, caused by an epidemic of unhealthy habits, including improper diet, inadequate exercise, smoking, and alcohol abuse.[3] Thus, the vast majority of disease is preventable.[4]

Incredibly, Republicans and Democrats consistently ignore proven prevention-oriented approaches to health, and Medicare specifically bans funding for most preventive services.[5] Following the federal example, most private health insurance companies also refuse to cover prevention. No health care reform bills debated in Congress have focused on improving health; they have dealt only with problems in disease care financing and delivery, hoping to save money by streamlining and downsizing the system.

Spiraling health care costs have dramatically increased the cost of health insurance, and at least 40 percent of U.S. citizens are now inadequately covered or have no medical insurance. Health care expenditures have also placed a heavy burden on American businesses; if employee insurance costs continue to rise, many companies will collapse by the end of the decade.

THE SOLUTION

By focusing on the prevention of disease and the promotion of health, the Natural Law Party offers a solution to the health care crisis that is comprehensive, cost-effective, and scientifically proven.

Our health care platform has two aspects.

> **1.** We support health strategies that focus on prevention and strengthen the general health of the nation, thereby shifting our national focus from disease care to health care. These programs include prevention-oriented health education, including strategies to modify unhealthy behaviors, and prevention-oriented natural medicines. These preventive strategies have been shown by extensive research to create healthier citizens and to cut health care costs by 50 to 70 percent.
>
> **2.** We support the introduction of financial incentives that will help prevent abuse of the health care system and ensure high-quality care. These incentives include (a) medical savings accounts for Medicare and Medicaid subscribers, which will provide financial rewards for good health,[6] and (b) vouchers enabling Medicare and Medicaid subscribers to choose any insurance plan or health care provider they desire, thereby promoting competitive costs and quality of care among medical providers. Such financial incentives will re-

duce demands for unnecessary care and prevent overuse of the health care system by giving greater financial control and responsibility to individual subscribers.

Through our two-pronged approach of preventive health care and financial incentives, we can rescue Medicare and Medicaid from bankruptcy, save the nation approximately five hundred billion dollars a year in health care costs, and prevent untold pain and suffering.

To structure meaningful health benefits options for all Americans without disastrously increasing the federal budget deficit, we must responsibly decrease health care outlays per person—a particular challenge as the population ages. The most effective and humane way to achieve this goal is to prevent disease in the first place by strengthening the human immune system and eliminating the imbalances that ultimately cause disease.

The prevention programs supported by the Natural Law Party incorporate the most up-to-date knowledge of nutrition, exercise, and stress reduction, as well as the use of natural herbal preparations, natural dietary supplements, and alternative medical treatment modalities. Americans favor such approaches. There are now more visits to alternative medicine practitioners than to conventional doctors.[7] Research has consistently shown that the prevention programs endorsed by the Natural Law Party significantly reduce the need for conventional medical treatment by empowering individuals to take better care of their own health.[8]

Our national health care debate has degenerated into an argument over who should pay for whose disease, with little attention given to preventing disease and improving health. Funding for proven prevention services has been denied to Americans, largely because the lobbying influence of more than one thousand medical political action committees (PACs) has shaped legislation and preserved the status quo.[9]

The Natural Law Party, which does not accept PAC contributions, is committed to changing this unethical and inhumane situation. During the past four years Dr. John Hagelin and Dr. Mike Tompkins, 1996 Natural Law Party candidates for president and vice president, have worked closely with the U.S. Congress to introduce wording into health care bills in both the House and the Senate that would provide coverage for any scientifically verified, cost-effective, proven preventive program. This proposal has such commonsense appeal that it has gained the support of conservative and liberal members of Congress alike.

The Natural Law Party's approach to health care provides a unifying influence in the political debate by transcending surface bickering over money and solving the health crisis at its basis: by improving the health of Americans. The enormous savings generated by the Natural Law Party's prevention-oriented programs, coupled with the financial incentives created by medical vouchers and savings accounts, will allow the government to extend high-quality health care realistically to tens of millions of uninsured Americans.

The programs of preventive health education advocated by the Natural Law Party are also unique in raising health care to a new level: development of the full potential of every citizen and reduction of individual and societal stress by promoting life in accord with natural law. This approach goes beyond behavioral modifications, such as smoking cessation, which have low compliance and cannot be enforced in a free society. Research shows that stress is responsible for the persistence of life-damaging habits despite overwhelming medical evidence and governmental warnings. By neutralizing individual and social stress, the Natural Law Party can improve the effectiveness of such behavioral modification programs by significantly enhancing compliance. In this way we can achieve a lasting social transformation toward more life-supporting, health-promoting behavior among our citizens.

The Natural Law Party is unique in offering high-quality health care for all while providing a net *cost savings* for the nation.

Education

The solution to all our national problems lies in proper education. The Natural Law Party advocates scientifically proven educational programs that can unfold the full creative potential of every student and produce ideal citizens capable of fulfilling their highest aspirations while contributing maximum to the progress of society. By harnessing America's greatest resource—the unlimited creativity of our 260 million citizens—the Natural Law Party can bring fulfillment to education and ensure America's competitiveness and continuing leadership in the family of nations.

THE PROBLEM

Education in America is not working. Even though the United States spends more money per student than any other country, its students still rank far behind most of their international peers in math and science—and well behind U.S. test scores of twenty years ago. Twenty-eight percent of our high school students drop out—the highest rate of any industrialized nation—and those who graduate are often ill prepared to enter the workforce.[1]

Each year 3.7 million children suffer substantial injury at school, resulting in an estimated $3.2 billion in medical spending and $115 billion in good health lost.[2] Drug and alcohol abuse continues to undermine our nation's students and rob them of their mental clarity, motivation, self-esteem, and ability to focus.[3] Moreover, juvenile violent crime, especially gang and school violence using guns, has increased markedly during the past decade.[4] According to the Centers for Disease Control, American youths are twelve times more likely to die by gunfire than their peers in other nations.

The culturing of inner values has all but disappeared from our nation's schools. Yet James Madison observed in the *Federalist Papers* that democracy cannot function unless our leaders and citizens are "in a higher degree of virtue than any other form" of government.

America's problems are human problems: crime, drug abuse, domestic violence, and declining health. Only through the full development of our human resource can we rise above the reach of problems. Yet research has shown that students graduating from our current educational system use at most 5 to 10 percent of their full mental potential.[5] A new and effective approach to education is clearly needed.

THE SOLUTION

Education is for enlightenment—the full development of mind, body, and behavior. The Natural Law Party promotes proven educational programs that directly increase intelligence and creativity and simultaneously improve moral reasoning, self-reliance, and mental and physical health and well-being. These programs include sound educational approaches to nutrition,[6] natural, preventive health measures,[7] effective drug prevention programs,[8] and innovative curriculum development, including programs to develop the full mental potential of students.[9]

While focusing on dissemination of knowledge, current approaches to education ignore the most fundamental component of learning: the consciousness or intelligence of the student, which is the basis of gaining knowledge. Today's educational approaches provide no knowledge of consciousness and no scientifically proven technology to develop it. This fundamental failure is the ultimate source of the problems afflicting education today. Even current proposals to improve education most often focus on information technologies, such as computer access to the Internet, that offer larger and larger volumes of data. However, without an educational approach that can develop more than 5 to 10 percent of a student's full mental potential, no amount of information will ever produce truly educated, ideal citizens.

The consciousness-based approach to education advocated by the Natural Law Party develops full human potential while providing mastery of the technical skills necessary to compete in today's society. This approach combines the most advanced and successful curriculum innovations with the most thoroughly researched educational program to develop the full potential of consciousness, the Transcendental Meditation program.[10] This integrated approach to education develops knowledgeable, highly creative citizens who can fulfill their own goals while simultaneously promoting the interests of society.

The Natural Law Party proposes to upgrade the U.S. Department of Education to a Department of Educational Excellence, which would charter several federally funded model schools in which educational innovations of all kinds could be implemented and researched. On the basis of the success of these programs, parents and educators across the country could choose the ones they thought would be most appropriate and effective in their neighborhoods. Rather than dictate educational curricula at the local level, the federal government could thereby play a crucial research and leadership role in expanding educational choices for parents and students, improving educational outcomes across the nation.

The Natural Law Party also supports federally funded vouchers to cover 100 percent of tuition to increase parental options for school choice and to foster competition among schools. These vouchers could be used to pay for any school of the parents' choice—public, private, or parochial—provided that the school maintains high academic performance on standardized national tests. The free market competition that this voucher system will engender will help reverse declining educational outcomes in America.

The Natural Law Party also supports the following initiatives:

- Fully fund the Head Start program, to give all eligible children an opportunity to excel from an early age.
- Provide financial support for every student who wants to go to college. The Natural Law Party does not support the scaling back of Pell grants and student loans for higher education. Government loans should be repaid after graduation—if necessary through mandatory salary deductions or community service.
- Establish higher national standards and the practical means to achieve them. Other parties have called for higher standards but have offered no effective strategies to accomplish this goal.
- Lengthen the school year and increase the number of required subjects in high schools, as recommended by the 1984 National Commission on Excellence in Education.
- Establish ties with teachers' organizations, schools, and community interest groups to develop policies and programs that upgrade the status and skills of teachers.

- Add computer support to the National Literacy Act of 1991, to provide research and help implement computer-aided instruction, including Internet instruction, in literacy programs.
- Increase the nutritional value of school lunches, a simple but essential change that has been shown to improve educational outcomes in economically disadvantaged neighborhoods.
- Establish community centers of knowledge where parents can receive the latest understanding of health and nutrition for their children.
- Create national apprenticeship programs by bringing together business, labor, and educational leaders to develop a system that offers training in a valuable skill for students who are not college bound.

Most of the educational programs promoted by the Natural Law Party have been successfully applied in diverse educational settings worldwide[11] and have therefore been the subject of extensive scientific research. The results of such programs include the significantly improved educational outcomes mentioned above—increased intelligence, creativity, motivation, academic performance, moral reasoning, psychological maturity, and social responsibility—as well as a higher quality of life among students and faculty.

Crime and Rehabilitation

The Natural Law Party envisions an America free of crime, where all citizens live fully in accord with both natural law and national law, where people freely move on the streets without fear, and where Americans live and work together harmoniously for both their own fulfillment and the national good.

THE PROBLEM

Crime costs Americans $450 billion annually.[1] Despite two decades of "get tough" policies—with longer, often mandatory prison sentences—the rate of violent crime in America is high compared with that of other developed nations.[2] Of gravest concern, juvenile violent crime, especially urban gang and school violence using guns, has spiraled during the past decade.[3] According to the Centers for Disease Control, American youths are twelve times more likely to die by gunfire than their peers in other nations. An FBI crime report concluded that "every American has a realistic chance of being murdered because of the random nature [that] crime has assumed."

America's criminal justice system is under constant strain. Courts, police, probation and parole agencies, and prisons are overworked and inadequate to deal with the high level of crime.[4]

Clearly, a "get-tough" policy is not enough. *Effective crime prevention* is also crucial. Yet despite the dismal track record of get-tough approaches, Republican and Democratic legislators ignore proven preventive strategies and press for more police, more prisons, and stiffer punishment. Consider the following:[5]

- BUILDING MORE PRISONS HAS NOT WORKED. Since 1971 the U.S. prison population has increased sixfold to more than 1.2 million—645 of every 100,000 Americans—incarcerated in fifteen hundred state and federal prisons and three thousand jails. The United States now has the largest percentage of its citizens behind bars apart from Russia.[6] Incarceration acts like a quarantine, preventing a faster acceleration of crime, but fails to eradicate the source of the crime epidemic.
- THE THREAT OF PUNISHMENT IS NOT ENOUGH. Most violent crime is "an impulsive response to an immediate stressful situation," often committed under the influence of drugs or alcohol, not a rational, considered action.[7]
- MANY EXPERTS BELIEVE THAT PRISONS TRAIN INMATES TO BE BETTER CRIMINALS.[8] Most violent crime is com-

mitted by hard-core repeat offenders: the majority of all prisoners commit new crimes and are arrested within three years of release.

- MORE POLICE ON THE STREET DO NOT LOWER CRIME. Published reports indicate that increased police patrols in major U.S. cities have had little effect on crime rates.[9] Washington, D.C., for example, has the highest police/population ratio in the nation—and one of the highest violent crime rates. The twenty-five-billion-dollar crime bill designed to deploy one hundred thousand more police represents merely a drop in the bucket and is hardly effective or cost-effective.

Increasing recognition of the need for prevention has led to experimental approaches such as Drug Abuse Resistance Education (DARE) and midnight basketball. Unfortunately, long-term scientific studies have found no significant effects on crime and drug abuse from such programs.[10]

THE SOLUTION

The Natural Law Party believes that these Band-Aid approaches do not work because they fail to address the root cause of crime: the epidemic of stress throughout society. During the past two decades medical science has documented the alarming rise of such stress-related illness as hypertension, stroke, and heart disease. This same buildup of stress is responsible for a similar rise in social illnesses: crime, drug abuse, domestic violence, and family disintegration.

Current crime prevention programs overlook the psychological and physiological devastation wrought by constant, traumatic stress. Stress causes a complex psychophysiological chain reaction that makes the nervous system hyperexcited and unstable.[11] Chronic, acute stress leads to serious physiological malfunction. Among other effects, the body's neurochemical balance is distorted, producing abnormally high levels of cortisol (a primary stress hormone) and low levels of serotonin (a key neurotransmitter).[12] This out-of-balance biochemistry has been linked with anxiety, fear, anger, impulsive violent behavior, and substance abuse.[13]

Moreover, the combined stress of all the individuals in society builds up and creates a dangerous, criminal atmosphere in the whole community. This societal stress and tension become a breeding ground for more crime and violence. Thus, to reduce crime, stress must be reduced in at-risk individuals and throughout society.

REDUCING SOCIAL STRESS. In addition to a tough penal code as a deterrent to crime, the Natural Law Party offers systematic, scientifically proven programs to reduce stress in the individual and throughout society, thus eliminating the root cause of crime. At least one such program, the Transcendental Meditation program, has been scientifically shown (1) to reduce individual and social stress; (2) to reduce cortisol and increase serotonin production in the body, thus counteracting the neurochemical imbalances produced by stress; and (3) to decrease anxiety, hostility, and anger, and improve psychological development and moral reasoning.[14]

Forty-three published scientific studies have shown that large groups practicing the Transcendental Meditation and TM-Sidhi program in one location reduce social stress and violence. These studies, which have investigated the impact of such groups on communities, cities, and entire nations, have consistently found decreases in crime, war deaths, and other negative social indicators, as well as improvements in economy and national mood.[15] This innovative approach offers a highly cost-effective, scientifically proven strategy to eliminate the fundamental cause of crime through reducing individual and societal stress.

EFFECTIVE PRISON REHABILITATION. The most cost-effective prevention strategy is to target those individuals who are at highest risk for crime: the current prison inmate population, 90 percent of whom will be released from prison. A five-year Harvard study investigated the effects of the Transcendental Meditation technique in a maximum security prison. Inmates who learned the practice decreased significantly in stress, aggression, and mental disorders. Violence throughout the prison decreased, and the rate of return to prison among participating inmates was 30 to 35 percent less than for four other treatment groups.[16] Similar studies in twenty-eight other maximum security prisons have shown equally impressive results.[17] (Current rehabilitation strategies put the cart before the horse. They try to reeducate and reform inmates without first changing inmates from within by ridding them of the stress that makes them uninterested in education or incapable of being reformed.[18])

COMMUNITY POLICING. In New York City a new initiative called computer-assisted community policing has been credited with reducing crime by 40 percent over two years. In this approach, police are assigned to high-crime neighborhoods identified by computer tracking, work closely with these neighborhoods, and are rewarded for *preventing* crime. According to statistics from the New York Police Department, murder in New York City dropped 31 percent during the first half of 1995 compared with the first six months of 1994, with similar reductions in other categories of violent crime. This striking improvement led one journalist to refer to New York as "the suddenly safer city."[19]

URBAN REVITALIZATION. Our overcrowded, decaying urban centers obviously contribute to the rise of stress and crime. Any program to reduce crime must involve a comprehensive plan to revitalize the inner cities, as laid out in our Revitalizing Our Inner Cities section.

DRUG AND ALCOHOL REHABILITATION. A high proportion of crimes are committed under the influence of alcohol and drugs. A recent study of crime in New York City found that tobacco, alcohol, and drug abuse cost the city's taxpayers and corporations twenty billion dollars in 1994—twenty-one cents of every tax dollar.[20] The Natural Law Party would introduce programs proven to reduce drug dependency, eliminate stress, and promote mental and physical health.[21]

PREVENTING YOUTH CRIME. School dropouts are at highest risk for crime and drug abuse. The Natural Law Party strongly supports more effective educational programs to keep children in school, off the streets, and out of the reach of crime. Our proven educational programs unfold greater creativity and intelligence and develop ideal citizenship by raising life to be in accord with natural law and national law (see our Education section). The Natural Law Party's strong educational focus is the true, long-term solution to the pervasive problem of crime.

The Natural Law Party is the only political party with a truly comprehensive, scientifically proven strategy to reduce crime. Our approach is the most hard-hitting since it focuses on scientifically proven programs that work. Our prevention-oriented approach will save the nation hundreds of billions of dollars and prevent immeasurable anguish and suffering in the lives of millions of Americans who are victims of crime each year.

Energy and Environment

The Natural Law Party will create a future in which renewable, nonpolluting, inexpensive energy is abundantly available, the air in our cities is pure and clean, and our rivers and lakes are free of pollution. We foresee a time when waste is efficiently managed; when the needless destruction of forests and species diversity has ceased; when there are many more parks, gardens, and fountains; when new jobs have been created to develop renewable energy sources, conserve energy, and protect the environment; and when global cooperation ends environmental threats to the future of humankind.

THE PROBLEM

The standard of living and the economic vitality of the United States depend on the increasing availability of inexpensive, clean, renewable sources of energy.

Until now the United States has relied mainly on fossil fuels. Coal, oil, and natural gas account for the majority of energy used for electricity, heat, transportation, and industry. However, these fuels are nonrenewable and limited in supply. Their use results in air pollution, acid rain, pollution from mercury and other contaminants, the threat of global warming, and other environmental hazards that may endanger future generations with irreversible global changes. Air pollution kills sixty-four thousand Americans a year—a higher death toll than for auto accidents.[1,2] The indirect costs of burning fossil fuels—health care, damage from acid rain, the impact on tourism and quality of life, etc.—are incalculable.[3]

Oil imports are responsible for almost 50 percent of our trade deficit. America's dependence on foreign oil creates economic vulnerability and political instability between the United States and the Middle East. For example, Desert Storm, with its enormous attendant costs, was largely to protect America's critical oil interests in the Middle East. The costs of such military operations must be added to the high health and environmental costs of fossil fuels.

By subsidizing these costs with taxpayer dollars, the federal government artificially suppresses the cost of fossil fuels relative to sustainable alternatives, such as wind and solar, which are not subsidized. The government thereby perpetuates our continued dependence on fuels that are environmentally and economically unsustainable.

In addition to the environmental hazards posed by current energy use, toxic agricultural and industrial chemicals threaten the health and safety of all Americans. Recent estimates indicate that exposure to such chemicals is responsible for 75 percent of all cancer cases in the United States.[4]

Shortsighted environmental policies contribute to alarming reductions of earth's nonrenewable resources. Approximately 93 percent of the virgin forests in the Pacific Northwest have been cut, and most of the remainder is scheduled to be cut in the next few years—nearly all of it on public lands. Biodiversity is being threatened at an alarming rate, not only in our vanishing forests but in the oceans. Hundreds of thousands of sea mammals are being exterminated by drift net fishing. Approximately 50 percent of our wetlands that provided habitats for wildlife have been destroyed, and overgrazed prairie lands are being increasingly eroded.

At the recent summit in Kyoto, Japan, where all nations assembled to address global environmental concerns, the U.S. government took a stand to protect economic interests that it perceived to be in conflict with environmental interests. Protecting the environment was equated with loss of jobs, increased costs of goods, and loss of economic vitality. Today America's environmental protections are being further eroded by a Congress held captive to special interest groups.

THE SOLUTION

The Natural Law Party is committed to increasing both energy efficiency and the use of renewable, safe, and nonpolluting energy sources. This approach will protect our environment, create energy self-sufficiency, and add to the economic prosperity of the nation. Through programs that will create new jobs and new industries in energy conservation and renewable energy sources, the Natural Law Party will move away from the hazardous and wasteful use of fossil fuels in ways that will simultaneously benefit the environment and save the nation hundreds of billions of dollars.

To improve energy efficiency and self-sufficiency, the Natural Law Party will:

- Support basic research on energy efficiency, energy storage (both for large- and small-scale applications), and fuel cells, in addition to electric, hydrogen, and highly energy-efficient vehicles.
- Provide financial incentives for homeowners and industry to use available energy efficiency measures, such as insulation and compact fluorescent lighting.
- Set performance standards for energy-consuming and pollutant-emitting products in order to encourage adoption of state-of-the-art technologies and to protect responsible and innovative manufacturers from being undercut by those who produce cheaper but dirtier products. By increasing efficiency, the United States can significantly reduce energy consumption—with substantial economic and environmental benefits for the nation.[5]

The Natural Law Party also supports the development of new energy sources, such as solar, wind, and biomass, which could be cost-competitive now if government stopped subsidizing fossil fuels. The Natural Law Party is committed to increasing the proportion of renewable, environmentally clean energy sources by the year 2000. To achieve these goals, the Natural Law Party will:

- Remove federal subsidies for fossil fuels and nuclear energy. Require that construction of new electrical power plants take into account all long-term costs to the nation, such as environmental protection and health costs.
- Progressively implement a tax on fossil fuels to reflect their real cost to the nation, including environmental

cleanup, medical costs, and security costs in the Persian Gulf.

The Natural Law Party does not support the development of nuclear energy. At present municipalities subsidize nuclear plants and the federal government funds nuclear reactor construction with tax-deductible bonds. But no one can safeguard for ten thousand years the highly toxic wastes generated by these reactors, which is what the federal government has agreed to do. (The government's efforts to clean up these wastes is yet another subsidy for pollution-generating energy sources.) In addition, the known worldwide reserves of low-cost, high-grade nuclear fuel are running low, and this will soon necessitate a transition to the next generation of nuclear power plants: advanced converters and breeder reactors. These reactors have the technological advantage of producing their own fuel, but they also produce bomb-grade fissionable materials as unavoidable by-products. With the widespread availability of bomb-grade material, nuclear containment becomes effectively impossible. Therefore, for both economic and security reasons, the Natural Law Party does not support further development and construction of nuclear energy plants.

It is vitally important for America to clean up its polluted air, rivers, lakes, beaches, wetlands, and oceans. When businesses are forced to stop polluting, they frequently come up with innovative ways to make use of their polluting by-products. In Scandinavia, for example, businesses in any given region collectively decide how to use polluting wastes from one business as part of the manufacturing process of another, with the goal of zero pollution.

To eliminate toxic waste, the Natural Law Party supports research into innovative technologies such as the plasma torch, a cost-effective process that cooks contaminated soil into inert, harmless glassy rocks suitable for road gravel. A similar technology, devised for liquid nuclear waste, drains out water and salts and turns the remainder into glass logs that are safer for long-term storage.

America should lead the global effort to prevent the destruction of the earth's forests, the decimation of the diversity of species, and the potential damage from ozone depletion and the greenhouse effect. A moratorium should be declared on cutting timber in national parks, national forests, and national monuments until a sustainable management plan for cutting is instituted.

To make these changes requires flexibility and ingenuity in the development of new environmentally sound technologies—not giving up the present standard of living but raising it through developing energy sources, industries, and modes of transportation that are in harmony with nature.

The programs supported by the Natural Law Party for cleaning up the environment and protecting it from irreversible damage will stimulate the economy, actually paying a dividend of increased energy efficiency and economic vitality. Cleaning up polluted rivers and lakes will increase fishing industries, tourism, and revenues from outdoor recreational activities. Cleaning the air will reduce the medical costs of respiratory disease and lung cancer. Protecting forests and reducing exhaust emissions will avert the potentially disastrous expenses of adapting to climatic changes resulting from global warming.

Since pollution is primarily caused by human behavior, bringing the individual and the nation into harmony with natural law will greatly facilitate implementation of the above programs. The Natural Law Party therefore supports educational programs that promote broad comprehension and "pollution-free behavior"—behavior that is in accord with natural law and does not create problems for society or the environment.

Agriculture

The Natural Law Party envisions a time when American farmers will farm in full accord with the laws of nature, fully utilizing nature's creativity to yield abundant, healthy food, while protecting the environment and ensuring a vigorous, diversified, sustainable agricultural economy.

The PROBLEM

The future of agriculture depends on its sustainability—that is, the ability of agricultural policies and practices to preserve and strengthen the farming economy, ecology, and community for future generations.

The recently passed Federal Agricultural Improvement and Reform Act of 1996 (FAIR) has been heralded as a major change of direction for U.S. agriculture. But it has left many wondering whether crucial, fundamental changes have really been made in agricultural policy and whether FAIR is fair—especially for small family farms and for the environment. FAIR does not go far enough to ensure agricultural practices that are sustainable—financially, environmentally, and socially.

1. FINANCIALLY UNSUSTAINABLE

- Recent projections of increasing international demand for food, coupled with rapidly shrinking global food reserves, suggest that consumers will pay even more for food in the future and that poor countries will receive less U.S. food aid. Despite these realities, current U.S. farm programs restrict America's agricultural production (for example, thirty-six million acres have been taken out of production) while encouraging competitors to plant more.[1,2]

- The new farm subsidy program of FAIR, although formalizing the phasing out of government subsidies over the next seven years, continues to favor the nation's largest farms.

- The growing consolidation and control of food production by a few very large corporations jeopardize the survival of small family farms. U.S. Department of Agriculture policies and regulations are biased against small farm operators and enforce a form of corporate welfare that drives small farms into bankruptcy so that they can be bought by huge agribusinesses.

- From 1988 to 1993 even the most economically profitable farms averaged only a 3 to 5 percent return on stockholder equity; food manufacturers, on the other hand, averaged 16.5 percent.[3] Clearly, farmers receive little of the value-added profit accruing to food manufacturers that process farm goods for the market. Farmers, especially those working small family farms, and their surrounding communities cannot survive without diversification of farm activities that keeps more of these profits close to home.

2. ENVIRONMENTALLY UNSUSTAINABLE

- Conventional agriculture erodes and degrades soil; it requires large-scale use of chemical pesticides and fertilizers that pollute groundwater and are unhealthy for consumers and farmers. These agrichemicals pose real threats to water quality, wildlife, and human health. Recent scientific research indicates that common pesticides are estrogen-mimicking and implicates them in the high incidence of breast cancer and prostate cancer in America and in the striking decline in male sperm count. Yet FAIR continues to support chemically intensive cropping practices.
- Federal agencies have decided that some genetically engineered plant and animal products (such as recombinant bovine growth hormone [rBGH], which boosts milk production) are safe and may be commercialized, despite the concerns of some scientists. Virtually all European nations have banned rBGH and other hormone treatment in livestock. Many products similar to rBGH are under review. In addition, many foods that have been genetically engineered with pig, insect, virus, or bacteria genes are already being sold in supermarkets. Yet these genetically altered foods are not labeled as such—despite well-documented health risks from some genetically engineered foods, including:

   Toxic Tryptophan. This genetically engineered food supplement killed thirty-seven people and permanently disabled fifteen hundred more.

Allergenic Soybean. This soybean, genetically altered with a Brazil nut protein, caused a marked reaction in many people allergic to Brazil nuts.

- Some leading scientists believe that alteration of DNA, the most fundamental level of plant and animal physiology, is likely to have profound negative impacts on the environment and human life.[4] For example, altered genes from cultivated food crops may be released to wild relatives, thus compromising the "gene pool" upon which breeders of domestic crops must draw to enhance resistance to pests and disease. Unlike other products, a genetically engineered organism that has been released into the environment can never be recalled.

- The explosion of factory hog farms, cattle feedlots, and poultry operations during the last few years has increased livestock concentrations, confinement housing, and separation of animals from their natural environments. As a result, these animals are more prone to disease; therefore, they need more antibiotics; and consequently, their wastes become a health hazard instead of a natural aid to soil fertility.

- In addition, to ensure maximum weight gain in their livestock, farmers commonly inject antibiotics into healthy animals. Many scientists suspect that this practice helps create bacteria and viruses that are resistant or immune to antibiotics. Since antibiotic-resistant germs have become a major health problem in America, this practice should be stopped immediately.

3. SOCIALLY UNSUSTAINABLE

- Experts believe that conventional agriculture has led to "decaying communities [in] rural America that continue to lose population, business, and even their reason to exist as farms consolidate into larger units and farm families leave."[5] Small towns are a reservoir of enterprise and traditional values that Americans cherish, and they should not be lost.

- Corporate-owned factory hog farms, cattle feedlots, and poultry operations, as well as the corporations that supply them, are becoming increasingly vertically integrated, pushing family farms and rural agribusinesses out of business and reducing farmers to corporate laborers.

- The challenges of farming today are making new demands on farmers and their families. The farmer must take into account many complex factors in making production decisions, including the weather, quality of the soil, threat of pests, available financial resources, and changing agricultural markets. Economic pressures cause stress, which affects health and well-being. Research has found that farmers are also at high risk from exposure to chemical pesticides.[6]

THE SOLUTION

Agriculture is more than a business; it is a way of life. The food produced by farmers is basic to our health and national security, and farmland itself is an irreplaceable resource vital to sustenance of life. Therefore, government must help ensure the long-term viability of agriculture.

The Natural Law Party supports legislation that will ensure true social, economic, and environmental sustainability of agriculture while balancing the following goals: (1) ensuring an economical and healthful supply of high-quality food for consumers; (2) promoting health and longevity in farmers and in the population as a whole; (3) protecting natural resources and the environment; (4) cushioning farmers from the natural and financial instability unique to agriculture; (5) enabling farmers to pursue financial profitability better; and (6) restoring the vitality of rural communities.

The Natural Law Party has identified solutions to the problems faced by U.S. agriculture:

1. Given the far-reaching ecological and health impacts of genetic engineering, a moratorium should be imposed on the release of genetically engineered organisms until the safety of such organisms can be firmly established. In addition, to protect the public's right to know, labeling of genetically engineered foods should be mandatory.

2. Farm policies should be redirected to expand opportunities for new and existing farmers to prosper using sustainable, organic systems that will enhance the health of the farmers and the population as a whole. Training and apprenticeship programs, loans, grants, and other incentives should be devised to assist conventional and entry-level farmers to adopt organic or more sustainable systems. Demonstration farms, farmer-to-farmer networks and field tours, and studies of successful alternative farming systems should be used to hasten the adoption of more sustainable practices.

3. The United States should change its policy focus from cheap food for the consumer to quality food for the consumer on a sustainable basis. Through research and education, the U.S. Department of Agriculture is in a unique position to influence (a) practices of farmers and the food production industry and (b) the food choices and demands of consumers.

a. Field-tested techniques supported by scientific research, such as integrated pest management, integrated crop management, and organic farming, already exist for farming profitably on a low-input, sustainable basis.[7] On this basis, agrichemical use could be reduced 50 percent by the year 2000. The USDA should initiate and fund research into further development of alternative and chemical-free sustainable agricultural practices, with an emphasis on the development of systems and technologies that can be integrated economically and completely into all agricultural production. In addition, economists have developed accounting techniques that incorporate the costs of pollution and natural resource depletion into agriculture's balance sheet.[8] Government legislation should make it a priority to disseminate these practices and techniques to the entire food production industry, showing farmers, producers, and consumers that sustainable food production practices are more cost-effective in the long run.

b. Consumer demand drives agricultural supply. Changes in consumer preferences will create a shift toward less resource-intensive food production and a healthier food supply. The USDA should initiate and fund research investigating the impact of dietary change on health and longevity and then launch campaigns to educate the public. For example, government should fund vigorous programs to inform consumers that chemical-free food is possible now, at a reasonable price. Moreover, scientists have recently concluded that substantial public health and environmental benefits would likely result from more widespread use of vegetables, fruit, and plant-based protein in the diet.[9] The government should educate the public about the health and environmental value of these foods in the diet.

Land grant universities and extension services should also take the initiative to develop and disseminate sustainable agricultural practices and healthier dietary approaches.

4. Farm communities should seek new ways to keep value-added processes and profits as close as possible to the farm. Public policy should promote cooperative development of local processing facilities and diversification into the production of higher-value, specialized crops, including chemical-free production.

5. Family-size farms should be protected and strengthened through more programs such as FAIR's Fund for Rural America, which supports value-added incentives, assistance for minority and beginning farmers, and other initiatives to empower farmers and rural communities to work toward revitalizing rural life. Even removing farm payment loopholes for large corporate agribusinesses would favor the viability of family-size farms. Programs such as the Fund for Rural America should be given high priority and full funding.

6. For the above recommendations to be successful, however, it is necessary—for the individual farmer and society as a whole—to develop consciousness and gain more support of natural law. The Natural Law Party therefore recommends educational programs to develop the consciousness of the farmer and thereby reduce stress, improve the farmer's health and well-being, and promote the skills to meet new management challenges. Such programs will enable farmers spontaneously to make better decisions and better use of the environment and will bring them greater support of natural law in all their activities. Similarly, the reduction of stress in the collective consciousness of society, combined with the Natural Law Party's focus on education, will influence consumer choices toward higher-quality food, better health, and more life-enriching behavior, life in accord with natural law.[10] These programs will help ensure that the natural resources upon which agriculture depends will be available far into the future.

Strengthening Democracy

Our nation's founders strove to create a democracy that would guarantee fundamental human rights and hold the government accountable to the people. The Natural Law Party is committed to restoring this vision to the American political process and overcoming the bipartisan conflict and special interest control that has paralyzed and subverted our government.

The Natural Law Party supports long-overdue election and campaign reforms to ensure (1) equal access to the ballot, the media, and the public for all qualified candidates, (2) the elimination of PAC and soft-money funding of campaigns, and (3) a shift toward public sponsorship of campaigns in order to reduce the undue influence of special interest money on election outcomes. Such reforms will fulfill every American's right to complete information about all candidates and their platforms while freeing elected officials to focus on serving their country rather than seeking campaign contributions.

The Natural Law Party envisions a future in which elections are a time of national celebration, free of negative campaigning, a time when the nation takes pride in its achievements and plans collectively for the future.

Election Reform

THE PROBLEM There is no constitutional basis for America's current two-party system. In fact, George Washington and Thomas Jefferson specifically warned against political parties, which they feared would become entrenched as elitists and servers of special interests, unresponsive to the needs and desires of the people.

Today we find ourselves in this very situation. Frustrated by political gridlock, many Americans think that government has grown into a self-serving, self-perpetuating partisan body that neither reflects nor recognizes their desires. Recent polls indicate that 86 percent of Americans believe that their elected officials will never solve the nation's problems, partly because political infighting has frozen the machinery of government. Consequently, the United States has the lowest voter turnout of any country in the world.

Over 60 percent of Americans favor the formation of a new major political party. Americans want change and are deeply frustrated with both Republican and Democratic candidates. Traditionally, third parties have introduced important new ideas, such as women's suffrage and the abolition of slavery, into our national political debate. As former Chief Justice Earl Warren commented, "All political ideas cannot and should not be channeled into the programs of our two major parties. History has amply proved the virtue of political activity by minority, dissident groups, which innumerable times have been in the vanguard of democratic thought and whose programs were ultimately accepted. The absence of such voices would be a symptom of grave illness in our society."[1]

Yet the Republican and Democratic parties continue to exert an effective stranglehold on the political process, preventing crucial new ideas from emerging via third parties and their candidates.

Current campaign laws unfairly discriminate against independent and third-party candidates. In 1996 Republicans and Democrats received $148 million in taxpayer dollars to run their general election campaigns, including $25 million to hold meaningless presidential nominating conventions, while independent and new-party candidates typically receive nothing. In most cases, access to the ballot is automatic for Republicans and Democrats, but independent and third-party candidates face the most rigid, discriminative, and unwieldy procedures in the world. For example, it is more difficult for a new party to get on the ballot in Florida than it is in all the countries of Europe, Australia, New Zealand, and Canada combined.[2]

The present ballot access barriers for third parties blatantly violate the 1990 international Helsinki Accords that guarantee universal and equal suffrage to all adult citizens "without discrimination," including equal access to the ballot and the media. Ironically, the United States is the world's foremost proponent of these accords.[3]

THE SOLUTION   The Natural Law Party supports election reform that returns American democracy to the high ideals envisioned by our nation's founders, a democracy that fairly represents the views of *all* its citizens and candidates. To achieve this, the Natural Law Party supports the following initiatives:

- Ensure ballot access fairness. Every political party and candidate should have the same requirements in every election for getting on the ballot. Incumbents should no longer have privileges over challengers with new ideas.
- Promote campaign fairness. It is the right of the American people to hear the views of every candidate on the ballot. All candidates who meet ballot access requirements should have the same access to their constituencies, including equal media access through a series of publicly sponsored televised forums, debates, and infomercials, as well as publicly sponsored mailings of voter education materials. To qualify for these privileges, candidates would be required to comply with voluntary spending limits. This structure would favor voter education over privately funded media advertising and would thereby help eliminate special interest influence on the election process.

- Encourage all Americans to vote. Election day should be made a mandatory national holiday, as in most other nations, so that everyone has time to vote. Voter registration should be facilitated by creating uniform laws that allow same-day registration or even automatic registration.
- Shorten the campaign season. The campaign season should be reduced to four months—two months for parties to choose their candidates and two months for the general election.
- Abolish the electoral college. Under the current system, a presidential candidate can receive a majority of the votes and still lose the election. The president should be elected by the people through direct popular vote.
- Allow national initiatives. The public initiative process, already enacted and in operation in twenty-three states, should be expanded to the national level. This process allows the collective will of our citizens to initiate legislative reform and thereby shape governmental policy more directly.
- Consider proportional representation. This political system, as opposed to the winner-take-all process, has been effective in countries around the world and more fairly represents the true will of the people.

Campaign Finance Reform

THE PROBLEM   The election process is far too long and expensive. Elected representatives spend too much of their terms fund-raising and campaigning for reelection. The United States has the longest campaign season, yet the lowest voter turnout, of any country in the world. The exorbitant cost of campaigns favors wealthy candidates and those who receive large contributions from political action committees (PACs) and other special interest groups. Research has shown that 90 percent of all campaigns are won by the candidate who spends the most. Consequently, government has become a hostage to special interests rather than responsive to the people.

In 1994 the Republicans supported campaign finance reform and won a landslide victory. However, once they became the majority party, the Republicans became the majority beneficiaries of PAC funds. Now they are the biggest recipients of special interest money in history, and the recent Republican filibuster ensured that no campaign finance reform will take place during the 1998 Congress.

The savings and loan crisis is a prime example of what happens when government is financed and controlled by special interest groups. The savings and loan deregulation was brought about by the influence of the powerful savings and loan lobby, which furnished large campaign contributions to the president and to Congress. The effects of this S&L deregulation and the consequent irresponsible handling of depositors' funds have cost taxpayers hundreds of billions of dollars—thousands of dollars for every taxpayer.

Campaign finances have usurped the focus of our elected leaders by forcing them to attend to fund-raising rather than doing their jobs and solving the nation's problems.[4] For example, it can take as much as ten million dollars or more to run an effective Senate campaign; consequently, incumbents must raise five thousand dollars every day they are in office. Hence the lure of PAC funding becomes too compelling to resist.

Unlike the major party candidates with PAC funding, independent and third-party candidates encounter formidable financial obstacles to media access. In addition, the frequent exclusion of these candidates from participation in televised debates, because of the stranglehold of the two major parties on the democratic process, prevents new ideas and new solutions from entering the political process.

THE SOLUTION The Natural Law Party will promote fairness in campaign financing through public sponsorship of election campaigns and will support legislation to correct injustices through the following campaign finance reforms:

- Eliminate PACs. When candidates run for Congress,
  they turn to lobbyists and PACs for contributions. Con-

sequently, when drafting legislation, they often feel
more accountable to special interests than to the people
they were elected to serve. This system amounts to legalized bribery. The elimination of PACs and special interest control of the political process would make our
elected representatives responsive to the people once
again.

- Eliminate soft money. This loophole circumvents the legal limits on what individuals or corporations can do-
nate to campaigns, limits that are flagrantly violated
today. Since current donation limits apply mainly to the
election of federal officials, unlimited funds can be do-
nated to nonfederal party accounts, whose administrators can then apply the money as they choose,
including, indirectly, to federal campaigns. Special interest groups often use such soft money to buy support for
their cause, thus sacrificing the best interest of the
American people.[5]

- Restrict lobbying. Strictly limit the ability of former
public servants to lobby on behalf of domestic and foreign interests.

- Limit congressional privileges. Public servants should
abide by the same laws as every American citizen. Free
mailings, congressional pensions, and other special privileges should be limited.

Revitalizing Our Inner Cities

The Natural Law Party supports a comprehensive, cost-effective
plan to revitalize our inner cities. Our plan includes proven programs
for education; job, technical, and management training; crime prevention; drug rehabilitation; urban revitalization; social welfare; economic development; and the development of a stronger sense of
community. To guarantee the plan's success, we would supplement
all these programs with scientifically validated technologies to re-

duce social stress and unfold the full creative potential of people of all ages.

THE PROBLEM

America's decaying urban centers are monuments to decades of flawed public policies. Billions of dollars are wasted on programs that fail to revitalize our cities because they do not go to the root of the problem. They fail to unlock the inner creative genius of the people, and they fail to reduce the alarming rise of stress in society, which is at the basis of the widespread epidemic of crime, violence, alcohol and drug abuse, and disease. For example, a recent report from the U.S. Justice Department noted that 81 percent of weapons arrests take place in cities and that teenagers account for 23 percent of these arrests. University of Cincinnati criminologist Frank Cullen commented in *USA Today* that this trend relates "to an absence of family and social structure to support them. Together, that's a lethal combination."

Without addressing the root causes of stress at the basis of urban decay and unrest, all other efforts for economic recovery and urban renewal are destined to fail.

THE SOLUTION

The Natural Law Party offers something new, something that has been shown by scientific evidence to work. This approach involves two steps: (1) reduction of built-up social stress, followed by (2) implementation of practical programs to improve community life and solve costly social problems.

To reduce stress, the Natural Law Party supports the establishment of coherence-creating groups practicing the Transcendental Meditation and TM-Sidhi program. Extensive research, published in leading scientific journals, has found that when a small proportion of a population collectively practices this program, there is a significant reduction in negative tendencies, such as crime, violence, sickness, and accidents, and a strengthening of positive social and economic trends in the population as a whole. Such programs will prevent the accumulation of stress and frustration that has erupted as violence in cities across the nation. In the more harmonious atmosphere generated by these programs, a deeper and more integrated sense of community will emerge as the best security against inner-city crime and decay.

After reducing social stress and creating a more coherent social atmosphere, the Natural Law Party would introduce practical solutions to costly social problems and specific programs to promote progress in every city:

- ECONOMY. In addition to effective vocational training and management training programs, the Natural Law Party supports the use of federally guaranteed loans to stimulate capital investment for start-up industries and urban enterprise zones. By targeting economically deprived urban areas, we can stimulate economic growth where it is most needed, thereby creating more jobs, a stronger sense of community, and the revitalization of our inner cities.

- HEALTH. To improve public health and curb rising health care costs, the Natural Law Party would support prevention-oriented health education and natural medicines that have been shown scientifically to prevent disease, promote health, and cut health care costs in half (see the Health section).

- EDUCATION. To improve education, the Natural Law Party would support programs that develop the inner creative genius of all students, along with the ability to conduct their lives in accord with natural law. Only education that is perceived as directly relevant to the student's own life, education that unfolds full mental potential and the ability to fulfill desires in harmony with natural law, can prevent students from becoming dropouts, who become the primary targets of inner-city crime and drug abuse (see the Education section).

- PUBLIC SAFETY. To improve public safety, the Natural Law Party would support proven, cost-effective programs that have been shown to rehabilitate criminal offenders; prevention programs that target at-risk youth

before they become involved in crime; effective programs to prevent and cure alcohol and drug abuse; and
a permanent coherence-creating group to reduce stress
and create a more harmonious social atmosphere
throughout the city (see the Crime and Rehabilitation
section).

- CITY PLANNING. To rebuild the inner city, the Natural
Law Party would help plan urban infrastructure and
housing that improve health, reduce crime, and restore
a sense of community. The Natural Law Party would
promote the development of nonpolluting automobiles
and public transportation, human-scale housing that discourages crime and supports neighborhoods in which
families can grow and prosper, and the development of
more parks and green spaces (see the Energy and Environment section).

Drug Abuse

The most effective defense against drugs is proper education, education that directly unfolds intelligence and creativity, builds self-
confidence, eliminates stress, and raises life to be in harmony with
natural law, thereby eliminating the tendency toward drug dependence.

To be effective, education must be deeply satisfying and directly
relevant to a person's life. Such education will eliminate functional
and technological illiteracy and also prevent students from becoming dropouts, who become the principal targets for drugs and drug-
related crime (see our Education section).

For those currently suffering from drug dependence, the Natural
Law Party promotes programs that have been shown to reduce drug
dependency dramatically and to eliminate stress and restore balance
in an individual's physiology and psychology (see our Health and
Crime and Rehabilitation sections).

The responsibility for stemming the drug trade currently belongs
to numerous federal agencies, including the Drug Enforcement Administration, the Border Patrol of the Immigration and Naturaliza-

tion Service, and the Federal Bureau of Investigation, as well as many state and local agencies. This fragmented approach inevitably results in overlapping and at times self-defeating investigations, apprehensions, and prosecutions. These conflicts make administration inefficient and sometimes result in senseless anomalies that allow known criminals to escape prosecution altogether.

The Natural Law Party therefore supports procedures that will promote cooperation and coordination among the various law enforcement agencies responsible for interdicting, apprehending, and prosecuting individuals and organizations engaged in illegal drug and narcotics activities.

Upholding the Rights of Women and Minorities

The rights of all American citizens are guaranteed by the U.S. Constitution, and the Natural Law Party would support any legislation deemed necessary to uphold these constitutional rights for women and for minorities. At the same time, the Natural Law Party recognizes the difficulties in "legislating" equality; equal rights legislation has not succeeded in eliminating discrimination.

Government cannot be present at all times and in all places to ensure that people treat one another fairly. Instead the Natural Law Party intends to reduce prejudice and bigotry in society through more effective educational programs that develop broad comprehension, increased intelligence, and improved moral reasoning and by reducing social stress that leads to fear and divisiveness. These programs will help create a unifying influence among our citizens and throughout society.

Natural law is that basic element in the universe that constantly nourishes the life of every individual and every living species. The Natural Law Party is the only political party that is based on this universally nourishing quality of natural law. Until now democracy has been willing to compromise the interests of the minority for the sake of the majority. This is because democracy has so far been based on limited principles of man-made law, which are not sufficiently comprehensive to be simultaneously nourishing to everyone.

When such principles compromise the interests of the minority, inevitably some segments of our population remain unfulfilled. The result is an increase in stress and frustration, which inevitably erupts as crime, sickness, and other problems throughout society.

By basing its administration on the most universal principles of natural law, the Natural Law Party's comprehensive, prevention-oriented solutions to America's problems are capable of providing universal nourishment, protection, and fulfillment to all citizens of the nation, including all the diverse groups that compose the richness and plurality of our great society.

We believe that increased participation in government by women and by minorities will bring greater strength and balance to the administration. In this context, we note that approximately a third of the candidates running for office with the Natural Law Party are women or minority candidates.

Abortion

The Natural Law Party is committed to substantially reducing the number of abortions in America. However, the Natural Law Party holds that the best way to reduce abortions is through education, not through legislation.

The Natural Law Party supports proven educational programs to bring individual and national life into harmony with natural law. These programs develop intelligence and creativity, improve moral reasoning, and promote farsighted thinking and actions that do not create problems. Such education alone can produce the changes in behavior that will reduce unwanted pregnancies. Only the Natural Law Party's strong educational approach, by changing attitudes and behaviors from the inside out, can offer prevention on a realistic basis.

Our nation's history shows that it is difficult to legislate morality. Laws forbidding the manufacture and sale of alcohol during Prohibition had little effect on alcohol consumption. Instead they led to the birth of the underground and the most murderous epoch in our nation's history. Similarly, legislation to outlaw abortions will simply lead to illegal abortions.

For this reason, the Natural Law Party believes that it is counterproductive for the federal government to outlaw abortion. Furthermore, the Natural Law Party holds that the moral responsibility for this decision should be left in the hands of those whose lives are affected most—the mother, the family, and the doctor—not the federal government.

At the same time, the Natural Law Party encourages a shift from public to private funding of abortion—specifically, private charity by those who wish to make abortion accessible for women who cannot afford it. Over time the government should eliminate the use of taxpayer dollars to fund abortion as a method of birth control, especially because such use of public funds is morally offensive to millions of taxpayers. The Natural Law Party would allow public funding of abortions in cases of rape, incest, or life-threatening medical necessity.

The Natural Law Party further believes that private charity to fund abortions could be better used to support proven, community-based programs such as CareNet, which reaches out to women with crisis pregnancies to offer them both material and emotional support, and the One Church, One Child adoption initiative founded by Father George Clements, which has enabled over fifty thousand children to find loving parents and a nurturing home environment.

The Natural Law Party's "antigovernment" stance regarding abortion—neither subsidizing abortions nor legislating them away—is the only defensible position from the standpoint of the U.S. Constitution, which states in the Tenth Amendment that "The powers not delegated to the United States by the Constitution, nor prohibited by it to the States, are reserved to the States respectively, or to the people."

The Natural Law Party's prevention-oriented approach to reducing the number of abortions will produce a much-needed unifying influence on our nation, which has been deeply torn by this highly divisive issue. Our policy serves the interests of both those who are prolife and those who are prochoice by (1) decreasing the number of abortions more effectively than legislation and (2) leaving moral responsibility in the hands of those whose lives are affected most. Only the Natural Law Party can solve the problem of abortion at its basis and thereby fulfill the goals of all Americans, those who emphasize the sanctity of life and those who uphold the sanctity of individual freedom.

Family Values

The Natural Law Party is deeply committed to strengthening the well-being of every American family by restoring the fundamental moral values that have sustained the minds and hearts of our citizens for generations. Such universal family values include honesty, integrity, responsibility, industriousness, self-discipline, compassion, generosity, and mutual respect. By bringing individual and family life into accord with natural law, we can largely erase the present epidemic of family breakdown and moral decay and create a society in which parents, children, families, and society mutually nourish and strengthen one another in their growth toward fulfillment.

THE PROBLEM

American families today are under unprecedented financial, social and environmental stress, making it difficult for parents to create loving, stable homes for their children.

- FINANCES. Real wages for average American workers have decreased since 1973. Because of the much higher cost of living in 1997, most two-parent families require two incomes to maintain a reasonable existence. In addition, the average American now works more hours than at any time since World War II—close to fifty hours weekly. Not surprisingly, this economic stress, coupled with the strain of long work hours, has resulted in increased tension within families, a rise in domestic violence, and an almost 50 percent divorce rate for new marriages. As a result, many children no longer receive the love, attention, and guidance from their parents that previous generations took for granted as essential for moral development.

Families with only one parent face even greater challenges. Over 25 percent of American children in single-parent families live in poverty, yet the rate of childbirth among unmarried women has been increasing, up to 32.4 percent in 1996. Despite the devotion and hard work of many single parents, some studies indicate that children in single-parent families are at greater risk for crime, for drug and alcohol abuse, and for dropping out of school.

- SOCIAL ENVIRONMENT. Parents today have little control over the negative influences assaulting their children: school shootings, drug and alcohol abuse, gangs, premature sexual activity, and the risk of AIDS and other sexually transmitted diseases. In addition, children now watch an excessive amount of television, time that used to be spent with parents, teachers, or other role models. Our educational system fails to instill core values in students, such as honesty, mutual respect, civility, and social responsibility.

- PHYSICAL ENVIRONMENT. Parents can no longer guarantee the quality of even the most basic necessities for their families: food, air, and water. The dramatic increase in poisons and toxicity in our environment—pesticides on crops, air and water pollution, and the potential harm from genetically engineered foods—all constitute a serious threat to the health of family members (see the Agriculture section).

These financial, social, and environmental challenges that parents face today have given rise to an increase of stress in family life. These rising levels of stress throughout society undermine the harmony and integrity of family life, so important to the growing stability and vitality of our nation. Other political parties decry domestic violence, child abuse, divorce, and the breakdown of morality, but they have been unable to offer effective solutions to these problems.

THE SOLUTION

The Natural Law Party offers proven programs that address the root cause of the breakdown of family life today: epidemic stress levels throughout society, especially in our densely populated urban centers. Medical researchers report an alarming rise in stress-related illness, including stroke, hypertension, and heart disease. This same epidemic of stress is responsible for the widespread growth of "social disease": domestic violence, child abuse, family decay, crime, and drug abuse. The most effective solution is therefore to reduce accumulated stress in the whole population, so that all individuals, and especially parents, are able to make the most life-supporting decisions in their personal lives and decisions that are most nourishing to the lives of their children.

The Natural Law Party would therefore support the permanent establishment of coherence-creating groups on the national, state, and local levels to dissolve communitywide tension and negativity. These programs of the Natural Law Party have been scientifically demonstrated to reduce crime, violence, and negative trends throughout society and to create a harmonizing influence in collective consciousness, enabling diverse individual interests and tendencies to coexist without creating conflict between family members and in society as a whole.

In addition, the Natural Law Party's cost-effective solutions to the nation's problems and progrowth economic policies will create jobs, stimulate growth, and ease the financial strain experienced by so many American families (see the Economy section). The Natural Law Party believes that primary-care parents should not be forced by economic necessity to work since their role as parents is vital for the strength and stability of future generations.

The Natural Law Party also strongly supports the role of the senior, most experienced members of our society as the source of wisdom and guidance for all other members of the family and the community and regards the widespread isolation and loneliness of our senior members as a significant loss to America. The Natural Law Party supports mentor and housing programs that can reverse this trend and maintains a deep commitment to protecting the lives and rights of our country's senior members.

Most important, the strong educational programs endorsed by the Natural Law Party will significantly support and strengthen family unity and the natural unfoldment of each member's full potential. These programs have been scientifically shown to develop intelligence, emotional maturity, moral reasoning, and harmonious relationships and to reduce anxiety, substance abuse, and antisocial behavior (see our Education section). Such outcomes will help different generations of a family to live together, to nourish each other, and to establish the harmony, respect, and mutual enrichment that are the ideal of family life.

The family is the source of life for every individual and as such is the primary training ground for social behavior. The quality of the home determines the quality of civilization.

By strengthening and reenlivening the family from the inside, and by eliminating the stress attacking the family from the outside, the Natural Law Party gives parents the opportunity to reawaken universal family values in their children and thus secure a bright future for our nation.

Foreign Policy

The end of the Cold War era has brought the international community to the threshold of a new era of global peace and harmony. The Natural Law Party believes that the United States should lead the world forward in creating new relationships governed by mutual friendship and cooperation and freed from aggression and armed conflict. America is faced with a historic opportunity to help create a new world order, in which peace is perpetual and every nation upholds the flag of every other nation.

THE PROBLEM

From 1946 to 1993 the United States spent $439.6 billion on foreign aid, 35 percent of which was military aid. These expenditures have not brought peace, economic stability, or greater economic cooperation to the family of nations. We continue to live in a dangerous world troubled by widespread violence and regional conflicts, as evidenced by Desert Storm, the ethnic violence in Bosnia, and continuing terrorism in the Middle East. Moreover, as a major supplier of the world's armaments the United States has directly contributed to such conflicts.

In addition, no real consensus exists concerning the purpose, allotment, and amount of foreign economic aid now that the historical goal of containing communism is no longer an issue. There is an urgent need to address America's deteriorating relations with China, the strained relationship and multibillion-dollar trade deficit with Japan, and economic competition with Western Europe. These relationships are especially troubling in view of the continuing U.S. financial commitment to defending Japan, as well as Germany and Western Europe.

Americans naturally wish to help the emerging democracies of the former Soviet Union and Eastern Europe, yet protest substantial funds given directly to Russia and other republics because of so many pressing priorities at home. U.S. aid to developing countries has also been criticized because of countless instances in which funds either were wasted on projects that did not help the people or failed to reach the people because of misuse by the recipient governments.

THE SOLUTION

The Natural Law Party would create an immediate shift in U.S. foreign policy away from military aid toward a more life-supporting policy based on the exportation of U.S. know-how. American expertise and technical assistance in such critical areas as business administration, entrepreneurship, education, sustainable agriculture, and environmental technologies, supplemented where necessary with economic support, should replace military aid as a principal instrument of U.S. foreign policy.

This new type of life-nourishing assistance will allow many developing countries to become financially self-sufficient and thereby to eliminate hunger and poverty. Such a policy would contribute to a more affluent and flourishing global trade and a more prosperous family of nations.

Since the end of the Cold War, America's security interests have begun to shift from military concerns to global economic and environmental issues. America is called to leadership in developing a foreign policy that most intelligently meets this challenge.

This foreign policy must respect and honor the diversity of cultures, religions, races, and economic and political systems of the world, while promoting the value of unity, so that every nation will respect and uphold the sovereignty and cultural integrity of every other nation in an unprecedented flow of economic cooperation and goodwill.

Above all, we must ensure that our precious national resources are applied effectively and not wasted through inefficiency, mishandling, or inappropriate allocation. Foreign aid decisions must be made in consultation with the people of recipient countries, from both the government and nongovernmental citizens' groups.

Fundamental to the success of all these initiatives is the continued lessening of Cold War–era tensions throughout the world. To alleviate remaining global and regional tensions quickly, the Natural Law Party would support the establishment of groups practicing the Transcendental Meditation and TM-Sidhi program in key areas of the world. These programs have been uniquely effective in dissolving social stress and preventing the outbreak of armed hostility and war.[1] By generating coherence in collective consciousness, they create an atmosphere in which diplomacy and other peaceful methods of conflict resolution can succeed. Such groups, established either within the United States or dispatched as a U.S. or UN peacekeeping force to specific trouble spots, could help prevent the senseless destruction and human suffering resulting from regional conflicts.

In a peaceful and harmonious world family, we can conceive of reducing our own military expenditures and realizing a significant "peace dividend," directing some of our enormous defense expenditures toward our own social programs, including investment and development as an economic superpower.

Defense

With the end of the Cold War era the United States has an unprecedented opportunity to lead the world in creating a stable and permanent peace, free from fear of aggression and war, in which every nation enjoys invincibility and friendship with every other nation.

THE PROBLEM

Despite the declining threat of superpower confrontation, uncertainty and fear still dominate U.S. defense thinking. History has shown that neither treaties nor arms can ensure peace and security. Regional and ethnic conflicts in the Middle East and Eastern Europe have demonstrated that even small nations can imperil world peace and stability. They can hold other nations hostage through terrorism, ecological warfare, and weapons of mass destruction.

No viable defense against nuclear weapons exists. Nuclear tests in China and the resumption of nuclear testing by France have stirred fears in the international community of runaway nuclear proliferation. At least forty-six nuclear weapons are thought to be missing from the former Soviet arsenal.[1] Arms experts fear that rogue nations and terrorist groups might opt for "backpack" nuclear weapons carried by foot soldiers. Even after substantial reductions in our own arsenals, thousands of nuclear weapons remain. The military faces huge environmental cleanup costs for its unused arsenals and bases.

Similarly, biological and chemical weapons pose a mounting threat to national security. Their relatively low-cost, easily accessible technology, and low-tech applications make them especially dangerous as weapons of mass destruction in the hands of terrorist groups or even individuals.

The United States remains one of the world's biggest arms suppliers. This global arms peddling has tarnished our reputation as a promoter of peace, fostered deep-seated international ill will, and led to a dangerous world in which our own soldiers are forced to confront American weapons on the battlefield. On the domestic front, Congress continues to fund expensive pork barrel defense contracts that the Pentagon does not even want.[2]

Finally, military personnel continue to face major health concerns, including problems with stress,[3] alcohol, and a higher rate of cigarette smoking than the civilian population.[4] Posttraumatic stress syndrome, a continuing problem for veterans, is virtually ignored because of the lack of solutions, and Gulf War syndrome has underscored the insidious influence of environmental toxins on our primary-level military personnel.[5]

THE SOLUTION

The changing global political landscape mandates a broad reassessment of the purpose, scope, strategy, and financial requirements of U.S. defense. The Natural Law Party believes that these crucial issues must be decided on the basis of a revised set of priorities reflecting America's realistic defense requirements, not on the basis of short-term political considerations and pork barrel politics.

The Natural Law Party recognizes the need to maintain the alertness of our nation's armed forces. Between 1993 and 1996, the U.S. military defense budget has been cut by 9 percent. Since the world remains dangerous and unstable, the Natural Law Party believes that the United States should not implement further major reductions of defense expenditures at this time. However, we believe that a smaller, more flexible force coupled with greater economic and security cooperation will serve the nation's security interests and provide the basis for a more stable world. We therefore emphasize human rather than material resources.

For example, the Natural Law Party believes that funding for costly, wasteful, and ineffective weapons systems could be rapidly scaled down. As part of this downscaling, we would (1) accelerate the decrease of U.S. nuclear arsenals, which cost twenty-five billion dollars annually to maintain, (2) immediately and permanently halt all U.S. nuclear testing and nuclear weapons research, and (3) reduce the U.S. presence in NATO and the Pacific Rim, encouraging Western Europe and Japan to contribute more toward the defense of those regions. The role of America should be to foster peace and prosperity in the family of nations, rather than to act as the world's policeman.

To strengthen our security further, the Natural Law Party offers a peace-promoting technology that will help neutralize international tensions and conflict and promote stability and harmony within the family of nations. Through this peace-promoting technology, which is based upon groups of experts collectively practicing the Transcendental Meditation and TM-Sidhi program, the Natural Law Party can help to ensure a peaceful world. Only through the addition of this technology to reduce global stress and to generate an actual, physical influence of peace among the family of nations can a political party responsibly cut defense spending and divert the precious resources of the nation toward more life-supporting and humane programs at home and abroad.[6]

Therefore, the Natural Law Party supports the immediate creation of a "prevention wing" within the military, a group whose primary purpose would be to prevent the outbreak of war and to preserve and strengthen national and international peace. By training even 1 percent of U.S. military personnel in the proven programs advocated by the Natural Law Party to reduce stress in individual and national life, America can create a genuine peacekeeping force that can maintain a powerful, integrated, coherent national consciousness and thereby prevent the emergence of an enemy.

The Natural Law Party also supports new priorities for the U.S. Department of Defense. Selected military personnel and resources could quickly adapt to roles such as drug interdiction and border defense. We believe that economic growth, leading to new industries and jobs, is the best way to help the defense industry adjust to military downsizing. There is strong statistical evidence that more jobs are created through domestic programs than through military spending. In addition, we favor incentives to stimulate investment of private sector funds and expertise to help industries diversify into nondefense markets.

Finally, the Natural Law Party supports prevention and rehabilitation programs that have been shown to reduce military stress, decrease alcohol and drug abuse, alleviate posttraumatic stress syndrome, promote better health, and enhance physical and mental performance.[7]

Gun Control

The Natural Law Party holds that the current debate over gun control overlooks the root cause of this issue. The climate of fear and tension pervading America's cities and towns is largely responsible for the proliferation of guns and their use in acts of violent crime. The Natural Law Party is the only political party to offer scientifically proven programs to reduce built-up social stress and thereby reduce crime and violence (see our Crime and Rehabilitation section).

Within six months of the implementation of these programs, the Natural Law Party anticipates a dramatic reduction in crime rate as stress is neutralized and the whole population spontaneously becomes more in harmony with both natural law and national law. In this improved atmosphere, the perceived need for, and the actual use of, weapons will naturally diminish.

At the same time, the Natural Law Party believes that the widespread availability of guns is in itself a significant contributing factor to the rise of violent crime. The Natural Law Party therefore upholds existing gun control legislation and believes that such legislation represents a suitable balance between public safety and the constitutional right to bear arms.

Capital Punishment

Given current levels of crime in America, capital punishment has gained broad popular support as a hoped-for deterrent to the most severe crimes. Unfortunately, experience shows that capital punishment neither effectively deters crime nor saves taxpayer money. Although the Natural Law Party supports a strong penal code, especially for specific, highly egregious violent crimes, the current effort to extend the death penalty to include a wide range of crimes is a desperate public (and highly political) reaction arising from deep frustration with present, ineffective crime-fighting strategies.

The Natural Law Party supports highly effective, proven crime prevention programs that have been shown to lower crime significantly (see our Crime and Rehabilitation section). We believe that the national mood will shift away from an outcry for the harshest possible punishment and toward more compassionate solutions once violent crime has been significantly reduced through the Natural Law Party's prevention-oriented approach.

Notes

CHAPTER 2: RUMINATIONS OF A THIRD-PARTY OPERATIVE

1. On May 18, 1998, the U.S. Supreme Court, by a vote of 6–3, turned down the petition from Ralph Forbes. Leaders of third parties and legal experts expressed shock and disappointment at the decision, and vowed to continue the fight for equal access to debates for all qualified candidates.
2. Ben Bagdikian, *The Media Monopoly* (Boston: Beacon Press, 1997).
3. Robert Roth, *Transcendental Meditation* (New York: Donald I. Fine, 1994).
4. The Natural Law Party was founded in 1992 by a dozen TM meditators—medical doctors, business executives, and lawyers. They started the party out of frustration with government leaders who, either because of a lack of information or for reasons of political expediency, were ignoring the effectiveness of the TM technique in health care, rehabilitation, and education. They were also frustrated that government was ignoring the effectiveness of many other crucial programs that could be of enormous benefit to society, such as natural medicine, renewable energy technologies, organic agriculture, etc. Thus the Natural Law Party was founded with a broad-based platform that has since attracted widespread support—whether or not voters are personally interested in meditation—and the party has now become the fastest-growing political party in America. In fact, John Hagelin estimates that just a small fraction—much less than 1 percent—of party voters practice the TM technique. The founding of the party by TM meditators

naturally led members of the press to ask for more knowledge about Maharishi Mahesh Yogi, the founder of the TM technique. For more than forty years Maharishi has worked to develop programs that harness nature's intelligence to solve critical problems in health care, crime, education, etc. and thereby raise the quality of life in society. The Natural Law Party supports these programs because they have been shown by independent scientific research to work, just as it supports all the other programs in its platform that have been similarly proven to work. Maharishi himself has no role in the running or building of the Natural Law Party, and the party has never received any financial contributions from the nonprofit TM organization.

CHAPTER 5: "THE BEST-KEPT SECRET IN AMERICA"

1. Michio Kaku and Jennifer Thompson, *Beyond Einstein: The Cosmic Quest for the Theory of the Universe* (New York: Anchor, 1995), and F. David Peat, *Superstrings and the Search for the Theory of Everything* (Chicago: Contemporary Books, 1988).

CHAPTER 7: GENETICALLY ENGINEERED FOODS: THE HAZARDS OF TINKERING WITH NATURAL LAW

1. Ruth Hubbard and Elijah Wald, *Exploding the Gene Myth* (Boston: Beacon Press, 1997).
   Dr. Mae-Wan Ho, *Genetic Engineering: Dream or Nightmare?* Bath, UK: Gateway Books, 1998.
2. Marion Nestle, "Allergies to Transgenic Foods—Questions of Policy" *New England Journal of Medicine* 334 (1996): 726–728.
3. A. N. Mayeno, G. J. Gleich, "Eosinophilia-Myalgia Syndrome and Tryptophan Production: A Cautionary Tale" *Trends in Biotechnology* 12 (1994): 346–352.
   P. Raphals, "Does Medical Mystery Threaten Biotech?" *Science* 249 (1990): 619.
   D. E. Brenneman, S. W. Page, et al., "A Decomposition Product of a Contaminant Implicated in L-Tryptophan Eosinophilia-Myalgia Syndrome Affects Spinal Cord Neuronal Death and Survival through Stereospecific, Maturation and Partly Interleukin-1-dependent Mechanisms," *Journal of Pharmacology and Experimental Therapeutics* 266 (1993): 1029–1035.
   P. Raphals, "EMS Deaths: Is Recombinant DNA Technology Involved?" *Medical Post* November 6 (1990): 16.

CHAPTER 8: PUTTING HEALTH BACK INTO OUR DISEASE CARE SYSTEM

1. G. F. Anderson, "In Search of Value: An International Comparison of Cost, Access, and Outcomes" *Health Affairs* 16 (1997): 163–171.

2. G. J. Schieber, J.-P. Poullier, L. M. Greenwald, "Health System Performance in OECD Countries" *Health Affairs* 13 (1994): 100–112.

3. J. M. Fries, C. E. Koop, et al., "Beyond Health Promotion: Reducing Need and Demand for Medical Care" *Health Affairs* 17 (1998): 70–84.

4. D. M. Eisenberg, R. C. Kessler, et al., "Unconventional Medicine in the United States: Prevalence, Costs, and Patterns" *New England Journal of Medicine* 328 (1993): 246–252.

5. For example, there are numerous scientific studies that document increased deaths and costs in the U.S. from medical errors:

   D. P. Phillips, N. Christenfeld, L. M. Glynn, "Increase in US Medication-error Deaths between 1983 and 1993" *Lancet* 351 (1998): 643–644.

   D. C. Classen, S. L. Pestonik, et al., "Adverse Drug Events in Hospitalized Patients" *Journal of the American Medical Association* 277 (1997): 301–306.

   D. W. Bates, N. Spell, et al., "The Costs of Adverse Drug Events in Hospitalized Patients" *Journal of the American Medical Association* 277 (1997): 307–311.

   T. S. Lesar, L. Briceland, D. S. Stein, "Factors Related to Errors in Medication Prescribing" *Journal of the American Medical Association* 277 (1997): 312–317.

6. C. Hoffman, D. Rice, H.-Y. Sung, "Persons with Chronic Conditions: Their Prevalence and Costs" *Journal of the American Medical Association* 276 (1996): 1473–1479.

7. Ibid.

8. L. L. Leape, "Error in Medicine" *Journal of the American Medical Association* 272 (1994): 1851–1857.

   D. W. Bates, D. J. Cullen et al., "Incidence of Adverse Drug Events and Potential Adverse Drug Events" *Journal of the American Medical Association* 274 (1995): 29–34.

9. Ibid.

   L. L. Leape, A. G. Lawthers, et al., "Preventing Medical Injury" *Quality Review Bulletin* May (1993): 144–149.

10. A recent study found that drug reactions from medications that were *properly* prescribed by doctors rank between the fourth to sixth largest cause of death in the United States, accounting for more than 100,000 unnecessary fatalities a year. This number does not even take into account deaths from errors in drug prescribing or fatalities associated with invasive procedures and surgery (J. Lazarou, B. H. Pomeranz, P. N. Corey, "Incidence of Adverse Drug Reactions in Hospitalized Patients: A Meta-analysis of Prospective Studies" *Journal of the American Medical Association* 279 [1998]: 1200–1205).

11. L. L. Leape. "Error in Medicine" *Journal of the American Medical Association* 272 (1994): 1851–1857.

A REASON TO VOTE

D. P. Phillips, N. Christenfeld, L. M. Glynn, "Increase in US Medication-Error Deaths Between 1983 and 1993" *Lancet* 351 (1998): 643–644.

J. Lazarou, B. H. Pomeranz, P. N. Corey, "Incidence of Adverse Drug Reactions in Hospitalized Patients: A Meta-analysis of Prospective Studies" *Journal of the American Medical Association* 279 (1998): 1200–1205.

M. García-Martín, P. Lardelli-Claret, et al., "Proportion of Hospital Deaths Associated with Adverse Events" *Journal of Clinical Epidemiology* 50 (1997): 1319–1326.

12. R. J. Williams and D. L. Heymann, "Containment of Antibiotic Resistance" *Science* 279 (1998): 1153–1154.

13. S. B. Levy, "The Challenge of Antibiotic Resistance" *Scientific American* March (1998): 46–53.

14. R. W. Pinner, S. M. Teutsch, et al., "Trends in Infectious Disease Mortality in the United States" *Journal of the American Medical Association* 275 (1996): 189–193.

15. F. C. Tenover and J. M. Hughes, "The Challenges of Emerging Infectious Diseases: Development and Spread of Multiply-Resistant Bacterial Pathogens" *Journal of the American Medical Association* 275 (1996): 300–304.

16. L. L. Leape, A. G. Lawthers, et al., "Preventing Medical Injury" *Quality Review Bulletin* May (1993): 144–149.

J. Lazarou, B. H. Pomeranz, P. N. Corey, "Incidence of Adverse Drug Reactions in Hospitalized Patients: A Meta-analysis of Prospective Studies" *Journal of the American Medical Association* 279 (1998): 1200–1205.

M. García-Martín, P. Lardelli-Claret, et al., "Proportion of Hospital Deaths Associated with Adverse Events" *Journal of Clinical Epidemiology* 50 (1997): 1319–1326.

D. C. Classen, S. L. Pestonik, et al., "Adverse Drug Events in Hospitalized Patients" *Journal of the American Medical Association* 277 (1997): 301–306.

D. W. Bates, D. J. Cullen et al., "Incidence of Adverse Drug Events and Potential Adverse Drug Events" *Journal of the American Medical Association* 274 (1995): 29–34.

17. Harvard Reports on Cancer Prevention, Cancer Causes and Control 7 (1996): S3–S59.

18. J. C. Bailar III and H. L. Gornik, "Cancer Undefeated" *New England Journal of Medicine* 336 (1997): 1569–1574.

T. Beardsley, "A War Not Won" *Scientific American* January (1994): 130–138.

S. S. Epstein, "Losing the War Against Cancer: Who's to Blame and What to Do About It" *International Journal of Health Services* 20 (1990): 53–71.

19. J. McGinnis and W. Foege, "Actual Causes of Death in the United States" *Journal of the American Medical Association* 270 (1993): 2207–2212.

U.S. Department of Health and Human Services. *Healthy People 2000: National Health Promotion and Disease Prevention Objectives* (Washington, DC: Government Printing Office, 1991).

20. The approach is based on Vedic medicine, the world's oldest and most complete system of natural health care, reformulated in a scientific, systematic framework by Maharishi Mahesh Yogi, along with leading medical doctors and Vedic physicians, and now known as Maharishi Vedic Approach to Health (Tony Nader, *Human Physiology: Expression of Veda and the Vedic Literature* [Vlodrop, Holland: Maharishi Vedic University, 1995]).

    H. Sharma and C. Clark, *Contemporary Ayurveda* (New York: Churchill Livingstone, 1998).

21. H. Sharma, *Freedom from Disease* (Twin Lakes, Wis.: Lotus Press, 1997);

    H. Sharma, *Awakening Nature's Healing Intelligence* (Twin Lakes, Wis.: Lotus Press, 1997).

22. D. Menzies and J. Bourbeau, "Building-Related Illness" *New England Journal of Medicine* 337 (1997): 1524–1531.

23. P. B. Fontanarosa and G. D. Lundberg, "Complementary, Alternative, Unconventional and Integrative Medicine: Call for Papers for the Annual Coordinated Theme Issues of the AMA" *Journal of the American Medical Association* 278 (1997): 2111–2112.

CHAPTER 9: BEYOND SUSTAINABLE AGRICULTURE: GOING ORGANIC

1. D. Pimental, L. McLaughlin, and A. Zepp, "Environmental and Economic Effects of Reducing Pesticide Use," *Bioscience* 41:6 (1991): 402–9.

2. D. Pimental, L. McLaughlin, and A. Zepp, "Environmental and Economic Costs of Pesticide Use," *Bioscience* 42:10 (1992): 750–60.

3. A. Blair and S. H. Zahm, "Agricultural Exposures and Cancer." *Environmental Health Perspectives* 103: Suppl 8 (1995): 205–208.

   K. Cahow, "The Cancer Conundrum." *Environmental Health Perspectives* 103 (1995): 750–760.

   T. J. Woodruff, A. D. Kyle, F. V. Bois, "Evaluating Health Risk from Occupational Exposure to Pesticides and the Regulatory Response." *Environmental Health Perspectives* 102 (1994): 1088–1096.

4. T. Colborn, D. Dumanoski, and J. P. Myers, *Our Stolen Future: Are We Threatening Our Fertility, Intelligence, and Survival?* (New York: Dutton, 1996).

   Sandra Steingraber, *Living Downstream: An Ecologist Looks at Cancer and the Environment.* (Reading, Mass.: Addison-Wesley, 1997).

   E. Carlsen, A. Giwercman, et al, "Evidence for Decreasing Quality of Semen During Past 50 Years" *British Medical Journal* 305 (1992): 609–613.

   M. Holloway, "Dioxin Indictment" *Scientific American* 270 (1994): 25.

5. D. L. Davis and H. L. Bradlow, "Can Environmental Toxins Cause Breast Cancer?" *Scientific American* October (1995): 166–172.

   D. L. Davis, D. Axelrod, et al, "Environmental Influences on Breast Cancer Risk" *Science and Medicine* May/June (1997): 56–59.

D. L. Davis, N. T. Teland, et al, "Medical Hypothesis: Bifuctional Genetic-Hormonal Pathways to Breast Cancer" *Environmental Health Perspectives* 105: Suppl 3 (1997): 571–576.

6. Colburn et al., op. cit.
7. The federal government does not screen farm chemicals for safety before they are marketed. The chemical manufacturers are given the responsibility for determining if their own products pose health or environmental risks. D. Fagin and M. Lavelle *Toxic Deception: How the Chemical Industry Manipulates Science, Bends the Law, and Endangers Your Health* (Secaucus, N.J.: Birch Lane Press, 1996).

CHAPTER 10: AMERICA'S ENERGY FUTURE—A SOLID BASIS FOR OPTIMISM

1. Michael C. Brower, Michael W. Tennis, Eric W. Denzler, and Mark M. Kaplan, *Powering the Midwest* (Union of Concerned Scientists, Cambridge, Mass. 1993): 2–3.
2. Devra Lee Davis and the Working Group on Public Health and Fossil-Fuel Combustion, "Short-term Improvements in Public Health from Global-Climate Policies on Fossil-Fuel Combustion: An Interim Report" *Lancet* 350 (1997): 1341–1349.
   J. J. Romm and C. A. Ervin, "How Energy Policy Affects Public Health" *Public Health Reports* 111 (1996): 390–399.
3. *Climate Change, 1995, Contribution of Working Group I to the Second Assessment Report of the Intergovernmental Panel on Climate Change* (Cambridge, U.K.; Cambridge University Press, 1995).
4. R. Monatersky, "Planet Posts Temperature Record for 1997" *Science News* 153 (January 17, 1998): 38.
5. Robert Watson, Marufu Zinyonwera, Richard Moss, and David Dokken, *Climate Change 1995: Impacts, Adaptations and Mitigation of Climate Change: Scientific-Technical Analysis Contribution of Working Group II to the Second Assessment Report of the Intergovernmental Panel on Climate Change* (Cambridge, U.K.; Cambridge University Press, 1996) 1–19.
6. Christopher Flavin and Seth Dunn, *Rising Sun, Gathering Winds: Policies to Stabilize the Climate and Strengthen Economies* (World Watch Paper 138; November 1997).
7. Tom Factor, "A GIS Wind Resource Map with Tabular Printout of Monthly and Annual Wind Speeds for 2,000 Towns in Iowa" Proceedings of the American Wind Energy Association (Washington D.C., 1997): 561–570.
8. Michael C. Brower, Michael W. Tennis, Eric W. Denzler, and Mark M. Kaplan,

Powering the Midwest (Union of Concerned Scientists, Cambridge, Mass. 1993): A 19.

9. Christopher Flavin and Seth Dunn, *Rising Sun, Gathering Winds: Policies to Stabilize the Climate and Strengthen Economies* (World Watch Paper 138; November 1997).

10. Seth Dunn, "CO_2 Cuts Not Difficult" *Wind Energy Weekly* 16 (December 22, 1997): 5.

11. Thomas R. Karl, Neville Nicholls, and Jonathan Gregory, "The Coming Climate: Meteorological Records and Computer Models Permit Insights into Some of the Broad Weather Patterns of a Warmer World" *Scientific American* (May 1997).

CHAPTER 11: THE ROOTS OF NATURAL LAW IN AMERICAN HISTORY

1. Basil Willey, *The Eighteenth Century Background: Studies on the Idea of Nature in the Thought of the Period* (New York: Columbia University Press, 1969) gives a rich feeling for the intellectual character of the century and the key role played by natural law ideas in its thought.

2. Quoted in Catherine Drinker Bowen, *Miracle at Philadelphia: The Story of the Constitutional Convention, May to September 1787* (Boston: Little, Brown, 1966).

3. In *The Works of John Adams*, ed. Charles Francis Adams (Norwalk, Conn.: Easton Press, 1992).

4. Quoted in *The Records of the Federal Convention of 1787*, ed. Max Ferrand (New Haven: Yale University Press, 1966).

5. Of the pre-Socratic philosophers, Heraclitus of Ephesus is known for his exposition of the *logos*. See *Heraclitus: The Cosmic Fragments*, ed. G. S. Kirk (Cambridge, U.K.: Cambridge University Press, 1954). The literal meaning of *logos* is something akin to *word*. Western readers are familiar with this translation of *logos* from its use in the first verse of the Gospel according to Saint John. A parallel description from the system of knowledge of ancient India is found in Veda, which denotes the eternal, primordial sounds of nature—natural law—at the unmanifest basis of creation.

6. A review demonstrating the central importance of natural law philosophy in Western thought, from Plato and Aristotle to the European philosophers of the eighteenth century, is provided in John Wild, *Plato's Modern Enemies and the Theory of Natural Law* (Chicago: University of Chicago Press, 1953).

7. In *De republica*, the statesman, orator, and essayist Marcus Tullius Cicero sums up what natural law was for the Romans: "True law is right reason conformable to nature, universal, unchangeable, eternal, whose commands urge us to duty, and whose prohibitions restrain us from evil. This law cannot be contradicted by

any other law, and is not liable either to derogation or abrogation. Neither the senate nor the people can give us any dispensation for not obeying this universal law of justice. It needs no other expositor and interpreter than our own conscience. It is not one thing at Rome and another at Athens; one thing today and another tomorrow; but in all times and nations this universal law must forever reign, eternal and imperishable. It is the sovereign master and emperor of all beings. God himself is its author, its promulgator, its enforcer." The Roman emperor Marcus Aurelius, reigning at the peak of the *pax romana* in the second century A.D., was also, for the following centuries, one of the best-known exponents of natural law. See Marcus Tullius Cicero, *De republica, de legibus* (Cambridge: Harvard University Press, 1928) and *The Meditations of the Emperor Marcus Aurelius*, ed. A. S. L. Farquharson (Oxford: Clarendon Press, 1944).

8. Ernest Barker gives a brief overview of the concept of "a Law of Nature" at the basis of the Western tradition of law in his introduction to Otto Gierke's definitive *Natural Law and the Theory of Society, 1500 to 1800* (Cambridge, U.K.: Cambridge University Press, 1934).

9. In the writings of several of the Fathers of the early Christian Church, notably St. Augustine of Hippo, scholars have noted an implied distinction between the eternal natural law of God and a more relative natural law of man. Writing nearly a millennium later, St. Thomas Aquinas, in Questions 90–97 of his *Summa theologica*, distinguished four kinds of law: the *lex eterna*, the eternal law, "the rational governance of everything on the part of God as ruler of the universe"; the *lex naturalis*, the natural law, "the participation in the eternal law by rational creatures"; the *lex divina*, the divine law, God's commandments to man; and the *lex humana*, the human law, the positive or man-made laws of societies. Aquinas maintained that if the human law disagrees with the natural law, "it is no longer a law, but a corruption of law." See *Thomas Aquinas, Treatise on Law*, ed. Stanley Parry (South Bend, Ind.: Regnery/Gateway, 1979).

10. One primary work carried the influence of Roman law throughout the Christianity-dominated Middle Ages, the *Corpus Juris Civilus* of the Emperor Justinian. Completed in 534 A.D. by a group of Byzantine lawyers, it comprised three works: the *Institutes*, the *Digest*, and the *Codex*. The jurist Gratian, in his famous *Decretum Gratiani*, which was the major source book for Christian Church law in the 12th and 13th centuries, borrowed from the introductory passages of the *Digest* in stating, "Natural law is the law common to all nations." Gratian began the *Decretum* with these words: "Mankind is ruled by two laws: Natural Law and Custom. Natural Law is that which is contained in the Scriptures and the Gospel."

11. The modern period of natural law thinking began in the late 16th and early 17th centuries with the so-called Late Scholastics, particularly the Spanish Jesuit scholar Francisco Suárez. The theory of the modern state took further shape with the political philosophers Jean Bodin in France and Thomas Hobbes in England; with the Dutch jurist Hugo Grotius, considered a principal founder of international law theory; and with the German professors Johannes Althusius, who elaborated the

compact theory of the state, and Samuel Pufendorf, who developed the theory of federalism. American clergymen throughout the seventeenth and eighteenth centuries, notably Thomas Hooker in Connecticut, Roger Williams in Rhode Island, and John Wise in Massachusetts, adapted the work of the European thinkers to the American case. English political activists John Milton and Algernon Sidney had a significant influence on the American colonists, as did the English Utopian thinker James Harrington and the English philosopher John Locke. In the eighteenth century, writings by the French jurist the Baron de Montesquieu and the Swiss jurists Emmerich de Vattel and Jean Jacques Burlamaqui and the American pamphleteer Thomas Paine all helped rationalize the American revolution and the new American state. For a history of the American republic from the perspective of constitutional law, see Alfred H. Kelly and Winfred A. Harbison, *The American Constitution: Its Origin and Development* (New York: W. W. Norton, 1948).

12. James Madison succinctly argued for the efficacy of these new features of democratic government in perhaps the most famous of the *Federalist Papers*, number 10. See the original McLean edition of these classic essays by Madison, Alexander Hamilton, and John Jay, reprinted in *The Federalist*, ed. Henry Cabot Lodge (New York: G. P. Putnam's Sons, 1904).

CHAPTER 12: SCIENCE, CONSCIOUSNESS, AND PUBLIC POLICY

1. Maharishi University of Management, formerly known as Maharishi International University, was founded in 1971 "to make education complete—to combine academic excellence with systematic programs to develop consciousness and creativity," according to the university's president, Dr. Bevan Morris. The North Central Association of Colleges and Schools, the oldest and largest accrediting body in the United States, awarded the university's bachelor's and master's accreditation in 1980 and doctoral accreditation in 1982. Today the university offers twenty-nine degree programs, including doctoral programs in physics, neuroscience, physiology, and management, and master's programs in mathematics, business administration, computer science, education, and English.

2. Among John Hagelin's more than sixty scientific publications, the following are considered especially important because they set new directions of research in the fields of elementary particle theory and cosmology.

- "Weak Symmetry Breaking by Radiative Corrections in Broken Supergravity," *Physics Letters* 125B (1993): 225, with J. Ellis, D. V. Nanopoulos, and K. Tamvakis

    Written up in *Current Contents* as a "core paper" and as "one of the most cited references in the physical sciences" for 1983, this paper solves the problem of the origin of mass and dimension in the universe. Specifically, it shows how quantum effects (in the form of strong radiative corrections) trigger weak symmetry breaking and generate particle masses from a theory that is otherwise fundamentally massless and dimensionless, and to generate these masses at a realistic scale that is exponentially smaller than the Planck scale.

- "Supersymmetric Relics from the Big Bang," *Nuclear Physics* B238 (1984): 453, with J. Ellis, D. V. Nanopoulos, K. Olive, and M. Srednicki

  Written up in *Current Contents* as a "core paper" and as "one of the most cited references in the physical sciences" for 1984, this paper establishes that supersymmetric particles are natural candidates for the missing dark matter that, according to many theorists, forms the dominant matter content of the universe. This work extends previous theoretical work by Steven Weinberg (which pertained to Dirac particles) to majorana fermions characteristic of today's supersymmetric theories. It sets forth the essential phenomenological features of a viable dark matter candidate and identifies the lightest supersymmetric particle (e.g., the photino), which is typically stable, invisible, and of naturally suitable cosmological abundance, as a likely dark matter candidate. Since publication, supersymmetric dark matter has achieved mainstream attention both within the professional particle physics/astrophysics community and in the popular press.

- "Flipped SU(5)×U(1) Revitalized," *Physics Letters* 194B (1987): 231, with I. Antoniadis, J. Ellis, and D. V. Nanopoulos

  This paper established a new grand unified theory of the fundamental forces of nature. The paper shows a previously all but overlooked symmetry group, SU(5)×U(1), is by far the most viable unifying symmetry principle needed to link the fundamental forces. The resulting theory, known as Flipped SU(5), solved severe technical problems of previous grand unified theories (GUTs), including the so-called gauge hierarchy problem, and sparked a renaissance of GUT model building and new experimental searches, some of which are still under way.

- "The Effects of Dark Matter on Standard Big Bang Nucleosynthesis," *Nuclear Physics* B329 (1984): 464, with R. Parker

  This paper introduced the concept of eternal annihilations, that dark matter inevitably modifies the cosmological abundances of the primordial elements (hydrogen, helium, lithium, etc.) through its continual annihilations—annihilations that persist throughout the nucleosynthesis era, long after such annihilations had previously been neglected. This realization places stringent constraints on the nature and abundance of dark matter candidates, such as neutrinos, photinos, etc.

- "COBE and Susy" (published under the title "Supersymmetry Mechanism for Naturally Small Density Perturbations"), *Physical Review Letters* 71 (1993): 4291, with A. Deans and L. Connors

    This paper explains the small primordial density fluctuations of matter in the universe long anticipated by cosmologists and ultimately observed by the COBE (Cosmic Background Explorer) satellite. Specifically, it shows that all realistic supersymmetric theories (i.e., those containing an electron) naturally generate small density fluctuations of the order 10^{-5} because of the presence of a small quartic coupling constant proportional the square of the electron Yukawa coupling. Prior to this article, attempts to explain the small primordial cosmic asymmetry required ad hoc assumptions and technically unnatural potentials.

3. John Hagelin describes the laws governing the dynamics of the unified field which underlie and give rise to the diversified laws of nature governing every level of the physical universe as the Constitution of the Universe.
4. The unified field, according to ancient Vedic science—the complete science of consciousness—is described as the togetherness (*Saṁhitā*) of the knower (*Rishi*), the process of knowing (*Devatā*), and the known (*Chhandas*). Maharishi Mahesh Yogi, *Vedic Knowledge for Everyone* (Vlodrop, Holland: Maharishi Vedic University Press, 1995).
5. For a detailed mathematical analysis of the parallel structures of the unified field of physics and the field of consciousness, see John Hagelin, *Manual for a Perfect Government: How to Harness the Laws of Nature to Bring Maximum Success to Governmental Administration* (Fairfield, Iowa; Maharishi University of Management Press 1998): 40–70.

CHAPTER 13: QUIET TIME AT THE FLETCHER-JOHNSON SCHOOL

1. A study of other inner-city children (not at the Fletcher-Johnson School) found that through their regular practice of the TM technique, students increased in analytic intelligence, self-concept, and general intellectual ability. Presented at the ninety-eighth annual meeting of the American Psychological Association, Washington, D.C., August 1990. Other findings include improved learning skills (S. I. Nidich, R. J. Nidich, M. Rainforth, "School Effectiveness: Achievement Gains at the Maharishi School of the Age of Enlightenment" *Education* 107 [1986]:49–54, and R. W. Cranson, D. W. Orme-Johnson, et al., "Transcendental Meditation

and Improved Performance on Intelligence-Related Measures: A longitudinal study" *Personality and Individual Differences* 12 [1991]: 1105–1116).

CHAPTER 14: AN OPPORTUNITY TO MEDITATE

1. Jay B. Marcus, *The Crime Vaccine: How to End the Crime Epidemic* (Baton Rouge, La: Claitor's Publishing, 1996).
2. Ibid.
3. Ibid.
4. Ibid.
5. C. R. Bleick and A. I. Abrams, "The Transcendental Meditation Program and Criminal Recidivism in California" *Journal of Criminal Justice* 15 (1987): 211–230.
6. M. C. Dillbeck and A. I. Abrams, "The Application of the Transcendental Meditation Program to Correction" *International Journal of Comparative and Applied Criminal Justice* 11 (1987): 111–132.
7. Bleick and Abrams, op. cit.
8. Dillbeck and Abrams, op. cit.
9. C. N. Alexander, P. Robinson, M. Rainforth, "Treating and Preventing Alcohol, Nicotine, and Drug Abuse Through Transcendental Meditation: A Review and Statistical Meta-analysis," *Alcoholism Treatment Quarterly* 11 (1994): 13–87.
10. J. Marcus, op. cit.

CHAPTER 15: THE FORGOTTEN VICTIMS OF INNER-CITY STRESS

1. R. H. Schneider, F. Staggers, et al., "A Randomized Controlled Trial of Stress Reduction for Hypertension in Older African Americans," *Hypertension* 26 (1995): 820–827.
2. C. N. Alexander, R. H. Schneider, et al., "Trial of Stress Reduction for Hypertension in Older African Americans II: Sex and Risk Subgroup Analysis," *Hypertension* 28 (1996):228–237.

CHAPTER 16: CREATING A TRUE PEACEKEEPING FORCE

1. "Russia Is Top Arms Seller to Developing Nations," *New York Times* August 20, 1996.
2. H. R. 2159, Foreign Operations Appropriations Act for Fiscal Year 1998.
3. "Weapons Bazaar," *U.S. News & World Report* (December 9, 1996): 26–38.
4. "China Syndrome," *Wall Street Journal* April 14 (1998): A22. Leslie Wayne, "800-Pound Guests at the Pentagon," *New York Times* March 15 (1998): WK5.
5. "President Clinton, more than any of his predecessors, is helping private com-

panies sell military weapons overseas." "Top cabinet officials regularly tour the world to hawk American arms," according to Jennifer Washburn in her article "Lobbyist-in-Chief," which appeared in the *Progressive* in December 1997.

6. "Alleviating Political Violence through Enhancing Coherence in Collective Consciousness: Impact Assessment Analyses of the Lebanon War," Summary of paper presented at the Eighty-fifth Annual Meeting of the American Political Science Association, September 1989.

7. Several specific examples include:

- A day-by-day study of a two-month coherence-creating assembly in Israel in 1983 showed that on days when the number of participants in the assembly was high, war deaths in neighboring Lebanon dropped by 76 percent. During these two months, crime, traffic accidents, and fires all declined in Israel. Other possible causes (weekends, holidays, weather, etc.) were statistically controlled for (D. W. Orme-Johnson, C. N. Alexander, et al., "International Peace Project in the Middle East: The Effect of the Maharishi Technology of the Unified Field." *Journal of Conflict Resolution* 32 [1988]: 776–812).

- A two-and-one-quarter-year follow-up study examined the effects of seven successive coherence-creating assemblies on the Middle East war. During the seven assemblies, there were marked reductions in war deaths ($p<10^{-10}$), war-related injuries ($p<10^{-6}$), and levels of conflict ($p<10^{-6}$), and a significant acceleration of the peace process ($p<10^{-8}$) (J. L. Davies and C. N. Alexander, "Alleviating Political Violence Through Enhancing Coherence in Collective Consciousness: Impact Assessment Analyses of the Lebanon War" *Dissertation Abstracts International* 49 [1988]: 2381A).

- Coherence-creating assemblies in Manila, New Delhi, Puerto Rico, and Washington, D.C., all corresponded with statistically significant declines in violent crime. In these studies, alternative explanations were explored and could not account for the findings (M. C. Dillbeck, K. L. Cavanaugh, et al., "Consciousness as a Field: The Transcendental Meditation and TM-Sidhi program and Changes in Social Indicators" *The Journal of Mind and Behavior* 8 [1987]: 67–104).

- A study of a random sample of 160 U.S. cities found that increasing the numbers of Transcendental Meditation participants in the 160 cities over a seven-year period (1972–1978) was followed by reductions in crime rate. The study used data from the FBI Uniform Crime Index total and controlled for other variables known to affect crime (M. C. Dillbeck, C. B. Banus, et al., "Test of a Field Model of Consciousness and Social Change: the Transcendental

Meditation and TM-Sidhi Program and Decreased Urban Crime"
The Journal of Mind and Behavior 9 [1988]: 457–486).

- A study of weekly data from October 1981 through October 1983
found that increases in the size of a large group practicing the
Transcendental Meditation and TM-Sidhi program in Washington,
D.C., were followed by significant reductions in violent crime.
Weekly violent crime totals in Washington decreased 11.8 percent
during the two-year period. Time series analysis verified that this
decrease in crime could not have been due to changes in the percentage of the population who were of young-adult age, nor Neigh-
borhood Watch programs nor changes in police policies or
procedures (M. C. Dillbeck, C. B. Banus, et al. "Test of a Field
Model of Consciousness and Social Change: the Transcendental
Meditation and TM-Sidhi Program and Decreased Urban Crime"
The Journal of Mind and Behavior 9 [1988]: 457–486).

8. Criminologists and social scientists have been unable to explain adequately the
dramatic and widespread reduction in violent crime throughout the United States
during the past five years. The standard explanations—changing demographics,
increased police surveillance, community policing, stricter sentencing, reduced
crack cocaine usage, etc.—cannot account for such an unexpected decline after
decades of sharply rising crime rates. In fact, many experts do not believe the
drop in crime will last. They project a significant increase in violent crime within
the next ten years as the younger generation reaches adolescence. John Hagelin
disagrees with this dire projection and offers a different perspective. He predicts
that crime rates will continue to fall, even accelerate in their decline because the
reduction is not due, in the main, to any of the conventional crime-fighting approaches. Rather, the decrease is due to the reduction in the social stress brought
about by the many millions of people practicing these technologies of consciousness over the past many decades, including large groups of experts in the TM-
Sidhi program. Just as people who pollute the environment inevitably produce a
cumulative damaging influence on the whole environment, so too research shows
that individuals who reduce stress and create coherence in their own lives from
the level of the unified field produce a cumulative positive effect on society as a
whole. Hagelin adds that crime rates in America remain unacceptably high. To
address this problem fully—particularly for our lower-income citizens—requires
improved health care, educational and career opportunities, better housing, and
in the field of corrections, more effective rehabilitative measures as well as significantly reduced social stress. The Natural Law Party's crime platform would
accelerate this positive trend by addressing all levels of the problem.

9. There has been extensive discussion in the literature concerning the possible

physical mechanisms that underlie the society-wide influence of Transcendental Meditation. For short-range applications, auditory, visual, and even olfactory cues (e.g., pheromones) provide viable mechanisms for the spreading of social coherence. For intermediate and long-range applications, more fundamental physical mechanisms must be considered, including the possible role of long-range physical forces. Of the four known forces of nature, only two—electromagnetism and gravity—are potentially capable of long-range interactions. Of these, the force of gravity is orders of magnitude too weak to provide a viable mechanism for social interaction. And although electromagnetism is under investigation as a possible source of EEG entrainment among humans in close physical proximity, most neuroscientists believe that electromagnetism will prove unable to account for the experimental data on the effects of meditation across large geographical distances. Scientists in the field have thus been led to consider more fundamental mechanisms for correlations among individuals at the quantum mechanical, quantum field theoretic levels. For a detailed analysis, see Hagelin, *Manual for a Perfect Government*, and references therein.

10. D. W. Orme-Johnson and P. Gelderloos, "Topographic EEG Brain Mapping During Yogic Flying," *International Journal of Neuroscience* 38 (1988): 427–434;

F. Travis and D. W. Orme-Johnston, "EEG Coherence and Power During Yogic Flying," *International Journal of Neuroscience* 54 (1990): 1–12.

R. K. Wallace, J. Silver, et al., "Systolic Blood Pressure and Long-term Practice of the Transcendental Meditation and TM-Sidhi Program: Effects of TM on Systolic Blood Pressure," *Psychosomatic Medicine* 45 (1983):41–46.

J. L. Glaser, J. L. Brind, et al., "Elevated Serum Dehydroepiandrosterone Sulfate Levels in Practitioners of the Transcendental Meditation (TM) and TM-Sidhi Program," *Journal of Behavioral Medicine* 15 (1992):327–341.

S. I. Nidich, R. A. Ryncarz, et al., "Kohlbergian Cosmic Perspective Responses, EEG Coherence, and the Transcendental Meditation and TM-Sidhi Program," *Journal of Moral Education* 12 (1983): 166–173.

11. David Robert Leffler, "A Vedic Approach to Military Defense: Reducing Collective Stress through the Field Effects of Consciousness," doctoral thesis, Union Institute Graduate School, Cincinnati, Ohio, 1997.

APPENDIX: GOVERNMENT SUPPORTED BY NATURAL LAW

1. For example, W. Bennett, *The Book of Virtues* (New York: Simon & Schuster, 1993).

2. Maharishi Mahesh Yogi, *Maharishi's Absolute Theory of Government: Automation in Administration* (Vlodrop, Holland: Maharishi Vedic University Press, 1993).

3. J. Hagelin, *Manual for a Perfect Government: How to Harness the Laws of Na-*

ture to Bring Maximum Success to Governmental Administration (Fairfield, Iowa: MUM Press, 1998).

4. M. Peterson, *Atlantic Monthly* (December 1994): 114; B. Mayo (ed.), *Jefferson Himself* (Charlottesville, Va.: University Press of Virginia, 1942): 291.

5. Maharishi Mahesh Yogi, *Life Supported by Natural Law* (Fairfield, Ia.: MIU Press, 1986).

6. R. Sapolsky, *Stress, the Aging Brain, and the Mechanisms of Neuron Death* (Cambridge, Mass.: MIT Press, 1992); H. Weiner, *Perturbing the Organism: The Biology of Stressful Experience* (Chicago: University of Chicago Press, 1992).

7. *Alcoholism Treatment Quarterly* 11 (1994): 89–117; *Archives of General Psychiatry* 49 (1992): 429–35, 436–41; *Life Sciences* 33 (1983): 2609–14.

8. Maharishi Mahesh Yogi, op. cit., 64.

9. Ibid., 165–172.

10. For a summary of research, see *Scientific Research on Maharishi's Transcendental Meditation and TM-Sidhi Program: Collected Papers*, vols. 1–5 (Fairfield, Ia.: MIU Press, 1990). Studies on specific benefits listed include: (intelligence) *Personality and Individual Differences* 12 (1991): 1105–16; (creativity) *Journal of Creative Behavior* 13 (1979): 169–80; (posttraumatic stress syndrome) *Journal of Counseling and Development* 64: (1985): 212–15; (anxiety) *Journal of Clinical Psychology* 45 (1989): 957–74; (hostility) *Criminal Justice and Behavior* 5 (1978): 3–20; (aggression) *Dissertation Abstracts International* 43 (1982): 539b; (mental health) *Journal of Psychology* 124 (1990): 177–197; (physical health) *Psychosomatic Medicine* 49 (1987): 493–507.

11. *Psychosomatic Medicine* 49 (1987): 493–507.

12. *Alcoholism Treatment Quarterly* 11:1–2 (1994).

13. *Dissertation Abstracts International* 43 (1982): 539b.

14. *Dissertation Abstracts International* 51 (1991): 5048.

15. Maharishi Mahesh Yogi, op. cit., 45–47.

16. Maharishi Mahesh Yogi, *Creating an Ideal Society* (Age of Enlightenment Press, 1976): 91, 105.

17. *Perceptual and Motor Skills* 6 (1986): 731–38.

18. *Journal of Clinical Psychology* 42 (1986): 161–64.

19. *Psychosomatic Medicine* 45:1 (1983): 41–46; *Journal of Behavioral Medicine* 15:4 (1992): 327–41.

20. S. I. Nidich and D. W. Orme-Johnson, *Proceedings of the International Symposium on Moral Education*, Fribourg, Switzerland, September 3, 1982.

21. *International Journal of Neuroscience* 54 (1990): 1–12.

22. Much of this research is summarized in *The Maharishi Effect: Results of Scientific Research 1974–1990* (Fairfield, Ia: MIU Press, 1990); see also *Journal of Mind and Behavior* 9 (1988): 457–86. Some specific examples include the following:

- *Journal of Conflict Resolution* 32 [1988]: 776–812. See Chapter 16, note 7.
- *Dissertation Abstracts International* 49 [1988]: 2381A. See Chapter 16, note 7.
- *Journal of Mind and Behavior* 8 [1987]: 67–104. See Chapter 16, note 7.
- The most recent study, a National Demonstration Project conducted in Washington, D.C., from June 7 to July 30, 1993, tested the efficacy of groups of experts in the Transcendental Meditation and TM-Sidhi program for reducing crime and social stress and improving the effectiveness of government. In this carefully controlled experiment, a coherence-creating group increased from eight hundred to four thousand over the two-month period. Although violent crime had been steadily increasing during the first five months of the year, soon after the start of the study, violent crime (measured by FBI Uniform Crime Statistics) began decreasing and continued to drop until the end of the experiment (maximum decrease 20 percent, $p<.0001$), after which it began to rise again. The effects of the group could not be attributed to other possible causes, including temperature, precipitation, weekends, and police and community anticrime activities. (See Institute of Science, Technology and Public Policy, Fairfield, Iowa, Technical Report ITR-94:1, 1994.)

  A growing number of scientists support this research, in recognition of its rigor, scope, and statistical significance. According to D. V. Edwards, a member of the independent Project Review Board that monitored the 1993 Washington study, "the claim can be made plausibly that the promised practical societal impact of this research significantly exceeds that of any other ongoing social-psychological research program" (ibid., addendum).

ECONOMY

1. In its January 1996 report, the Kemp commission provides specifics about the enormous cost of tax compliance (*Unleashing America's Potential: A Pro-Growth, Pro-Family Tax System for the 21st Century*, National Commission on Economic Growth and Tax Reform, January 1996: 7). In 1991 the Tax Foundation reported that small corporations spent a minimum of $382 in compliance costs for every $100 they paid in income taxes. According to 1995 IRS estimates, businesses will spend about 3.4 billion hours and individuals will spend about 1.7

billion hours embroiled in tax-related paperwork. That means nearly three million people—more people than serve in the U.S. armed forces—work full-time all year just to comply with tax laws, at a cost of about $200 billion a year, according to the Tax Foundation.

2. Ibid., 5.

3. "The Dropout Problem: Can Schools Meet the Challenge?" *NASSP Bulletin* 78: 565 (1994): 74–80.

4. The Natural Law Party's flat tax proposal maintains charitable deductions but does not maintain the mortgage deduction. A mortgage deduction increases the tax on all Americans by at least 2 percent and unfairly penalizes those who use their earnings for other purposes—for example, to send their children to college. The mortgage deduction, pushed by the housing industry, amounts to a form of corporate welfare for that industry. The Natural Law Party believes that taxes should be used to finance government, not to shape social and economic agendas by favoring some businesses over others.

Our flat tax proposal would maintain charitable deductions to promote an increase in charitable giving. Local philanthropic activities are more effective, more rewarding, and less wasteful than federally administered, socialized charity. The Natural Law Party would therefore like to see a shift in the responsibility for charitable giving from the government back to the individual. More Americans will be inspired to give once they have more wealth as a result of lower taxes and our progrowth economic policies.

Capital gains (indexed for inflation) and interest will be taxed as normal income under the Natural Law Party's proposal, but double taxation (e.g., a tax on dividend income) will be avoided.

The Natural Law Party proposes a tax floor of $25,500 for a family of four, below which Americans would pay no taxes. While this floor is lower than that proposed by some others, the Natural Law Party believes that most citizens should contribute something to society—to our schools, our roads, and our national security. Most important, however, with our low 10 percent tax rate, all Americans will pay significantly less tax than they do today.

5. *Unleashing America's Potential*, 11–14.

6. A program designed by Dr. Dean Ornish and used in a number of American hospitals has consistently shown that systematic use of diet, exercise, and meditation, in combination, can clear clogged arteries, promising large savings over the average twenty- to fifty-thousand dollar cost of angioplasty and bypass surgery (see *Journal of the American Medical Association* 274 [1995]: 894–901; *Lancet* 336 [1990]: 129–33; and *American Journal of Cardiology* 69 [1992]: 845–53).

In addition, a five-year study of health insurance statistics on over two thousand persons practicing the Transcendental Meditation program found that their doctor visits and hospitalizations were less than half those of other groups of comparable age, sex, and profession. Improvements were observed in all disease categories, including an 87 percent drop in cardiovascular illness (*Psychosomatic Medicine*

49 [1987]: 493). A study on hypertension in elderly African-Americans found that TM was twice as effective in reducing high blood pressure as Progressive Muscle Relaxation and was comparable to medication (*Hypertension* 26:5 [1995]: 820–27). An eleven-year study of 693 subjects over age forty-five who utilized TM and other aspects of Maharishi Vedic Approach to Health showed overall hospitalization rates 91 percent below those of norms and 88 percent below those of matched subjects (*American Journal of Managed Care* 3:1 [1997]: 135–44).

7. Drug and alcohol abuse cost America an estimated $166 billion a year. Stress has a negative impact on personal and corporate productivity and costs U.S. business $150 to $200 billion each year. See "Healthy Mind; Healthy Organization—A Proactive Approach to Occupational Stress," *Human Relations* 47:4 [1994]: 455–71; and United Nations International Labor Organization, "Stress at Work," *World Labor Report* 6 (Geneva, Switzerland: United Nations International Labor Office, 1993).

8. A recent study found a sizable reduction in Okun's Misery Index—defined as the sum of the inflation rate and the unemployment rate—from implementation of the national coherence-creating program proposed by the Natural Law Party (American Statistical Association, Business and Economics Statistics Section [1987]: 799; [1988]: 491; [1989]: 565).

HEALTH

1. The "miracles" of modern medicine have been much less effective in producing health than most Americans have assumed, according to mortality and morbidity rates in the United States. Research published in the *Journal of the American Medical Association* estimates that 40 percent of the U.S. population—more than one hundred million people—suffer from at least one chronic disease. Despite a vast array of advanced medical technologies and medications, modern medicine has no cure for these chronic diseases, only palliation (*Journal of the American Medical Association* 276 [1996]: 1473–79).

2. Spiraling medical expenses are an urgent governmental concern. Cost-containment strategies, including managed care, have not been entirely successful in stopping medical cost growth. In 1998 the United States will spend approximately one trillion dollars on medical treatment, more than any other nation. Yet surprisingly, the United States has among the worst health outcomes of all industrial nations. Despite our high-tech medical treatments, Americans have comparatively poor life expectancies at birth: The United States ranks twentieth for males and eighteenth for females among the twenty-three OECD nations and has the fifth-highest infant mortality rate (*Health Affairs* 16:6 [1997]: 163–71; *Health Affairs* 3:4 [1994]: 100–12).

3. See *Journal of the American Medical Association* 270 [1993]: 2207–12; U.S. Department of Health and Human Services, *Healthy People 2000: National Health*

Promotion and Disease Prevention Objectives, DHHS Publication No. (PHS) 91-50212 (Washington, D.C.: Government Printing Office, 1991); and U.S. Department of Health and Human Services, *Healthy People 2000: Midcourse Review and 1995 Revisions* (Washington, D.C.: Government Printing Office, 1995).

4. Nearly 47 percent of premature deaths among Americans could have been avoided by changes in individual behaviors, and another 17 percent by reducing environmental risks, according to a 1994 assessment by the Centers for Disease Control and Prevention. In contrast, the study suggested that only 11 percent of premature deaths could have been prevented by improved access to medical treatment. (See CDC, *Ten Leading Causes of Death in the United States, Update* [Atlanta: Centers for Disease Control and Prevention, 1994]).

5. Only 1 percent of our health sector budget is used to avoid disease, while 99 percent is spent to treat illness after it occurs. Astonishingly, the federal government also subsidizes unhealthy influences on our nation. For example, even though tobacco use is known to cause four hundred thousand deaths per year, including three thousand from passive smoking, the U.S. government subsidizes the tobacco industry. Our government also provides funding for genetic engineering and supports the nonlabeling of genetically engineered foods—despite the potentially serious health risks of such foods and the absence of research on long-term environmental effects (see our Agriculture section). Furthermore, the current Congress cut funding for the Environmental Protection Agency by 27 percent in 1995 despite the link between industrial pollution and disease suggested by the rising high incidence of cancer in America and other industrialized nations.

6. This health care option would be available to Medicare and Medicaid subscribers under a voucher system. Medical savings accounts establish an annual sum to cover subscriber health care costs; any unused portion of the account is paid directly to the subscriber each year. These accounts thus encourage savings and discourage unnecessary use of the health care system. However, this health care option also provides for catastrophic coverage at rates similar to traditional insurance plans in order to protect subscribers facing unexpected health care costs.

7. *New England Journal of Medicine* 328 (1993): 264–52. See also *The Future of the Body* (New York: G. P. Putnam & Sons, 1992).

8. Real preventive health care averts disease before it arises, and recent studies indicate that specific programs of behavioral prevention produce large cost savings.

- A ten-year study by the University of Michigan at Steelcase Corporation reported that systematic programs of diet, exercise, and stress reduction, when targeted for subjects in high health risk categories, reduce total health care costs by 46 percent (see *Medical Tribune* 14 [February 10, 1994]).
- A program designed by Dr. Dean Ornish and used in a number of

American hospitals has consistently shown that systematic use of diet, exercise, and meditation in combination can clear clogged arteries, promising large savings over the average twenty- to fifty-thousand-dollar cost of angioplasty and bypass surgery (see *Journal of the American Medical Association* 274 [1995]: 894–901; *Lancet* 336 [1990] 129–33; and *American Journal of Cardiology* 69 [1992]: 845–53).

- A retrospective study of Blue Cross/Blue Shield health insurance data for 693 faculty, staff, and dependents at an Iowa university who used components of the Maharishi Vedic Approach to Health showed that the group had 92 percent fewer hospital admissions for cardiovascular disease compared with statewide norms. Subjects over forty-five years old had 91 percent fewer days in the hospital for all diseases and 88 percent fewer days than matched controls; total medical expenditures per person were 59 percent lower than norms and 57 percent lower than controls (*American Journal of Managed Care* 3:1 [1997]: 135–44).

- Research on the Transcendental Meditation program has consistently demonstrated both cross-sectional and longitudinal health benefits. A five-year study of two thousand subjects has shown that people who practice TM have health care utilization more than 50 percent lower than matched control groups. The reductions were greatest in the oldest age-group (averaging 67 percent lower) and in high-cost areas (the TM group needed 76 percent less surgery and suffered 87 percent less heart disease) (*Psychosomatic Medicine* 49 [1987]: 493–505).

- A study on hypertension in elderly African-Americans found that the TM technique was twice as effective in reducing high blood pressure as Progressive Muscle Relaxation and about equally as effective as medication, but without harmful side effects (*Hypertension* 26:5 [1995]: 820–27). A further study found that Transcendental Meditation was more cost-effective in the treatment of hypertension than any of five classes of hypertensive drugs studied (*American Journal of Managed Care* 2:4 [1996]: 427–37).

9. The AMA spent $8.5 million from January to June 1997 lobbying the federal government to influence national medical policy making (*Chicago Tribune* [March 7, 1998] section 1, p. 7). The American Medical Association political action committee, known as AMPAC, is one of the largest medical PACs. For a discussion of the insidious influence of such expenditures on legislation, see P. Starr, *The Social Transformation of American Medicine: The Rise of a Sovereign Profession and the Making of a Vast Industry* (New York: Basic Books, 1984) (winner

of the Pulitzer Prize for general nonfiction); H. Wolinsky and T. Brune, *The Serpent on the Staff: The Unhealthy Politics of the American Medical Association* (New York: G. P. Putnam's Sons, 1994); and R. M. Harmer, *American Medical Avarice* (New York: Abelard-Schuman, 1975).

EDUCATION

1. The United States spends over $270 billion per year on public and elementary education, and expenditures per pupil, adjusted for inflation, have increased more than 25 percent over the past ten years. Yet America is falling behind in the knowledge race. Recent National Educational Goals Panel statistics (see *U.S. News & World Report* [April 1, 1996]) included the following:

   - Among U.S. high school seniors, 60 percent could not meet suggested national educational standards; 76 percent spend less than five hours per week on homework, compared with 35 percent of seniors in Japan.
   - U.S. high school students spend less than half as much class time studying math, history, and science as do students in Japan, France, and Germany.
   - Only 4.4 percent of U.S. students pass advanced placement exams, compared with 33 percent in France, Germany, Israel, and Japan.
   - A comparison of Japan, Korea, Taiwan, Israel, Scotland, Canada, and the United States found that the United States has the shortest school year: sixty-two days shorter than Japan's.
   - Results from the recent Third International Mathematics and Science Study showed that in twenty-one countries giving twelfth-grade tests, U.S. high school seniors ranked sixteenth in general science knowledge, nineteenth in math, and last in physics (see *Wall Street Journal* (February 25, 1998): A22; and *U.S. News & World Report* [March 9, 1998]: 14).

2. *American Journal of Public Health* 88 (1998): 413–18.
3. A 1996 survey found that at least one-third of all schoolchildren have used an illicit drug other than marijuana or alcohol before graduation from high school. Furthermore, it is estimated that one out of four American high school students has a serious drinking problem.
4. According to the National Center for Juvenile Justice, murder arrests among ten- to seventeen-year-olds have doubled since 1983, and the actual murder rate among fourteen- to seventeen-year-olds has risen 165 percent since 1984. Crimes in and around American public schools have increased significantly; well over one hundred thousand students now carry guns to school. A recent U.S. Justice

Department report found that juvenile arrests for gun charges have doubled since 1985, and gunshot wounds have become the second leading cause of death among high school students.

5. Developmental psychologists have outlined specific, natural stages of psychological growth in children. The final stage, termed *formal operations* by Piaget, is associated with adolescence and represents the level of mental functioning in which abstract thinking becomes stabilized. Because of the inadequacies of our educational system, the majority of our students never achieve this stage of normal adolescent mental development across cognitive domains, let alone their full potential. (For a more comprehensive treatment of this topic, see Charles N. Alexander and Ellen J. Langer [eds.], *Higher Stages of Human Development: Perspectives on Adult Growth* [New York: Oxford, 1990].)

6. A series of recent studies has found a correlation between nutrition and academic performance (*Personality and Individual Differences* 4 [1991]: 343, 361). These studies found that in several hundred schools in New York, there was a 16 percent gain in academic performance resulting from improved nutrition. The study suggested that many students experience malnutrition that is too slight for clinical signs but that nevertheless affects their intelligence and academic performance. This impairment can be corrected through improved nutrition.

7. These prevention-oriented health care programs include Maharishi Vedic Approach to Health, a natural system of health care that promotes balance in mind, body, and behavior and that has been shown to reduce significantly medical utilization by producing better health in its practitioners. These programs strengthen mind and body and reduce anxiety, thereby enhancing receptivity and the capacity for learning.

8. Research confirms a marked improvement in student health and a reduction in drug abuse, alchol use, and cigarette use through programs proposed by the Natural Law Party (*Alcohol Treatment Quarterly* 11 [1/2, 3/4], 1994; *International Journal of Addictions* 12:729, 1977; *Bulletin on Narcotics* 40:50, 1988; *Journal of Addictions* 14:147, 1981; 26:293, 1991; *American Journal of Psychiatry* 131: 60, 1974).

9. Extensive scientific research on one such program endorsed by the Natural Law Party—the Transcendental Meditation program—has consistently demonstrated its capacity to unfold student potential and thereby fulfill the highest goals of education. For decades, IQ was thought to be static, a measured quantity that was fixed after a certain age. However, research indicates that the practice of Transcendental Meditation significantly increases IQ (*Educational Technology* 19 [1979]: 7; *Personality and Individual Differences* 2 [1991]: 1105; *College Student Journal* 15 [1981]: 140; *Perceptual and Motor Skills* 62 [1986]: 731). Other scientific studies have shown that practice of Transcendental Meditation increases learning ability, improves memory, and enhances orderliness of brain functioning (*Memory and Cognition* 10 [1982]: 205; *International Journal of Neuroscience*

14 [1981]: 147, *Psychosomatic Medicine* 46: 3 [1984]: 267); reduces stress and exam anxiety (*Journal of Clinical Psychology* 45 [1989]: 957); stimulates ego development, motivation, and moral reasoning (*Journal of Social Behavior and Personality* 6 [1991]: 189; *Journal of Moral Education* 12 [1983]: 166); and results in significant improvements in analytic intelligence, self-concept, and general school performance among inner-city youths ("Effects of the Transcendental Meditation Program with Low-Income Inner-City Children," presented at the 98th Annual Convention of the American Psychological Association, Boston, Massachusetts, August 1990).

10. Ibid.

11. In the United States model institutions incorporating educational programs endorsed by the Natural Law Party include Maharishi University of Management in Fairfield, Iowa, and its award-winning laboratory school from preschool to twelfth grade.

CRIME AND REHABILITATION

1. See *Victim Costs and Consequences: A New Look,* a comprehensive survey published in 1996 by the National Institute of Justice (the research branch of the Justice Department).

2. Federal Bureau of Investigation, *Crime in the United States 1996, Uniform Crime Reports,* (Washington, D.C.: U.S. Department of Justice, 1997).

3. According to the National Center for Juvenile Justice (1995), the murder rate among fourteen- to seventeen-year-olds increased 165 percent during the last ten years, and the number of arrests for violent crime among ten- to seventeen-year-olds doubled. In addition, according to *USA Today* ([November 13, 1995]: 1A), the number of teenage arrests on weapons charges has doubled since 1985.

4. America leads the industrialized world in murders—almost four times the annual U.S. casualty rate during the Vietnam War (see J. Wilson, *Commentary* [September 1994]: 25). The 1996 FBI annual crime statistics for the United States reported 19,650 murders, 95,770 rapes, 537,050 robberies, 1,029,810 aggravated assaults, and 2,501,500 burglaries. (See Federal Bureau of Investigation, op. cit.)

5. See S. R. Donziger (ed.), *The Real War on Crime* (New York: HarperCollins, 1996).

6. See *U.S. News & World Report* (March 23, 1997) 6:33. U.S. Department of Justice figures (press release, August 27, 1995) indicate that 5.1 million Americans are under some form of correctional supervision: prison, jail, parole, or probation.

7. See J. Petersilia, "Crime and Punishment in California: Full Cells, Empty Pockets, and Questionable Benefits," CPS Brief (Berkeley: California Policy Seminars, May 1993).

8. Ibid., 10; R. Sampson and C. Laub, *Crime in the Making* (Cambridge, Mass.: Harvard University Press, 1993): 255.

9. *The Newark Foot Patrol Experiment, 1981; The Kansas City Preventive Patrol*

Experiment: A Summary Report (Washington, D.C.: Police Foundation, 1974). See also James Q. Wilson, "What to Do about Crime," *Commentary* (1994): 215–234.

10. *Social Problems* 41:3 [1997]: 448–72. See also R. A. Mendel, *Prevention or Pork? A Hard-Headed Look at Youth-Oriented Anti-Crime Programs* (Washington, D.C.: Youth Policy Forums, 1995).

11. R. Sapolsky, *Stress, the Aging Brain, and the Mechanisms of Neuron Death* (Cambridge, Mass.: MIT Press, 1992).

12. *Alcoholism Treatment Quarterly* 11 [1994]: 89–117.

13. *Archives of General Psychiatry* 49 [1992]: 429–35, 436–41; *Life Sciences* 33 [1983]: 2609–14.

14. *Journal of Clinical Psychology* 45 (1989): 957–74; *Society of Neuroscience Abstracts* 18 (1992): 1541; *Journal of Neural Transmission* 39 (1976): 257–67; *Criminal Justice and Behavior* 5 (1978):3–20; *Dissertation Abstracts International*, 51 (1991):5048.

15. The most recent study, a National Demonstration Project conducted in Washington, D.C., from June 7 to July 30, 1993, tested the efficacy of groups of experts in the Transcendental Meditation and TM-Sidhi program for reducing crime and social stress and improving the effectiveness of government. In this carefully controlled experiment, a coherence-creating group increased from eight hundred to four thousand over the two-month period. Although violent crime had been steadily increasing during the first five months of the year, soon after the start of the study, violent crime (measured by FBI Uniform Crime Statistics) began decreasing and continued to drop until the end of the experiment (maximum decrease 20 percent, $p<.0001$), after which it began to rise again. The effects of the group could not be attributed to other possible causes, including temperature, precipitation, weekends, and police and community anticrime activities. (See Institute of Science, Technology and Public Policy, Fairfield, Iowa, Technical Report ITR–94:1, 1994.)

16. *Dissertation Abstracts International* 43 (1982): 539b.

17. The Transcendental Meditation technique has been successfully used in twenty-eight rehabilitation programs in fifteen U.S. states. Studies have shown that the Transcendental Meditation technique is highly effective in reducing recidivism (*Journal of Criminal Justice* 15 [1987]: 211; *International Journal of Comparative and Applied Criminal Justice* 11 [1987]: 111; *Dissertation Abstracts International* 43 [1982]: 539b). In 1987 and 1988 the African nation of Senegal applied this rehabilitation strategy nationwide. More than eleven thousand Senegalese prisoners and more than nine hundred prison officers were instructed in the TM technique. Recidivism dropped dramatically, the prison population was halved, prison violence declined, and several prisons closed while many others operated at well below capacity. See *New Horizons in Criminology and Penitentiary Science: The Maharishi Unified Field Based Integrated System of Rehabilitation in Senagalese Prisons*, Dacca, February 12–13, 1988.

18. For a fuller discussion of this approach to rehabilitation and crime prevention, see Jay B. Marcus, *The Crime Vaccine* (Baton Rouge: Claitor's Books, 1996).
19. C. Horowitz, "The Suddenly Safer City," *New York* (August 14, 1995).
20. See Joseph A. Califano, *Substance Abuse in Urban America: Its Impact on an American City, New York,* Center on Addiction and Substance Abuse, Cornell University, February 1996.
21. A recent meta-analysis of programs used in the treatment of substance abuse found that those endorsed by the Natural Law Party were highly effective in decreasing the use of alcohol, cigarettes, and a wide variety of nonprescribed drugs (*Alcoholism Treatment Quarterly* 11:1–2 [1994]: 13–87).

ENERGY AND ENVIRONMENT

1. Scott Allen, "Study: Air Pollution Killing Thousands," *Des Moines Register* (May 9, 1996): 1.
2. According to a 1995 report from the Department of Health and Human Services, environmental toxins are responsible for 14 percent of annual deaths in America.
3. If the real costs associated with the use of polluting fuels were appropriately distributed—for example, if the environmental costs of gasoline were included in its cost at the pump—the free market system would have eliminated fossil fuels long ago. In essence the government is blocking free enterprise and free market competition by subsidizing fossil fuels and not their nonpolluting competitors.
4. See *Environmental Health Perspectives* 103:8 (1995): 301–306, and *Journal of the American Medical Association* 270:18 (1993): 2207–12. Individuals with high body burdens of PCBs, DDT, and other such compounds have higher levels of cancer, liver damage, reproductive disorders, immune system suppression, and neurological problems (see *Annual Review of Public Health* 18 [1997]: 211–44; and *Environmental Health Perspectives* 100 [1992]: 259–68). Since such contaminants degrade very slowly in the environment, governmental attempts to control sources of exposure may not solve the problem.
5. According to a study by the Electric Power Research Institute, the introduction of energy conservation practices could reduce electricity use in the United States by as much as 55 percent (Romm, "The Economic Benefits of Combatting Global Warming," 1992).
    Further research shows that existing energy conservation technologies can cut the use of fossil fuels in half, eliminating dependence on foreign oil, the largest component of our trade deficit. One study, entitled *America's Energy Choices*, published by the Union of Concerned Scientists, concludes that the United States can dramatically reduce energy use and air pollution and increase the use of renewable technologies at a significant cost savings to the nation.
    The cost of energy to our nation is a substantial proportion of our gross national

product. We spent 15 percent of our GNP on energy in 1990, or a total of $847 billion. According to the schedule proposed by the Natural Law Party, we would spend only 10.2 percent by the year 2005, cutting hundreds of billions of dollars from the nation's energy bill.

AGRICULTURE

1. "Grain Prices Head Higher," *Business Week* (November 20, 1995): 38.
2. "Another Crisis in World's Future?" *Des Moines Register* (November 12, 1995): 1J.
3. W. Heffernan, cited in "U.S. Ag Called Feudal System," *Des Moines Register* (November 27, 1994).
4. One is Dr. John Fagan, discussed in "Biologist Returns US Grants to Protest Genetic Research," *Boston Globe* (November 16, 1994).
5. Northwest Area Foundation, *A Better Row to Hoe: The Economic, Environmental, and Social Impact of Sustainable Agriculture* (December 1994): 1; see also USDA/ERS:18.
6. *Scandinavian Journal of Work and Environmental Health* 18(1992): 209–215; *Journal of the American Medical Association* 256:9 (1986):1141–47; S. H., Zahm et al., Annual Meeting of the Society for Epidemiological Research, Vancouver, Canada, June 15–17, 1988.
7. National Research Council, Board on Agriculture, Alternative Agriculture (1989); Northwest Area Foundation, op. cit., 2.
8. *Paying the Farm Bill: U.S. Agricultural Policy and the Transition to Sustainable Agriculture*, World Resources Institute, 1991.
9. "Health Effects and Prevalence of Vegetarianism," *Western Journal of Medicine* 160 (1994): 465–71.
10. See Government Supported by Natural Law section.

STRENGTHENING DEMOCRACY

1. U.S. Supreme Court, *Sweezy v. New Hampshire*, 1957.
2. In 1996 the number of signatures required to get a presidential candidate on the ballot in all fifty states plus the District of Columbia was 25,500 for Democrats, 49,250 for Republicans, and 729,245 for a new party. In addition, to run a full slate of candidates in 1998, a new party would have had to gather 5.1 million signatures. Such discriminatory practices create an enormous financial obstacle for third parties trying to participate in our democratic process.
3. See the 1990 Document of Copenhagen Meeting of the Conference of Security and Cooperation in Europe (CSCE).
4. Getting elected to public office has never been more expensive. Total expenditures for the 1996 campaign were $2.1 billion. The average winning campaign for

the House of Representatives cost over $673,000 in 1996. That's a 30 percent increase from just two years earlier, when the average seat cost $516,000. Ninety-four candidates for the House spent more than $1 million to get elected. Six of them spent $2 million or more, and the most expensive campaign of all was the reelection effort of House Speaker Newt Gingrich, which cost nearly $5.6 million. In the Senate, the average seat in 1996 cost $4.7 million—only slightly more than it's been in recent years. Averages mean less in the Senate, though, since there are comparatively few races (only a third of Senate seats are up in any given election year) and since the costs in any one year depend heavily on which states are having elections. In 1996 neither California nor New York had Senate races. In 1998 both do, and those races will likely be expensive enough to push the averages up again. The race for the presidency is in a league by itself. Bill Clinton and Bob Dole each spent more than $100 million in their campaigns, but their respective parties poured in millions more to help them indirectly. Under federal campaign rules, funding for the fall presidential campaigns is supposed to come entirely from federal funds supplied by taxpayers who divert $3 of their taxes into the Presidential Election Campaign Fund. In reality, the general election campaign period is the most frenzied fund-raising season of all, with both parties acting as surrogates for their slates of candidates and raising as much money as they possibly can.

5. An editorial in the March 24, 1998, edition of *USA Today* reported on findings from the Center for Responsive Politics on how big money buys big favors. The editorial included the following:

- "Big Tobacco gave at least $4.2 million last year alone, and it wasn't even an election year. That helped get tobacco a 25% reduction in the size of the proposed tax increase. Tobacco lobbyists also were able to dictate a backdoor addition to the 1997 budget deal that was worth $50 billion to the industry. Fortunately, it was spotted after the fact and repealed by suddenly embarrassed lawmakers.

- "Cable TV and local telephone companies have given $22.8 million in political contributions since 1991, much of it to the members of the Commerce committees that write telecommunications legislation. Guess what? The 1996 deregulation law that was touted as making telecommunications more competitive and responsive to consumers instead seems to have spurred a wave of profitable consolidation and little of the proposed competition.

- "Brand-name drug makers have given more than $18.6 million over the same period. Congress responded by letting them hold on to their exclusive drug patents up to two years longer. The payoff: $6.2 billion in higher drug charges over the next 17 years, according to a University of Minnesota study."

FOREIGN POLICY

1. *Journal of Conflict Resolution* 32 (1988): 776–812; *Dissertation Abstracts International* 49 (1988): 2381A; *Journal of Mind and Behavior* 8 (1987): 67–104.

DEFENSE

1. G-2, *Military* 11:7 (1994): 3.
2. For example, Congress has apportioned $13.4 billion for additional B-2 bombers that the Pentagon doesn't want; legislators have funded the construction of four GS cruisers, although the navy requested only two; and the costly Seawolf project is currently funded for $700 million, even though the navy doesn't want it at all.
3. *Air Force Times* (May 27, 1996): 10.
4. *U.S. Naval Institute Proceedings* (July 1995): 73; *American Journal of Public Health* 81:7 (1991): 865–69; *American Journal of Preventive Health* 11:4 (1995): 245–50.
5. See *U.S. Naval Institute Proceedings* (January 1996): 64. Environmental dangers cited include inhalation of sand and other airborne particles, heavy metals, depleted uranium, chemical and biological agents, pollution from hydrocarbons, and genetic and cancer risks.
6. *Journal of Conflict Resolution* 32 (1988): 776–812; *Dissertation Abstracts International* 49 (1988): 2381A; *Journal of Mind and Behavior* 8 (1987): 67–104.
7. See our Health, Crime and Rehabilitation, and Education sections, and references therein. For research on posttraumatic stress syndrome, see *Journal of Counseling and Development* 64 (1985):212. However, we believe that a smaller, more flexible force coupled with greater economic and security cooperation will serve the nation's security interests and provide the basis for a more stable world. We therefore emphasize human rather than material resources.